The Inventor Handbook

How to Invent, Protect Yourself, Patent Your Invention, and Make Serious Money

Peter D. Keefe

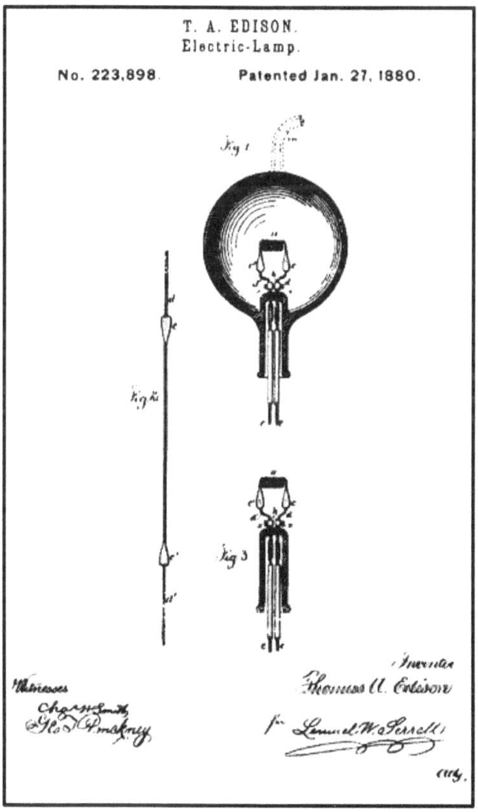

Image credit: USPTO.gov database.

Cover: The bulb portion of the Drawing page of Thomas Alva Edison's United States Patent 223,898 for the first practical incandescent light bulb.

The Inventor Handbook

How to Invent, Protect Yourself, Patent Your Invention, and Make Serious Money

Published by LMDSI, Eastpointe, Michigan

in association with PatentApplication.com.

Second Edition

Library of Congress Control Number:
2025916610

ISBN-13: 978-1-7326624-7-6

PURPOSE OF THIS HANDBOOK

In this second edition, as in the first, you will learn the art of inventing, the formalities of patenting and the dos and don'ts of marketing.

While inventing and marketing are largely do it yourself subjects, patenting is not.

The legal process of obtaining a patent is fraught with landmines that can blow-up any chance of your success. Yes, the U.S. Patent and Trademark Office (USPTO) accepts patent applications from unrepresented persons. But this is not who you want to be if your goal is to make serious money.

Hire a patent attorney to get a patent of the highest quality. Fear not, for this handbook will give you the insider information you'll need to ensure your patent attorney is optimally in your corner at every turn of the process.

FREE ONLINE SUPPORT

Exclusively available to readers of The Inventor Handbook, please visit the Reader Support portal at https://PatentApplication.com. Subject to change, you'll find:

- Handbook Updates;
- Patent News;
- Frequently Asked Questions;
- Keefe's Korner, the Author's I.P. blog;
- Quick Links to the QR Codes; and
- Filing a Provisional Patent Application.

https://PatentApplication.com

To access the Reader Support portal at PatentApplication.com, please enter the ten character password on page 78.

FOR MORE INFORMATION AND CONTACT

Please visit About Us at PatentApplication.com. There, you'll find:

- the PatentApplication.com story;
- the Author's biography; and
- the Reader Contact form, where the Author welcomes your comments and suggestions.

DISCLAIMER

The information provided in this book (The Inventor Handbook) does not constitute legal advice, all information being intended for general information purposes only.

Readers of this book should contact an attorney, accountant or other licensed/credentialed professional to obtain advice with respect to any particular legal, accounting, business or other matter arising from reading of the information. Only a professional can assess whether, and if so how, the information presented in this book is applicable to your situation. In no event does the purchase of this book create an attorney-client relationship between the reader and the Author (Peter D. Keefe).

The views expressed in this book are those of the Author. All liability with respect to any actions taken or not taken based on the information in this book is hereby expressly disclaimed. The information in this book is provided "as is;" while the Author has undertaken care in the preparation of this book, no representations are made that the information is error-free.

No representation is made that any online link is endorsed or affiliated with the Author, except PatentApplication.com. Please kindly note, readers visit each linked webpage/website, other than PatentApplication.com, at their own risk.

The Author may discontinue PatentApplication.com and/or modify, change or delete content of PatentApplication.com, including the Reader Support portal, at any time, with or without prior notice.

The title and subtitle of this book do not represent, nor do they constitute, any assurance of result, monetary or otherwise. There are no guarantees of any kind as to a reader's outcome from reading of this book.

"The Congress shall have Power ... To promote the Progress of Science and useful Arts, by securing for limited Times to Authors and Inventors the exclusive Right to their respective Writings and Discoveries;"

-- *Article I, Section 8 of the United States Constitution.*

The United States of America

The Director of the United States Patent and Trademark Office

Has received an application for a patent for a new and useful invention. The title and description of the invention are enclosed. The requirements of law have been complied with, and it has been determined that a patent on the invention shall be granted under the law.

Therefore, this

United States Patent

Grants to the person(s) having title to this patent the right to exclude others from making, using, offering for sale, or selling the invention throughout the United States of America or importing the invention into the United States of America, and if the invention is a process, of the right to exclude others from using, offering for sale or selling throughout the United States of America, or importing into the United States of America, products made by that process, for the term set forth in 35 U.S.C. 154(a)(2) or (c)(1), subject to the payment of maintenance fees as provided by 35 U.S.C. 41(b). See the Maintenance Fee Notice on the inside of the cover.

Director of the United States Patent and Trademark Office

Patent Grant Cover for the Author's U.S. Patent 9,410,730.

CONTENTS

THE PATENT PROCESS

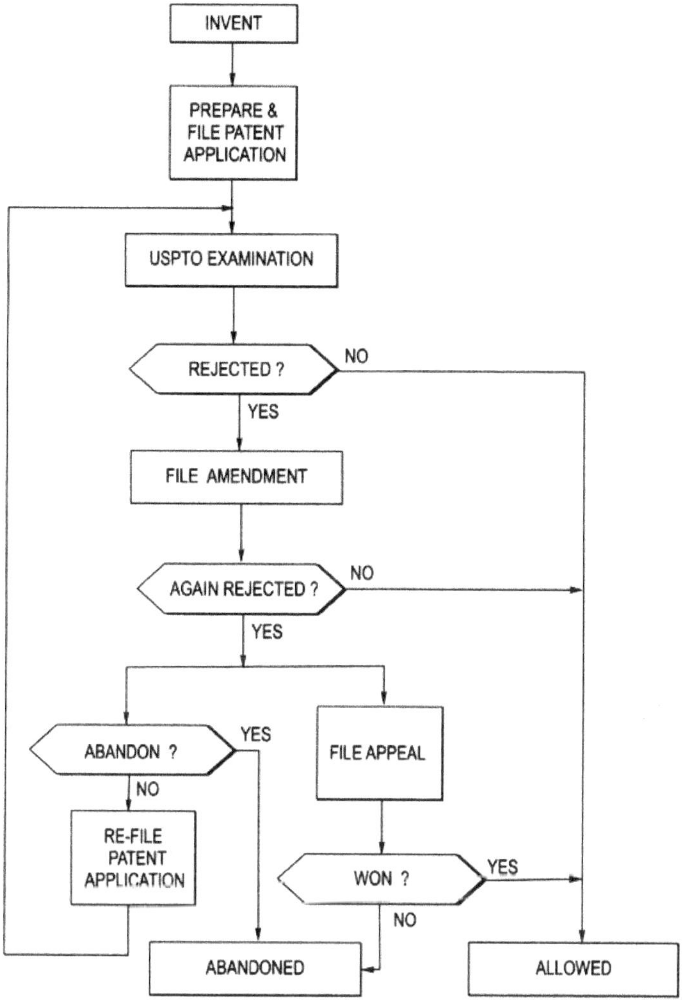

Patent Application Flow Chart

Once you have perfected your invention and filed a patent application with the U.S. Patent & Trademark Office (USPTO), your submission will be assigned to an Examiner, a technically qualified employee of the USPTO, who then reports back to you through your attorney on the patentability of your invention as defined by the "claims" in your patent application.

In the end, one of two possibilities will happen: either your patent application will be allowed because the USPTO has determined your invention is patentable and entitled under law to a patent grant, or, your patent application will be abandoned because, for all your good efforts, the USPTO has determined your invention is not patentable under law.

PREFACE

Invention Reflection

1968 was my inventive *annus mirabilis*. That year, I invented screw-in fluorescent light bulbs, auto-reversing tape recorders, hydraulic suspensions, pneumatic crash absorbing bumpers, circuit breakers in the shape of a screw-in fuse and passive acoustic noise cancellation systems. Yes, they were crude versions of today's products, but I grasped the concepts and worked diligently on embodiments. I'll never forget the day in late August of 1968 when I was driving my Mustang on Detroit's 8 Mile Road and heard on the radio, "Bell & Howell announces auto-reversing tape recorders." I almost wrecked the car! I was a kid who didn't know how to move ahead with my inventions. Perhaps, I was more worried about protecting myself and that's why my inventions went nowhere: I was crippled by ignorance, fear and uncertainty.

This is NOT going to happen to you. This handbook will guide you through every step, allowing you to march forward confidently and capably, knowing what will happen before it does and what to do before it's too late. You'll benefit, while preventing others from inappropriately benefitting off you.

While the emphasis in this handbook applies to inventors, it also applies to all the intellectual fruits of creative people.

* * *

True to my inventor roots, I majored in physics at the University of Detroit, obtaining a master's degree. To my delight, the department chairman, Gerhard Blass, agreed to be my thesis advisor. He offered me much advice, both in physics and in life.[1]

With patent law in my windshield and physics in the rearview mirror, I travelled down the road to law school. This was a financially

---

[1] Gerhard Blass received his Ph.D. from Leipzig University at the beginning of WWII. He went to work for Werner Heisenberg on the German atomic bomb program. This fascinating aspect of WWII history is recounted by me in "The Demon and the Quantum" by Robert Scully (with Endnotes by Marlan Scully), ISBN 978-3-527-40983-9, Wiley-VCH, Weinheim, Germany, page 117, (2010).

painless process, as the University of Detroit offered me remission of tuition if I would continue my teaching assistant position in the physics department.

My post 1968 inventive *raison d'être* was inspired by an epiphany that happened in an otherwise boring law school class. In that epiphany, I suddenly envisioned how superconductivity could be harnessed to extract ambient heat from the atmosphere and convert it into work to run an engine or provide electrical power. It was a visionary dream because it challenged the Second Law of Thermodynamics, but perhaps not so challenging because the fundamental process involved was entirely quantum mechanical. I filed a patent application, obtaining U.S. Patent 4,638,194. Many scientific conferences and Nobel Prize winner consultations later, with no progress being made in understanding the phenomenon, I eventually figured out on my own that sublime subtleties in the underlying physics did indeed save the Second Law.[2]

I apprenticed at two patent law firms, earning my wings when the senior partner at the second firm one day asked me how he should proceed on a difficult case. No longer was I the babe being told what to do, I was now an equal to the partner telling him what to do!

I had earlier accepted a teaching position in the physics department of the University of Detroit, which provided both the income and the flexibility I needed to establish my own patent law firm, Keefe and Associates.

Always the champion of the individual inventor, I created the *Inventors' Association of Metropolitan Detroit*, inviting a number of my colleagues and clients to join in. The monthly meetings, freely open to the public, featured speakers who provided focused assistance to aspiring inventors, while the monthly newsletter I wrote amplified on the theme. In those days, I was probably the busiest patent attorney in metro Detroit whose practice was devoted solely to helping individual inventors.

Through my close contacts in the profession, I became outside

---

[2] My culminating paper, "Magnetic Hysteresis in the First Order Adiabatic Phase Transition of Mesoscopic-size Type I Superconductors," published in The European Physical Journal Special Topics, ISSN: 1951-6355: Non-Equilibrium Systems and Foundations of Quantum Physics, V. 230, No. 4, 993-1001 (June, 2021), is available at DOI: https://doi.org/10.1140/epjs/s11734-021-00099-9.

See www.Keefengine.com.

patent counsel to General Motors Corporation. It would seem I did a reasonably good job for GM, for the director of the patent department one day confided in me that I was GM's "secret weapon," the company's go-to patent attorney who could handle anything thrown my way. He then smiled and said, "Pete you need to buy a car." I bought a Buick LeSabre Limited: its gentle ride, responsive engine and comfortable good looks won me over. Routinely visiting the Technical Center and the Proving Grounds, I continually came face-to-face with many engineer inventors whose inventions ranged across the spectrum from simple to complex, practical to whimsical, down-to-earth to stratospheric.

From my experience, there's one thing I want to emphasize at the outset: these professional inventors were not any more gifted than the individual inventors whom I had counseled and continued to counsel in my private law practice while I was with GM. So take heart all of you "basement inventors," you really do have a shot!

My forty plus years of experience in patent law has taught me that it makes no difference:

- what age, gender or race you are - incredible ideas come from all of us, perhaps largely because America inherently instills innovation in our collective intellects;
- whether you're an engineer, work on the line, mow grass, mind the kids or are retired - I have seen some of the best inventions come from moms and kids;
- the level of your education - I know of several occasions when a Ph.D. had trouble understanding the technical aspects of a high school dropout's invention; and
- the extent of your financial resources - if your invention is good, a way can always be found to take it to market.

On the other hand, my experience has taught me what does make a difference:

- keeping your eyes open to problems and envisioning solutions;
- being diligent - an idea is like a baby, it won't grow into adulthood without nurturing under constant care;
- recognizing that inventing is your realm, while patenting is the patent attorney's realm; and
- knowing when to dig in and fight, and when to give up and move on.

* * *

This handbook is intended to be an informative reference guide for inventors and entrepreneurs, revealing how to nurture your ideas, navigate the patent system and successfully market your innovations, all with the aim to make serious money. The teachings are crafted to effectively assist you in working with your patent attorney.

The Patent Process flowchart exemplifies how a typical patent application makes its way through the U.S. Patent & Trademark Office.

The Foreword by patent attorney Joseph P. Carrier, a former Patent Examiner, reflects his thoughts on the developing U.S. patent laws.

The Prologue provides an overview of the subject matter of this handbook.

Part I, *Inventing*, explores the subtleties of the process: how ideas originate, what characterizes a good idea, and how to turn that good idea into a perfected invention. To help you along the way, topics include the searching of prior art, assertions of co-inventorship, and claims of ownership by an employer.

Part II, *Patenting*, explains the arcane formalities necessary to obtain a patent. You'll understand what a patent is and is not; how the U.S. Patent Office works and how it fits into the international patent system; why patent applications are written according to a time tested standard; exactly what a patent claim is and how claims define the extent of your patent protection; how to find a patent attorney, know how to work with him/her and be on the lookout for practice, procedure and billing irregularities; and finally, the tricks, strategies and maneuvers that can win you a patent.

Part III, *Marketing*, reveals how to make money from your invention. Understanding the economic merits of your invention and recognizing how it fits into the marketplace is a challenge, but an achievable one. How this essential knowledge is then parlayed into a manufacturer match is key. You'll learn how to approach a prospect and navigate the maxims of marketing.

* * *

If you have difficulty accessing the QR codes with your cell phone camera, please go to the Reader Support portal at www.PatentApplication.com for clickable links to use with your computer.

FOREWORD

Thoughts on the U.S. Patent System

by

Joseph P. Carrier, Esq.

Many aspects of the U.S. and world patent law have radically changed over the last several decades. The world in general has also changed radically over this same time period, not always in step with patent laws. Regardless of the radical changes, the world moves forward based on advancements in technology, and there has been a significant shift in the value of businesses from physical assets including inventory and factories to intangible assets based on ownership of intellectual property including patents. For this reason the patent laws are essential because they help to establish the ownership and direction of technical advancement in the world. Mr. Keefe's new book is most helpful to understand the evolving patent laws and to get the most out of any new technology.

When I began working as an Examiner for the U.S. Patent & Trademark Office (USPTO) in the 1980s, the Patent Act of 1952 was in effect and the price of obtaining patent rights in the U.S. was much less than today on a relative scale. It was a simpler time, but the issues were not necessarily simpler. However, U.S. patent laws had a few important differences from other patent laws around the world, which mostly benefitted U.S. inventors, but created significant discrepancies in the patent disclosure and protection available under U.S. laws and foreign patent laws.

For example, the 1952 law designated the first person to invent to be the rightful patentee. This necessitated detailed record keeping on the part of the inventor to prove a date of conception followed by diligence toward a *reduction to practice*, which may be either "actual" by the making of the invention, or "constructive" by the filing of a patent application. Although it happened very infrequently, if two unrelated inventors each filed a patent application on the same invention they would need to go through a costly inter-parties legal process, known as an *interference*, to ascertain who was the first to invent and, ergo, the lawful first inventor. Another protection under the 1952 law, highly valued by inventors for multiple reasons, was the requirement that all patent applications be kept in secrecy unless and until a patent issued. This allowed inventors to continue to develop their inventions for market without giving competitors notice of what the inventors were seeking protection on until the inventors had secured patent rights on the inventions. Unfortunately, this seemingly benign facet also allowed some inventors to surprise competitors by artificially delaying issuance of patents on their invention by filing continuations of their pending applications while not paying an issue fee to maintain secrecy of their inventions many years beyond the expected pendency term of 2-3 years, and defeating the intended purpose of giving the public timely notice of inventions for which patents were being sought. Then after competitors had made great investments in doing research on related inventions and developing markets for their products without having any notice of the pending patent applications, these inventors would only then pay issue fees for their long-pending patent applications so that these applications would mysteriously surface as patent to the surprise of many large industries. The term *submarine patent* given to these types of patents was well deserved. This was the consequence of a 17 year patent term independent of the date of filing of the patent application under the existing law.

Fortunately, the 1952 law was not to remain the law of the land for much longer.

As a result of international negotiations that resulted in the "Uruguay Round Agreements Act of December 8, 1994," USPTO implementing rules went into effect on July 8, 1995. The most significant change to the patent laws as a result of the Agreements Act was to establish a patent term of no more than 20 years from the date of filing of the patent application—applying to the date of filing of a first patent application in a chain of related applications, rather than based on the date a patent issued. This was the end of submarine patents. At the same time, the USPTO came to the aid of inventors by affording the right to file a *provisional* patent application. While only effective for up to a year unless within that year a later filed *regular* patent application refers to it, it eliminated many onerous formal requirements to get a patent application on file, such as the omission of patent claims.

The U.S. Congress made additional tweaks to the 1952 patent law with the "*American Inventors Protection Act of 1999*." Most significant of these was the publication of utility and plant pending patent applications at 18 months from the date of filing (with limited exceptions), which the rest of the world was already doing. The new law also endeavored to fix shortcomings, such as a patent term extension in the event of patent issuance delay caused by the USPTO.

Today's law, the *America Invents Act of 2012* (AIA), was a sea change. What remained of the 1952 Act that was still afloat, was torpedoed by the AIA into a shipwreck. The first person to invent system was tossed aside in favor of a first person to file system, bringing U.S. patent law into compliance with the patent laws of foreign nations. Now it makes no difference who invented first, all that matters is who filed the patent application first—a harsh rule, but one that eliminates the insanely complex *interference* process. One of the additional aspects, unwelcomed by individual inventors but gladly welcomed by accused infringers as a good alternative to being sued for patent infringement in U.S. Federal Courts, is a post grant validity review process, which potentially places a patent in jeopardy of invalidation at the USPTO Patent Trial & Appeal Board (an Administrative Law Court within the USPTO) if a third party files an *opposition*.

I add one caveat relating to design patents. Unlike utility patents, design patents under the AIA remain *unpublished* until issued and enjoy a term of 15 years measured from the *issue date*. The practice of submarine design patents remains alive and well.

* * *

In my practice, I routinely assist both American and international inventors, and a plethora of authors, designers, artists and creators. From this perspective, the international intellectual property law system has evolved on two levels: on the one hand toward the simplification of issues, and on the other toward adoption of worldwide consistency.

The protection of your inventions, writings, artistic creations, trade names, trade dress and trade secrets are well defined in the law, albeit a lawyer is necessarily your most trusted counselor for keeping you out of trouble and maximizing your wealth.

Peter's handbook is *the* essential inventor guide that will enable YOU to make smart decisions, stay ahead of the curve, advantageously handle people (yes, "people" includes lawyers), and come out on top.

Joseph P. Carrier, Esq.
Managing Partner
Carrier, Shende and Associates, P.C., *Intellectual Property Attorneys*
Novi, Michigan

PROLOGUE

Ideas, Intellectual Property and Money

In order to parley your idea into money, that idea must be, or become, *all* of the following:

- Valuable;
- Intellectual Property; and
- Yours.

Valuable Ideas

It's clear that if something is worthless, no one will pay for it; and vice versa, if something has worth, people will pay for it. But is it really so clear?

Value is in the eye of the beholder, and as the saying goes, "One man's junk is another man's treasure." Here looms a danger for the aspiring inventor: never be deluded into thinking there is a market for an idea if just the right buyer can be found. Value declines exponentially in relation to the lack of potential buyers. Yes, there may be a small group of people who would pay handsomely for your idea, but even with the far reaching eyes of the internet, the overwhelming odds are that you will find yourself a Don Quixote on a quest for the *impossible dream*. Keep in mind the most valuable ideas are ones that satisfy a need or want that is shared by a large number of people.

Succinctly put, an idea is a thought, a concept, an inspiration that is not fleshed out in implementing detail—in other words, you don't know yet how to make and use it. Whereas, an invention transcends a mere idea in that it constitutes a completed knowledge set in which the inventor knows how to make and use it.

Ideas have little to no worth, unless you have a job that calls for you to be an "idea person," or, if you are lucky enough to find someone who is willing to pay a nominal "finder's fee" for it—with emphasis on the word "nominal" (as in "miniscule"). Why? Because what makes an idea valuable is the concrete completeness that engulfs it when it has been fashioned into an invention. Yes, the idea remains the heart and soul of the invention, but the value resides in the know-how necessary to enable making and using it.

Intellectual Property

Knowledge is legally protectable, rendering it potentially valuable, if it comes under at least one of the following forms of *Intellectual Property*:

- Patent;
- Copyright;
- Trademark; and
- Trade Secret.

While these may seem at first glance to have overlapping grey zones, to those trained in the law they are each starkly differentiated in black and white. To this end, the law protects each of these in a unique manner.

Patents are the domain of the United States Patent & Trademark Office, (USPTO) which issues patents according to laws and rules of practice. Patents protect inventions, not ideas, because the application for a patent must specify how to make and use.

Copyrights are the domain of the United States Copyright Office, which issues copyrights according to laws and rules of practice. Copyrights protect artistic expressions that have been affixed (completed in some tangible form). This could be the recording of a song, the filming of a movie, the creation of an artwork or the typing of a story. Copyrights protect expressions of ideas, not the ideas, themselves.

Trademarks are administered by the USPTO, as well as the states. The reason for this is that the U.S. Constitution specifically provides for patents and copyrights, but is silent regarding trademarks, a commercial concept that arose later on. While not expressly empowered in the Constitution, the USPTO regulates trademarks nationally under the Interstate Commerce Clause of the Constitution, meaning interstate trade must be involved. For trade within a state (intrastate), that state is empowered to regulate its intrastate trademarks. Trademarks protect indicators of the origin of goods or services, as identified by a name, mark, or other identifiable criteria (trade dress).

Trade secrets are valuable secret information (know-how). Protection of trade secrets is available through the various states (and the federal government under the Commercial Espionage Act of 1996).

Trade secret protection has no time limit so long as the information remains secret. Once the information becomes public, protection is lost. If the loss was by nefarious means, compensation may be available.

Ownership

An idea that you originate and develop into an invention all by yourself is yours. But is that always true?

Inventors, beware: someone who originates and develops independently of you and files a patent application before you file will own the patent, not you.

Similarly, you will not prevail in a copyright or trademark application if someone has already created your expression or used your mark. And, independent origination is *always* a destroyer of trade secret rights.

Added to this mix is the frequent situation when an idea is created by one person, but the invention is thereafter created with the assistance of others. This may introduce a "co-inventor" aspect in which each contributor to the invention must be named as an inventor on a patent application. Copyrights have a nuance called a "work for hire," where the hired writer is not named as an author. Yet another issue arises when your intellectual property is created during employment. This can be particularly vexing for engineers.

Turning Ideas into Money

The progression to making money from an idea is this:

- a raw idea is thought about until it becomes a good idea;
- this good idea is then fleshed-out into an invention by further thinking, research, etc.;
- the invention is then improved by prototyping, experimenting, etc. into a perfected invention;
- the perfected invention is then translated into a patent application which issues as a patent; and finally,
- the perfected invention is realized into a product optimally having a wide demand under protection of the issued patent.

* * *

Sometimes the realization of your invention into money is through a sale, where a transaction results in a sum paid for ownership of the invention; sometimes this is through a license, where a transaction specifies royalty payments based upon sales. There are many variations on this theme, some of which may additionally include the inventor being paid for consulting services.

While typical inventors do not have the wherewithal to market a product on their own, and as such, must seek existing industry to perform this all too important chore for them, there are exceptions. These exceptional individuals are uniquely poised to develop a marketable product, package it and sell it commercially or at retail.

> *The key to unlock riches from an idea is to configure your idea into an invention of maximum value.*

* * *

To bring this book to life, I will often refer to my personal experience regarding my own invention, the "Thawometer" (a.k.a. "Freezer Thaw Indicator"), which matured into U.S. Patent 9,410,730.

* * *

PART I

INVENTING

Chapter 1

Catching an Idea

Ideas are bit like viruses: they're all over the place, but you can't see them. Indeed, catching a cold is not so different from catching an idea. You're not sure you've got it until the symptoms become undeniable. In the case of catching an idea, the primary symptom is a mental grasp of something new, accompanied frequently by feelings of superiority, accomplishment, confidence, and happiness.

An idea can come at any time, you just have to catch it.

> *What is common to the catching of all ideas is an awareness of something new, however vague its implementation may be at the time.*

1. Dreams

While I was out of town one summer, there was a power outage. Though the power was back on when I got home and everything was frozen in the freezer section of my refrigerator, I wondered to what extent the food had thawed out. Was it okay to eat? I decided to throw everything out because even if it was frozen and looked to be okay, I had no idea as to the depth of the thaw. A minor amount of thaw might be okay, but a major amount of thaw would not be. There was simply no way for me to tell.

That got me to thinking whether there might be some reasonable solution to this problem.

Ideas came and went, but not a single one was practical. "Practical" for me meant a solution that was reliable, simple, cheap and easy to use. So after some time of thinking about it without making any progress, I let the quest for an idea disappear into the back of my mind and went on with other pursuits.

Then one night I went to sleep as usual, freezer thaw concerns being distantly out of my mind. I woke up in the middle of the night with a clear understanding of what I was to later call, the "Thaw-ometer." The dream-land vision vividly burned into my brain was for a cylindrical container half filled with water. In the middle was a screen bisecting the cylinder. I imagined a sequence in which if the liquid at the bottom was frozen in the freezer and then the container was flipped, the ice would be held up at the top by the screen. Now, if the power went out and the freezer warmed, then the ice would melt, collecting at the bottom of the container. When the power came back on, the water at the bottom would freeze. The amount of ice at the bottom would tell the story of how bad the thaw episode was. "Wow!" I thought. I couldn't sleep, so I got up.

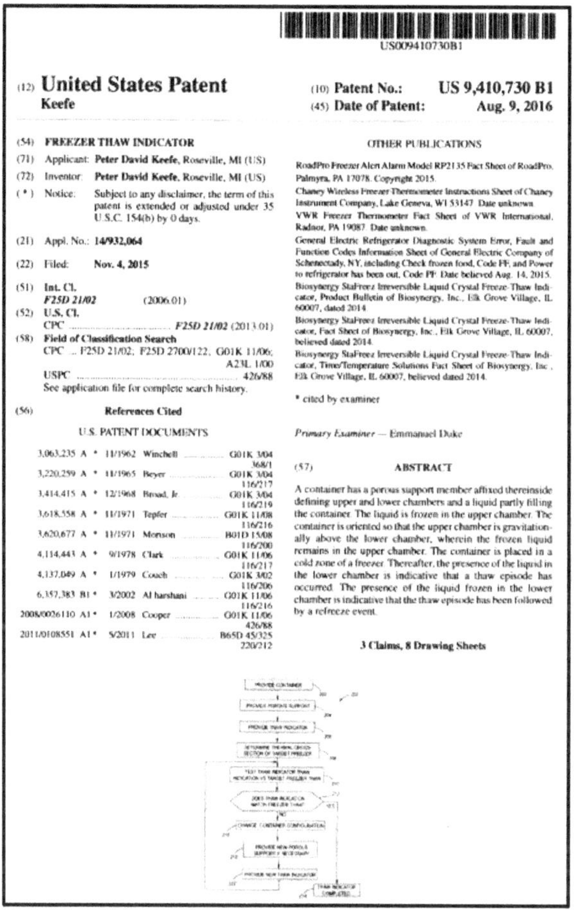
US009410730B1

(12) **United States Patent**
Keefe

(10) **Patent No.: US 9,410,730 B1**
(45) **Date of Patent: Aug. 9, 2016**

(54) **FREEZER THAW INDICATOR**

(71) Applicant: **Peter David Keefe**, Roseville, MI (US)

(72) Inventor: **Peter David Keefe**, Roseville, MI (US)

(*) Notice: Subject to any disclaimer, the term of this patent is extended or adjusted under 35 U.S.C. 154(b) by 0 days.

(21) Appl. No.: **14/932,064**

(22) Filed: **Nov. 4, 2015**

(51) **Int. Cl.**
F25D 21/02 (2006.01)

(52) **U.S. Cl.**
CPC ***F25D 21/02*** (2013.01)

(58) **Field of Classification Search**
CPC ... F25D 21/02; F25D 2700/122; G01K 11/06; A23L 1/00
USPC 426/88
See application file for complete search history.

(56) **References Cited**

U.S. PATENT DOCUMENTS

3,063,235 A * 11/1962 Winchell G01K 3/04 368/1
3,220,259 A * 11/1965 Beyer G01K 3/04 116/217
3,414,415 A * 12/1968 Broad, Jr. G01K 3/04 116/219
3,618,558 A * 11/1971 Tepfer G01K 11/08 116/216
3,620,677 A * 11/1971 Morison B01D 15/08 116/200
4,114,443 A * 9/1978 Clark G01K 11/06 116/217
4,137,049 A * 1/1979 Couch G01K 3/02 116/206
6,357,383 B1 * 3/2002 Al harshani G01K 11/06 116/216
2008/0026110 A1 * 1/2008 Cooper G01K 11/06 426/88
2011/0108551 A1 * 5/2011 Lee B65D 45/325 220/212

OTHER PUBLICATIONS

RoadPro Freezer Alert Alarm Model RP2135 Fact Sheet of RoadPro, Palmyra, PA 17078. Copyright 2015.

Chaney Wireless Freezer Thermometer Instructions Sheet of Chaney Instrument Company, Lake Geneva, WI 53147. Date unknown.

VWR Freezer Thermometer Fact Sheet of VWR International, Radnor, PA 19087. Date unknown.

General Electric Refrigerator Diagnostic System Error, Fault and Function Codes Information Sheet of General Electric Company of Schenectady, NY, including Check frozen food, Code FF, and Power to refrigerator has been out, Code PF. Date believed Aug. 14, 2015.

Biosynergy StaFreez Irreversible Liquid Crystal Freeze-Thaw Indicator, Product Bulletin of Biosynergy, Inc., Elk Grove Village, IL 60007, dated 2014.

Biosynergy StaFreez Irreversible Liquid Crystal Freeze-Thaw Indicator, Fact Sheet of Biosynergy, Inc., Elk Grove Village, IL 60007, believed dated 2014.

Biosynergy StaFreez Irreversible Liquid Crystal Freeze-Thaw Indicator, Time/Temperature Solutions Fact Sheet of Biosynergy, Inc., Elk Grove Village, IL 60007, believed dated 2014.

* cited by examiner

Primary Examiner — Emmanuel Duke

(57) **ABSTRACT**

A container has a porous support member affixed thereinside defining upper and lower chambers and a liquid partly filling the container. The liquid is frozen in the upper chamber. The container is oriented so that the upper chamber is gravitationally above the lower chamber, wherein the frozen liquid remains in the upper chamber. The container is placed in a cold zone of a freezer. Thereafter, the presence of the liquid in the lower chamber is indicative that a thaw episode has occurred. The presence of the liquid frozen in the lower chamber is indicative that the thaw episode has been followed by a refreeze event.

3 Claims, 8 Drawing Sheets

Image credit: USPTO.gov database.

If I had gone back to sleep, would I have remembered it?

Keep a pad and paper near your bed to record any ideas sprouting from the nocturnal environment.

2. Problems

Problems come in all sizes. Some you can deal with and some you cannot. It's when you cannot that an idea can sprout out of your frustration. What you need to do is keep in mind that solutions are out there.

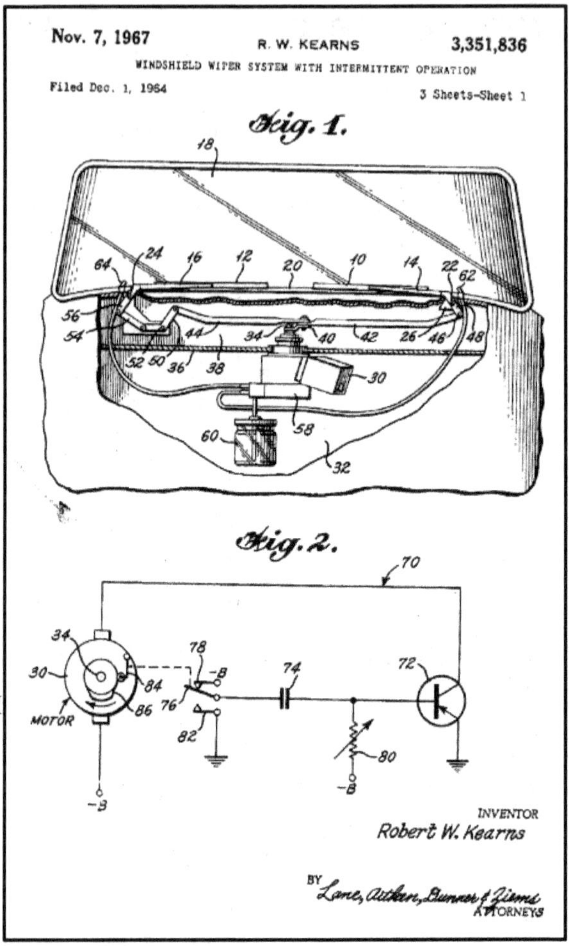

Image credit: USPTO.gov database.

Consider wiper blades wiping a windshield at only two speeds, fast and slow. That's the way it had always been, and for all the automotive engineers in the world, this was just the way it was—perhaps, the way it "should be."

In a drizzle, even with the wipers at slow speed, the wiper blades move across the windshield too frequently for the sparse amount of moisture, resulting in blade squealing. That problem annoyed Robert Kearns. So much so, that he got an idea: intermittent wiper movement. Just how to do that required the Detroit engineer to tinker away. As recounted by Robert's son, Dennis, at a meeting of the Inventors Assoc. of Metro Detroit, no sooner had he perfected the device, he installed it on his car and then drove to the main gate of the Ford Rouge Complex. After some interaction with guards and engineers, he was invited to drive inside. Ford was anxious to be the first manufacturer to offer intermittent windshield wipers, and indeed it was with the 1969 Thunderbird. Kearns had meanwhile filed for a patent. But he didn't want a royalty, he wanted Ford to set him up in business. This conflict resulted in litigation, eventually affecting virtually every car manufacturer in the world at that time.

When something annoys you, smile. An idea is in the offing.

3. Epiphanies

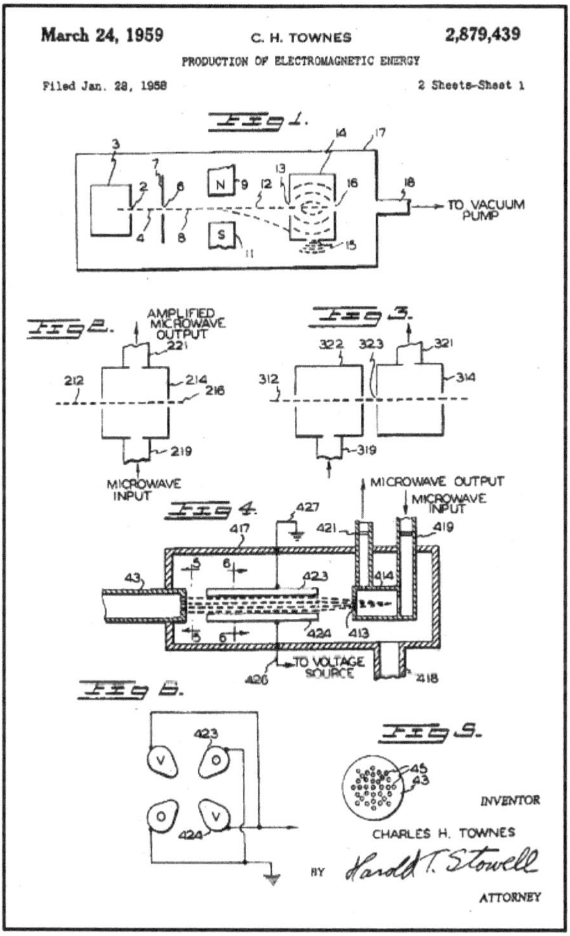

Image credit: USPTO.gov database.

Also referred to as a "flash of genius," epiphanies are characterized by an unexpected mental connection that suddenly erupts without a trigger into a transcendent awareness of an idea. Whereas an idea arising from a dream or a problem is usually an improvement, an idea arising from an epiphany is quite likely to be pioneering. That is, a completely new idea having no derivation from anything else.

Nobel laureate Charles Townes is known as the father of the laser, which he co-invented with fellow Nobel laureate Arthur Schalow when at Bell Labs (first called the "optical maser"). But his true claim to fame was his earlier invention of "microwave amplification by stimulated emission," the maser. While he didn't have that name in mind when he filed his patent application, the idea for the maser came to him in an epiphany.

As recounted by Townes,[1] he wanted to create wave resonance at very high frequencies of light (microwaves), but it seemed impossible. "Then I suddenly recognized the possibility. … I realized there was a way of getting amplification out of molecules and atoms, by avoiding thermodynamic equilibrium. … On the back of an envelope I quickly worked out a possible way of obtaining an oscillator at high frequency."

I spoke with Charles Townes at the yearly physics conference *Physics of Quantum Electronics* in Snowbird, Utah.[2] Between our plenary talks on January 4, 2006, I asked him if he ever made any money on his maser and laser patents. He laughed, saying, "When your invention is pioneering, nobody knows how to seriously use it until after the patent's expired."

> *Try what you will, hypnosis, soul searching, getting a Ph.D., nothing you can do will induce an epiphany. It is, as Townes put it, "a gift from God."*

* * *

Chapter 2

Idea to Invention

Once you've got an idea, the first thing you need to do is decide if it is any good. This may seem obvious, but there's usually some emotion involved that can fog your vision. No one should throw away a good idea, but that just begs the question, "What is a good idea?" You're probably expecting me to give you a subjective answer, but I'm going to give you a definitive answer, "It's a good idea if it has value."

Value comes in different flavors: money, fame, altruism, self-satisfaction. But none of those flavors will be tasted until the idea is

---

[1] *Making Waves* by Charles H. Townes, AIP Press, Woodbury, NY, ISBN 1-56396-334.5, pg. 18.

[2] This wonderful conference, the brainchild of Marlin O. Scully of Texas A&M, attracts physicists the world over. Townes' talk was entitled "Early Non-linear Optics and Beyond," the Author's was entitled "Intellectual Property for Scientists."

transformed into an invention. Think of it as you using seasonings and cooking techniques to transform raw food into a delicious meal. If you're a cook, you'll transform your idea into a passably edible invention. But if you're a chef, then you'll have yourself a ravenously delicious invention. Yes, it's really just like that.

> *Raw ideas need culinary artistry to turn them into savory inventions.*

The first thing you should do is write down your idea, or otherwise affix it in some tangible form, as for example using a word processor on your computer. Most of the time an idea can only be fully expressed in terms of drawings. So you'll need not only to write a description of your idea, but include one or more drawings that you make reference to in your write-up. At this stage of the game, the description is likely to be sketchy and the drawings crude. That's completely okay. In fact, it's the usual situation that most inventors find themselves.

Now, read it over and think about it. Does it make sense? Are there aspects you left out? Is there a better way to do it? Does the write-up shout at you that the idea is dumb, ho-hum or ingenious?

> *Whatever your thoughts, sleep on it. The mind has surprising ways of figuring things out during a deep sleep.*

Assuming you've decided the idea is a good one, then it's time to make it into an invention. Not all ideas can become inventions. Some are beyond technology, some are beyond your talents and some are just plain too "out there."

The process of converting an idea into an invention entails figuring out how to make and use. In essence, it is the transmogrification of something worthless into something valuable. This can be easy, or it can be hard. The important thing is to complete the process from idea to invention.

Consider a plumber who, while repairing a homeowner's faucet, gets an idea for a washerless single handle faucet. With a deep grasp of the mechanics, it will take but little effort for Joe to figure out how to make and use it. By the time Joe's shift is over, he'll have processed in his head the path from raw idea to invention. He'll be thinking on his drive home which manufacturer would most likely buy it, fully confident of his mastery of how to make and use.

Consider now the case of a nurse who is driving in the mountains of West Virginia, frequently wondering what her altitude is. With no aforethought, the idea of an altimeter in her car suddenly jumps into Rita's mind. In view she knows medical devices, but has no idea how an altimeter works, the job to take her idea to an invention will require Rita to not only learn how altimeters work, but how one could be configured to fit into an automotive dashboard.

> *If your idea is in a subject you already know, then your path is as easy as getting a drink at the kitchen faucet. But if not, you've got mountains to climb.*

1. What is a good idea?

All good ideas have in common:

- Feasibility;
- Potential; and
- Uniqueness.

To consider this in some detail, let's consider Rita's idea for a car altimeter.

As she's driving, she has to concentrate on the road. But she's also going to steal, as often as possible, views of the many vistas that the mighty Allegheny Mountains offer. If the idea really struck her imagination, then she'll easily remember the idea, despite the mental distractions, even as she arrives at her parent's home for Christmas.

Rita embarks on her new avocation of inventor when she jots down the idea on some scrap paper while contemplating an altimeter on the dashboard of her Jeep. At this point, she has no clue as to whether her idea is any good, simply for the reason that she has no inkling as to whether or not her idea is feasible.

After saying good night to her mom and dad, Rita jumps onto her portable computer and Googles "altimeters." A pretty quick study, she quickly apprehends that altimeters are very well known and simply sense air pressure to indicate altitude.

Rita next Googles whether any car has an altimeter. She finds out that in all probability not a single car manufacturer offers it. She smiles thinking a car dashboard altimeter is feasible, has potential to make money, and is uniquely hers.

However, her smile fades as she learns after a deeper dive into the workings of altimeters that the local barometric pressure changes with the weather, typically lower in stormy skies and higher in clear skies. This makes her wonder whether or not a car altimeter is commercially feasible in that their variability in the altitude reading will adversely affect its potential for use by a car manufacturer.

Rita, undaunted, does some more Googling, finding out that GPS devices calculate altitude from data transmitted from the constellation of GPS satellites. Her face now sports a wry smile because she just took her raw idea and made it into a good idea: A motor vehicle dashboard GPS navigation unit having display of vehicle altitude.

> *You'll know you have a worthy idea because it stays with you. But you'll only know if it's a good idea after some soul searching.*

2. What is an invention?

To have an invention, you must comprehend how to:

- Make; and
- Use.

Let's continue with Rita's story to illustrate.

Now back at her home in Michigan, Rita begins to seriously research her idea. Googling has led her to conclude that navigation systems built into the dashboards of many cars are probably capable of indicating altitude.

"Probably" is the operative word here, for at this point she has no idea how to configure one of those navigation systems to calculate altitude from the incoming satellite data and then to display altitude on the screen. She has hit a wall.

But walls can be torn down, and Rita is determined to do just that. She has a friend whose sister, Abby, is an electrical engineer at General Motors.

When first meeting with Abby, Rita, who is a smart cookie, has Abby swear to secrecy by signing a non-disclosure agreement form she bought at an office supply store. Rita then tells Abby all she knows of her idea while showing her a write-up.

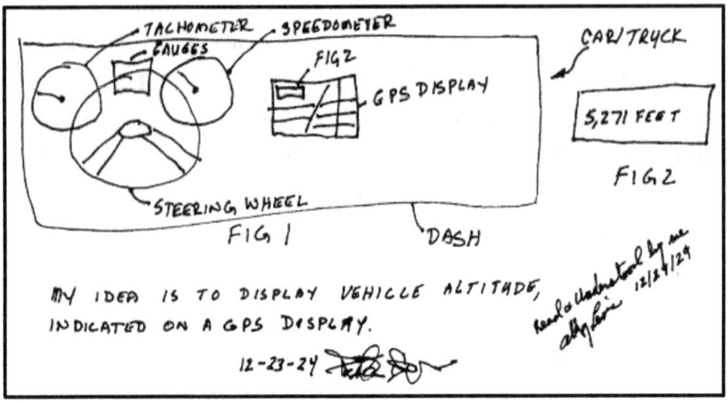

She asks Abby to sign her disclosure and to write "Read and understood by me" where she signed and dated it. This is the "old" way of doing things, when the first to invent would win the patent. Under the current patent law, the first to file wins the patent, so now the words are superfluous—but still, it serves to prove invention. Rita is careful not to encourage, in fact she discourages, Abby from offering a suggestion: she wants the invention to be hers alone at this stage of the process. Abby gets excited, saying she'll figure it out.

A month later, Abby meets with Rita. She shows Rita a circuit diagram with a circle showing where she modified a conventional automotive navigation system circuit to calculate and provide an output signal to the display. She also shows Rita a drawing of a navigation system display indicating the calculated altitude.

Now co-inventors, the ladies have a deep understanding of how to make and use an altimeter for a car dashboard: they have an invention.

If you know how to make and use, then you have an invention. You do not need to make a model. All you need is an ability to communicate clearly the configurational and operational details of your invention.

* * *

Let's next discuss how this applies to my development of the Thawometer.

While Rita needed Abby because of the high-tech nature of her invention, I conceptualized the Thawometer as a simply constructed and operated mechanical device. As soon as I awoke with the idea in mind, the invention, itself, had simultaneously stepped out of my dream world and into my conscious world.

The day after I got the idea, I thought about various configurations that would be easiest for a homeowner to use. Thinking of the cylinder as elongated relative to its cross-section, I considered placing a hook at each end to allow it to be hung from either end on freezer shelves that are constructed of closely spaced parallel rods. For panel shelves, I considered a squat cylinder without hooks, the larger cross-section in relation to the length of the cylinder assured either end could be placed on the shelf without tipping, an issue in view the ice at the top half would create a top heavy situation. This issue of top heaviness was overcome with either of the configurations.

As it turns out, I had an invention, but not a "perfected invention." Why? Though I had solved the cylinder tip over problem, I was oblivious to a more sinister problem: the operational suitability of the mid-section screen.

* * *

Chapter 3

Searching

The time-tested method to know whether or not your invention is yours, and yours alone, is a prior art search. Sometimes this is referred to as a patent search or a novelty search. While an investigation of closely related patent documents certainly is on the to-do list, that list also must include subject matter other than patents. I used the term "subject matter" on purpose, because the prior art can be all kinds of stuff, including documents, such as books, magazines and web pages, as well as things, such as products on the market.

1. Patent Searching

While a patent search is not required before filing a patent application, nor to market an invention, it's a good idea to have some command of the landscape before you traverse it.

Preliminary Patent Search

A so-called "preliminary patent search" is just that: a fast, simple and painless search of U.S. patent documents to get an idea of what's out there. To perform the search quickly, everything is done online. To keep it simple, the search is limited to U.S. patent documents (patents and published patent applications). It's painless because you take advantage of existing search engines designed for this purpose. The two best online search engines are independently provided by the USPTO and Google.

a) Google

The easiest and fastest search engine for novice inventors is undoubtedly Google Patents at https://patents.google.com. The search rules are simple. In addition, Google Patents allows for your search to include international patent documents and non-patent literature, via Google's "Google Scholar" search feature. Google Patents also allows "CPC classification symbol" searching, discussed below.

An example of a Google Patents search comes courtesy of a joke recently texted to me by my nephew, Chris, of a guy breathing in sewer gas through a toilet bowl to avoid breathing smoke in a hotel fire, supposedly patented in 1981.

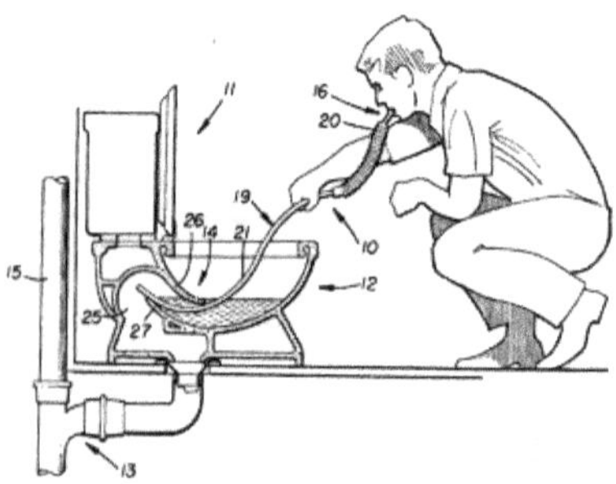

Was this really a joke? I went to Google Patents, where I typed into the text box:

Toilet breathe tube 1981

I did not check the box "Include non-patent literature (Google Scholar)," as this was unnecessary. I immediately got a hit (even if the patent date was actually 1982): U.S. Patent 4,320,756. Indeed, this figure formed part of the drawing on the face page of the patent.

Using Google Patents is just that easy for a preliminary patent search. Let your patent attorney do the heavy lifting associated with a professional patent search.

b) USPTO

For those who enjoy the art of searching, the USPTO website

search engine is for you. If you find reading this section tedious, just rely on Google Patents and skip to the heading: 2. Size-up the Marketplace.

The homepage of the USPTO website is located at https://www.USPTO.gov. Internet addresses change over time, but for the life of the internet, USPTO.gov has been its timeless address. However, the search page address has changed from time to time. At the time of publication of this handbook, the USPTO search page has this internet address: https://ppubs.uspto.gov/pubwebapp/static/pages/landing.html. To get there another way, go to the search box at the USPTO.gov entry page and type in "patent search." If you type in only "search" the website ignores you. From the response list, choose "Quick Search" or a similar term. This will take you to the Patent Public Search page. Now, since we are doing a preliminary patent search, click on "Basic Search."

You are not doing a patent document number search, so go to the "Basic Search" area. You are able to search using one or two words.

At the left, there is a search box which limits what portion of the patent document is to be searched, as for example an inventor's name. At this point, leave the box with its default "Everything," meaning the search will be conducted covering everything written in the documents. Drawings are not searchable.

At the right are the query boxes. These are limited to one word each, not one term. In the upper box, type in a word relevant to your idea/invention. While it might be possible to just go with a single word, most searches can be better performed with a second word. Type in a second word in the lower box.

In the first go-round, enter the two words that best describe your invention in its broadest sense. Be a bit creative (inventive) with what words you choose to use. If nothing comes back, it is extraordinary. Try a mix of other words; if nothing comes back, then more likely than not an angel just received his wings … but remember, this was only a preliminary patent search: it potentially missed documents a professional patent searcher might find and it ignored foreign patent documents, as well as other documents and products on, or previously on, the market.

By way of example, let's return to Rita's automotive altimeter idea. If her first inclination would be to type "automotive" and "altimeter," she would get some 2,000 returns. Going down the list of patent titles, some seem completely irrelevant. This result is not helpful; in fact it is so unhelpful that she decides to go for the "Advanced Search" option.

In Advanced Search, the searcher is in far better command—and that translates into both a more enjoyable and efficient searching process. Conveniently, there are three boxes on the screen, an upper left, a lower left and a right. The upper left box is where search queries are entered, the lower left box displays the search result listing, and the box on the right shows the listing item highlighted.

Rita firstly enters "automotive AND altimeter." Over 3,000 returns greet her. She tries a number of other queries. None of them get her anywhere. Finally, she tries, "dashboard AND "altitude indicator." Happily, she gets 38 returns. This is an easily manageable listing. She goes through each by highlighting the document number, then reading the text that appears in the right window.

She reviews document 20180066941 (a U.S. patent application publication, meaning it may or may not now be a patent, but during its pendency it has been published by the USPTO). The search words Rita used will be highlighted in the text, allowing her to quickly see if this patent document has revealed her invention. Scrolling down, at paragraph [0046] she sees the word "dashboard" highlighted. She reads the text surrounding it and recognizes it references a monitor that is, indeed, dash mounted. She blows this off, as most cars have dashboard mounted displays these days.

She scrolls down further. At paragraph [0156] she sees the words "altitude indicator" highlighted. She freaks, but quickly catches her breath.

She looks carefully and sees there's a modifier to the word "altitude," the word "relative." She settles down, thinking maybe this is something else, used for another purpose than knowing how high up a mountain road is.

Rita reads through the paragraphs on either side of [0156].

> *"[0154] FIG. 18 is an explanatory view of an output image of the sixth exemplary embodiment.*
> *[0155] The viewpoint image Glb is displayed as a background image on an output image Gout21, and the vehicle model image 40M for displaying a state (inclined state) of the vehicle 40 is displayed*

> *in a state of being inclined with respect to the horizontal surface Gr in front of the viewpoint image Glb which is the background image.*
> *[0156] A relative altitude indicator AIND for visually displaying an actual relative altitude of the vehicle 40 is displayed on the left part of the output image Gout21, and a vehicle icon 401 is displayed at a position corresponding to the actual relative altitude of the vehicle 40.*
> *[0157] Therefore, the user may visually and easily recognize the current relative altitude (e.g., a difference in uphill road altitude) of the own [sic] vehicle 40 with respect to the reference altitude."*

Rita contemplates, "Hey, I'm not doing that. This guy's doing something with off-roading." She decides she needs to look at the drawings. To do that, Rita has to go back to Basic Search and type in the patent document number. Now she's looking at the entire document as a pdf, which she can print or save if she wishes.

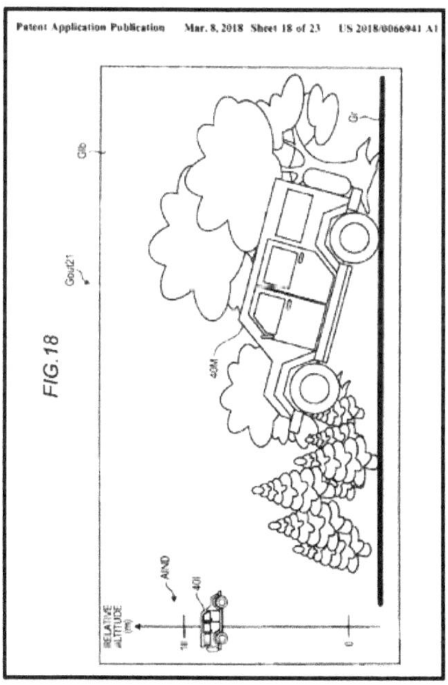

Image credit: USPTO.gov database.

She looks through the figures, noting the vehicle is jeep-like, doing daring off-road maneuvers. Rita stares at all important Figure 18.

She notes that the motor vehicle seems to be strangely tilted, with the front end off the ground. But what interests her more is the altitude displayed in the bottom, or left, of the figure. She notes that the "0" indication is at neither of the front or rear wheels. In any event, a representation of the vehicle appears on a vertical line above the "0" at a height below, but close to, "10." Near the arrow of the vertical line are the words "RELATIVE ALTITUDE (m)." She thinks, "Well, okay, the vehicle is at about 8 meters above some reference height." She then thinks some more, reading again paragraph [0157]; she exclaims, "Wait a minute, this thing is indicating local changes in road height, not absolute height above sea level like I'm doing. Hooray!" Her excitement will face a reality check when it comes time to patent her invention. For now, her sails are billowing, pushing her forward.

> *Definitely perform a preliminary patent search to avoid a walk down Primrose Path. Google Patents is my recommendation for independent inventors because it is so easy to use and comprehensive in its search results. Leave the patent search heavy lifting to your patent attorney.*

Professional Patent Search

While it is possible for inventors to perform a patent search of professional quality, it is an impractical exercise in terms of time and likelihood of missing one or more key documents. The biggest pitfall is for an inventor to become preoccupied with searching. I have encountered a number of inventors, mostly novices, who have devoted a year or more to their search rather than to invention improvement and filing of a patent application, for which, as I mentioned, a search is not required. Maybe a root cause is a fear of success, but I think the true cause is obsession.

> *As soon as you get an idea, the cards have already been shuffled and dealt. All inventors hope they're holding a winning hand. Just remember, another person holding a lesser hand can beat you to the Patent Office.*

Professional patent searchers may start with the Advanced Search, carefully examining the returned patent documents for how close their disclosure is to your invention, what is termed "relevance." They will look with particular attention at the faces of the most relevant patent documents. What they are looking for is the "classification" symbols (an arrangement of letters and numbers) assigned to that patent document. Another way a professional searcher will arrive at the most relevant classification symbols is to consult the Classification Resources page of USPTO.gov.

The USPTO developed its own patent classification code system, but so did other patent offices. In order to harmonize the classification codes assigned to patent documents, the USPTO and the European Patent Office developed the Cooperative Patent Classification (CPC) symbols scheme; it was adopted by the USPTO in 2015 and is retroactively applicable to earlier patent documents. The USPTO patents classification webpage is found at https://www.uspto.gov/web/patents/classification/.

The idea is simply this: if a relevant patent document has one or more CPC symbols assigned to it, then a searcher could, in theory, find all the relevant patent documents by an online search of those CPC symbols.

The classification system incorporates "classes" and "subclasses." The classes represent a large grouping, such as "hand tools," whereas the subclasses are much more specific, such as "screwdrivers," which could be subclassed further as "straight tip screw drivers" and "Phillips tip screw drivers."

For example, if your invention was for perforated discs for soil working by a tractor drawn tiller, you would search the CPC scheme for "soil working," obtaining CPC Class A01B. Going down the list of the scheme subclasses, you'll arrive at CPC Subclasses: "A01B 5/00 Ploughs with rolling non-driven tools, e.g. discs (with rotary driven tools A01B 9/00)," as well as "A01B 9/00 Ploughs with rotary driven tools (tilling implements with rotary driven tools A01B 33/00)." Thus, the searcher would search online for patent documents in CPC Class/Subclass: A01B 5/00, A01B 9/00 and A01B 33/00.

Let's now see how CPC symbols apply to Rita's patent document search. She uses patent application publication 20180066941 for her starting point.

The CPC classification system allows searchers to find relevant prior art references by reviewing all the patents assigned the same CPC symbols as that of a patent document closely related to the invention being searched.

The first page, or "face," contains a treasure-trove of information

(19) **United States**
(12) **Patent Application Publication** (10) **Pub. No.: US 2018/0066941 A1**
KUBOTA et al. (43) **Pub. Date: Mar. 8, 2018**

(54) **IMAGE PROCESSING SYSTEM FOR VEHICLE**

(71) Applicant: **AISIN SEIKI KABUSHIKI KAISHA**, Kariya-shi (JP)

(72) Inventors: **Naotaka KUBOTA**, Kariya-shi (JP); **Tetsuya MARUOKA**, Okazaki-shi (JP); **Yoji INUI**, Ama-gun (JP); **Takashi HIRAMAKI**, Nagoya-shi (JP); **Osamu KIMURA**, Nagoya-shi (JP); **Itsuko OHASHI**, Nagoya-shi (JP)

(73) Assignee: **AISIN SEIKI KABUSHIKI KAISHA**, Kariya-shi (JP)

(21) Appl. No.: **15/614,783**

(22) Filed: **Jun. 6, 2017**

(30) **Foreign Application Priority Data**

Sep. 8, 2016 (JP) 2016-175890

Publication Classification

(51) **Int. Cl.**
G01C 9/04 (2006.01)
G06T 17/05 (2006.01)

(52) **U.S. Cl.**
CPC *G01C 9/04* (2013.01); *G06T 17/05* (2013.01)

(57) **ABSTRACT**

An image processing system for a vehicle includes: a viewpoint image generating unit that generates a viewpoint image viewed from a predetermined virtual viewpoint when assumed that a surrounding image corresponding to surrounding image data is projected on a virtual projection plane whose arrangement position has been set in advance, based on inclination information corresponding to an inclination of the vehicle and the surrounding image data obtained by capturing an image of a periphery of the vehicle; and an output image generating unit that generates and outputs output image data in order to cause a display device to display an output image in which an own vehicle model image having an inclination according to an inclination of the vehicle corresponding to the inclination information is superimposed on the viewpoint image.

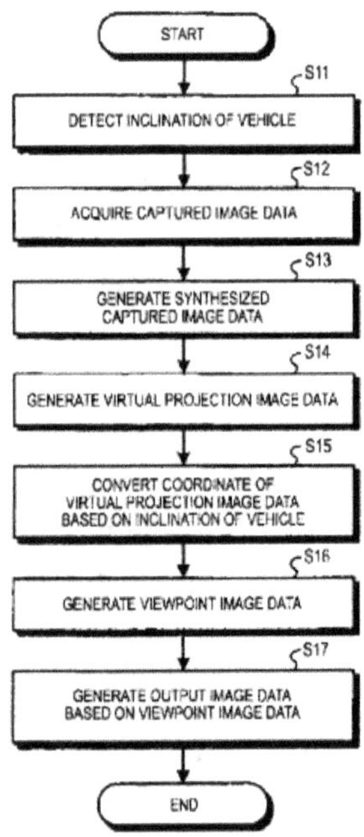

Image credit: USPTO.gov database.

for helping Rita further her search. At the top she sees what she already knew, that this is a U.S. Patent Application Publication. Just below that is the first named inventor Kubota, where "et al." means there are co-inventors. Sole inventors will see only their last name. To the right, is the

Publication Number (the first 4 numbers are the year of publication) and below that is the Publication Date (usually 18 months after filing). On the left is the Title, the Applicant (the corporate owner, who is also the assignee), a list of the co-inventors, the Application Number, date of filing of the patent application, and Priority Data (this application was earlier filed in Japan). On the right are the Classification Symbols. This is followed by an Abstract, which summarizes the gist of the inventive subject matter. Below these is a representative figure selected by the USPTO Examiner to indicate, at a glance, the inventive subject matter.

The arrangement of the face data can differ among various patent application publications. As for patents, a listing of prior art references considered by the Examiner will be listed (those found by the Examiner and those cited by the Applicant under "Duty of Disclosure."

For Rita's purposes just now, she takes note of the CPC symbols on the face. The bold numbers are the CPC symbols, whereas the parenthetic numbers refer to the U.S. Classification Numbers (rumored to soon go the way of the dinosaurs) for purposes of cross-referencing. She goes to the USPTO.gov "Lookup Symbol" page (see the QR code on page 35). She enters the classes, finding G01C applies to "Measuring distances, levels or bearings; Surveying; Navigation; Gyroscopic instruments; Photogrammetry or Video-grammetry," and G06T applies to "Image data processing or Generation, in general."

Rita further learns that G01C 9/04 refers to "Measuring Inclination, e.g. by clinometers, by levels," at subclass 9/00, and specifically at subclass 9/04 "Transmission means between sensing element and final indicator for giving an enlarged reading." She also learns, using the Lookup Symbol page, G06T 17/05 refers to "Three dimensional [3D] modeling, e.g. data description of 3D objects at subclass 17/00, and specifically at subclass 17/05 'Geographic models'."

To perform her CPC search, she returns to the Advanced Search page and enters "G01C9/04.cpc." without the quotes. She receives 142 results. She then looks at them on the viewer. Next she enters the search query "G06T17/05.cpc." again without quotes. She receives a daunting 5,413 results. At this point, she gives up and decides to concentrate on perfecting her invention, letting a professional do the search.

> *Not many inventors have time on their hands, so let your patent attorney do the searching beyond the preliminary patent search.*

2. Size-up the Marketplace

Now that the preliminary patent search is out of the way, and there's still some wind billowing your sails, it's advisable to go to the store and/or go online to see what's out there. This is going to be helpful to you in the future when it comes time to market your invention, and we will revisit this in Part III. Here, we're taking on the role of Sherlock Holmes, sleuthing around to see if anybody has beaten you to market. By the way, there are plenty of products out there that were never patented, nor published, anywhere.

In my practice, there was a smart lady who came to see me with an ingenious invention. She owned several cats and was sick and tired of changing the kitty litter. She explained to me a pan system to effortlessly get rid of the clumps, while keeping the "good" litter. Not only was this easy to perform, but it saved kitty litter. She had done a serious preliminary patent search at the local Patent Depository Library (in those days, searching online was unavailable). We discussed the idea from A to Z, and I was onboard with going ahead to file a patent application. A few days later she burst into my office holding back tears. Her invention was on the market at a local pet supplies store. That put the kibosh on the whole project. She saved having to pay any and all patent processing costs, but her deep disappointment far outweighed any thought that she had avoided her walk down Primrose Path. I felt her pain.

> *Market searching is an area of investigation outside the realm of professional patent searchers and patent attorneys; it's up to you to do it.*

3. Look Around for Non-Patent Documents

Most commonly, these will be magazine articles. Popular Mechanics is more likely to describe your bicycle invention than People, so a bit of common sense here saves time.

As a patent attorney who receives a lot of technically oriented magazines, there's been a time or three when I came across an article relevant to a client's invention. You may at first think, "Oh, if you didn't get so many magazines, this would have blissfully been overlooked." But a patent is only as strong as the examination it receives at the Patent Office. Citing the articles to the USPTO rendered each client's patent stronger, not weaker.

To uncover non-patent documents, Patent Examiners use two documents sources: Google Scholar (https://scholar.google.com) and ProQuest (https://ProQuest.com), an offshoot of University Microfilms.

> *If you see something, say something. The USPTO rules of practice require you to disclose information you are aware of that is relevant to the patent examination process.*

* * *

In the case of my Thawometer, I confidently figured no one could invent "so clever" an idea, so a patent search was not worth my time; I'd simply leave the job up to the USPTO. However, as I was to unceremoniously learn courtesy of the USPTO, a preliminary patent search is advisable.

I did, however, conduct a Google search, looking for products suggestive of the Thawometer. I found a number of electronic indicators and cited them in several Information Disclosure Statements, which I'll discuss under that topic. Happily, none of them anticipated the Thawometer. My confidence got an injection of adrenaline.

* * *

Chapter 4

Invention Perfection

It is enough to know how to make and use in order to obtain a patent. But this is the lowest bar—you want to achieve the highest bar, and that means you have an invention that will be both a hit in the marketplace and anticipate others modifying it. The former is imperative in order to make serious money, the latter is essential to prevent others from getting around you with some modification.

> *You have an invention when you can describe how to make and use it; you have a perfected invention when you've optimized it.*

1. Basic and Best Embodiments

An embodiment represents the essential essence of an invention. There may be any number of embodiments associated with a particular invention. An embodiment typically constitutes an operative structure (i.e., a device), matter (i.e., a chemical), or a manipulation of matter (i.e., a method). There is undoubtedly a rainbow of colorations that you can think of that will affect how you see your invention. Each color will shine upon an embodiment of your invention. Some of those views will be impractical, so concentrate on those views which show your invention in its best light.

Whether your invention is a Rube Goldberg contraption or something grabbed from Fibber McGee's closet, it is critical to distill your invention down to its most basic constituents that still enable your invention to work. This constitutes your basic embodiment: the minimal elements necessary to effect the make and use of your invention.

The basic embodiment is almost always not the best embodiment. The best embodiment usually adds some bells and whistles that result in a compellingly great invention. To achieve a best embodiment, elements of the basic embodiment are tweaked. For example, consider how a change of materials, configurations, components, interactions, etc., can be optimized to epitomize an embodiment that will make the most money with the least cost of production, while at the same time exhibiting a widest possible usefulness.

Generally speaking, most inventions will have a spectrum of embodiments, each a colorized version of the basic embodiment, with one being the most radiant, the best embodiment or "best mode" for carrying out the invention.

While the basic embodiment will be claimed to render broadest protection for your invention, the best embodiment, the best mode, is the embodiment that will be described and also claimed in your patent application. Not only is this required by the USPTO, it discloses the most likely embodiment to be introduced into the marketplace.

> *You need to consider different embodiments of your invention. It is essential to know both the basic and best embodiments.*

2. Arriving at a Best Embodiment—Best Mode

Once you have your idea upgraded to an invention, it's probably not too difficult to figure out the minimal aspects that are essential to make and use the invention: the basic embodiment. The best embodiment is another story altogether.

Let's return to Rita's automotive altimeter idea. She had to turn to Abby to make an invention from her idea. In view of that, Abby is probably the one of the two co-inventors who will decide on the basic and best embodiments. But, is there a way that Rita could have figured it all out on her own? The surprising answer is, yes!

One of the greatest friends of inventors is the flow chart. Flow charts constitute a diagram of rectangular and diamond blocks interconnected by flow arrows. The rectangles represent something being performed (a step), and the diamonds represent decisions (yes or no). The blocks are labeled so that the chart in combination with a written description describe how to make and use, taking the idea to invention—provided the blocks are understandable to someone of ordinary skill in the art. Here Rita is in luck, for although it will be hard, if not downright impossible, for her to describe to somebody on the street how to make and use her idea, she only has to make her idea clear to a person of ordinary skill in the GPS, altimeter and automotive arts.

Rita has drawing software on her computer and using it, she creates a flow chart of her invention. Of course, she could have simply drawn the chart by hand. Her patent readings have given her a "bit" of ability to describe her invention.

Rita labels the blocks and adds numbers so when she describes the blocks, the reader knows what she is talking about. She writes:

> *"200 is a flow chart of a GPS altimeter indication for an automotive dashboard. At execution block 202, the operator starts the vehicle. Thereupon, electronics of the vehicle initializes the in dash GPS at execution block 204, including altitude data at block 206. If navigation is not automatically displayed, the operator selects navigation at decision block 208. If the operator declines, the routine goes to execution block 210, where some other information is displayed, as for example audio or cabin HVAC. If the operator selects navigation, or it is automatically displayed, then at execution block 214 navigation information, such as a map, is displayed, including a*

display of vehicle altitude above or below sea level. If navigation was declined at decision block 208, but later selected at decision block 212, then execution block 214 is performed, otherwise the routine returns to execution block 210."

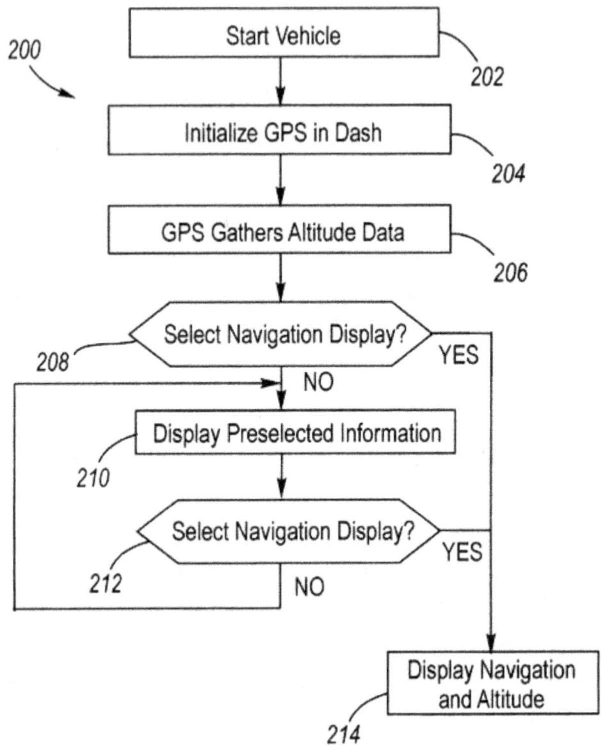

While Rita feels she has figured out her invention, in fact she hasn't. The reason is that while execution block 204 is clearly in the prior art and known to anyone of ordinary skill in the art, her execution blocks 206 and 214 are unique to her invention and she has no clue how to describe the details of carrying them out. Rita needs to teach this. But how?

Rita suddenly remembers patent application publication 20180066941, which revealed a lot of information on how to display a "relative altitude" using a display. Her patent searching has her pretty astute as to what flies. She adds to her description.

"At execution blocks 206 and 214 electronic processing is performed to achieve the indicated

> *result using known technology, as for example as disclosed by patent application publication 20180066941, hereby incorporated herein by reference."*

Rita's patent sophistication derived from her patent searching has introduced her to some magic words, "hereby incorporated herein by reference." Yes, you can use patent documents in your description to describe how something is performed, even though you, yourself, have no idea how to do it!

Your best embodiment will be the one you are happiest with, makes the most sense in terms of the prior art and the marketplace, and commands others to take note of it.

* * *

In the case of my Thawometer, even though the mechanics and physics were quite clear to me, I wasn't sure if it would work reliably. So I did some experimenting. Lucky for me, an issue with the screen suddenly roared to life in my first try.

I obtained a cylinder from a toothbrush travel holder. This was ideal because the cylinder separated into halves at the midpoint and was easy to seal. I plugged the air holes and glued a transverse screen to one of the halves at the midpoint of the holder. I then filled it half way with water and sealed the midpoint. I froze the bottom water, then removed it from the freezer, flipped it, and watched the thaw.

Even as the ice at the top melted, it did not drip to the bottom in defiance of gravity! Why? Because the surface tension of the melted water acted on the screen, retaining all the melt water in the upper half until almost all the ice had melted. At that point gravity overcame the surface tension, and the melt water gushed to the bottom.

In later experiments, I replaced the screen with a "support member" having large openings, and that did the trick. Now, surface tension was powerless, allowing gravity's pull to take any and all of the melt water to the bottom in real time.

I had gone from an invention to a perfected invention.

* * *

Chapter 5

Ownership Issues

Co-Inventors

While most times someone will catch an idea on his/her own, the road to an invention can be paved with a lot of input from other people. Whether these contributions toward the invention constitute one or more of these inputs arising to the level of co-inventorship, also referred to as joint inventorship, is often a murky affair.

The USPTO has long held its definition of inventorship, and this is presented in its Manual of Patent Examining Procedure (MPEP) at Sec. 2109:

> *"The definition for inventorship can be simply stated: The threshold question in determining inventorship is who conceived the invention. Unless a person contributes to the conception of the invention, he is not an inventor. ... A person who shares in the conception of a claimed invention is a joint inventor of that invention. ... one who suggests an idea of a result to be accomplished, rather than the means of accomplishing it, is not an coinventor..."*
>
> *Difficulties arise in separating members of a team effort, where each member of the team has contributed something, into those members that actually contributed to the conception of the invention, such as the physical structure or operative steps, from those members that merely acted under the direction and supervision of the conceivers. ... However, it is not essential for the inventor to be personally involved in carrying out process steps ... where implementation of those steps does not require the exercise of inventive skill. ... [(Such as the case where a] noninventor's work was merely that of a skilled mechanic carrying out the details of a plan devised by*

another.)

Pursuant to 35 U.S.C. 116, "[w]hen an invention is made by two or more persons jointly, they shall apply for patent jointly and each make the required oath, except as otherwise provided in this title. Inventors may apply for a patent jointly even though (1) they did not physically work together or at the same time, (2) each did not make the same type or amount of contribution, or (3) each did not make a contribution to the subject matter of every claim of the patent."

The inventive entity for a particular application is based on some contribution to at least one of the claims made by each of the named joint inventors. ..."

Section 2109.01 offers an interesting aspect of co-inventorship.

"A joint inventor or coinventor need not make a contribution to every claim of a patent; a contribution to one claim is enough."

So now that you've read the definition of inventorship straight from the horse's mouth, let's discuss what the horse had to say in plain English.

1. Conception

A co-inventor is someone who shares conception.

2. Ordinary Skill Versus Inventive Skill

After conception, a co-inventor is someone who contributes to the invention by going beyond "ordinary skill in the art." What this means is that routine knowledge or skill does not cut it. An ordinarily skilled mechanic, electrical engineer or chemist who exercises ordinary skill helping you with your invention does not arise to being a co-inventor.

Let's consider Rita's consultation with Abby. In that Abby did not contribute to conception, if Abby's re-design of the electrical circuit of a GPS navigation display was something any other electrical engineer could do straightforwardly, then Abby is not a co-inventor with Rita. On the other hand, if there were issues involved with the existing circuit that required Abby to solve problems, such as electronic integration issues that she had to get around going beyond ordinary skill, then Abby would be entitled to be named a co-inventor with Rita.

> *To be a co-inventor, you must conceive or solve a problem that routine skill in the art does not provide.*

3. Identifiable Contribution in at Least One Claim

A co-inventor post conception must provide an identifiable inventive solution to a problem that inhibits an idea from becoming an invention. As we shall see in Part II, inventions in patents are defined by a set of claims. If the contribution of the co-inventor is excluded from inclusion within the claimed subject matter of the patent, then that person loses co-inventorship status.

For example, let's say Abby went to her co-worker, George, who added the contribution of an on/off switch to allow a driver to select whether altitude is displayed, and that contribution had some problems to be overcome to make it work. If later, patent prosecution (the examination process in the Patent Office) leads the patent attorney to cancel the only claim that recited the switch, then George has been cancelled, too.

> *A co-inventor's contribution is co-conception, or later on, a contribution beyond ordinary skill that is both identifiable and recited in at least one claim of the patent application.*

To avoid future arguments, co-inventors should sign an agreement of understanding that resolves foreseeable issues.

* * *

Employment

Inventors can run into some very serious troubles when their employer gets wind of their inventive endeavors. While this issue arises most commonly with scientists and engineers whose job classification renders them "hired to invent," it can arise for any employee subject to an employment agreement, industry customs and practices, or situations where the invention was created using employer resources or know-how.

1. Engineers and Scientists

Engineers and scientists are hired by employers to use their expertise to create and perfect aspects of the business. This expertise is the skill necessary to perform their daily duties, being, at minimum, the ordinary (or routine) skill of the art, i.e., for chemical engineers and chemists, the art would be chemistry. Even with regard to management, the employer relies on its scientist/engineer managers to use, at minimum, ordinary skill in the art in the course of their managerial duties.

Companies, however, expect more from their engineers and scientists; they are expected to exceed from time to time the ordinary skill in the art: to invent. While the act of inventing is unpredictable and speculative, this is, nonetheless, an essential expectation of the employment arrangement. Even if there is no signed employment agreement, this is the industry standard practice.

The expectation of company ownership frequently extends beyond patents, including copyrights, trademarks and trade secrets (know-how). I once asked a former schoolmate of mine, who was then the chief patent counsel at one of the Big Three (other than GM), what his company expected to happen if an engineer posted pornography on the internet. He laughed, saying, "That engineer better post a notice of our copyright." That's a funny extreme, but it's not funny when your employer is claiming ownership of your invention. By the way, if you are hired to invent, that invention you got the idea for while on a hunting trip is almost certainly company property!

Engineers and scientists are hired to invent, frequently rendering their employer the owner of their inventions in return for their salary.

When a company claims ownership of your invention, while you will be named the inventor on the patent application, the employer will have you sign an assignment of your ownership rights to the company. You will likely get nothing more than your regular salary because you were hired to invent. Then again, your employment value will have increased and the next salary evaluation should result in a raise (let's hope!).

So, how can you overcome this hired to invent claim of

ownership of your invention by your employer?

This gets tricky, but here's the best approach.

Once your idea has congealed into an invention, coldly assess: is it your invention or the company's? If you invented at work for a work-related invention, it's your employer's—just be cooperative when the time comes to sign the assignment. But, if you invented something unrelated to your employer's business and did not use employer resources, then you can request an exception.

At the earliest stage of development, go to your supervisor and hand him/her your disclosure in an unpolished, but complete, form (I said this was tricky) with a request for the company to grant you full rights to your invention. He/she will then take your request to the appropriate company officials to write you a letter that officially states the company's position on its ownership claim to your invention. If it comes back that the company declines all ownership rights, then you're in the clear to proceed. If it comes back that the company retains its ownership rights, then go see a patent attorney for a best outcome. Keep all interactions businesslike, otherwise you could be considered a disloyal employee, subjecting you to discharge. The company will still claim its ownership rights despite the discharge. Oh, by the way, quitting for the purpose of getting around a company claim of ownership will not work.

> *Go through the unpleasant hassle of a sign-off early on. At the earliest stages of invention development, the road ahead is obscured by costs to patent, uncertainties of the marketplace, and lack of a quality disclosure. If you wait, the further along you are, the more likely an employer will retain its ownership rights.*

<u>2. Regular Employees</u>

The general rule is that a regular employee, someone who was not hired to invent, owns all of the rights to their intellectual property. Exceptions arise on a case by case basis.

If the employer provided an environment opportunistic to the act of invention by the employee and the invention is related to that environment, then it could be possible for the employer to assert a claim of ownership. The claim of company ownership will succeed the more the inventor-employee has interaction with the company in the inventing process. If the invention was derived from an idea happening at work and the development of the idea into an invention utilized company facilities, the company's assertion of ownership will be harder, but not necessarily impossible, to overcome.

If the employer has its employees universally sign an employment agreement that covers inventions made when at work, then that agreement will control.

By way of exemplification, I represented a client who worked for one of the Big Three in Detroit. His job was purely clerical and his time at work was exclusively in an office setting; he was not hired to invent. Frustrated with staple removers not always extracting staples, he got an idea for an improved staple remover that solved the problem. I advised him, in an abundance of caution and prudence, to get a sign-off from his employer, which he received with very little effort. He went on to get a patent and then license it to an office supplies manufacturer.

> *Regular employees can usually escape an employer's assertion of patent ownership.*

3. College Professors

Being hired to teach and/or research and publish, professors are a unique class of employees when it comes to retention of intellectual property rights. University's have rules of operation, referred to as "statutes." These control ownership of intellectual property created by professors during their employment.

Patents are almost always designated in university statutes as the property of the university. While some statutes may leniently allow the professor a royalty, the general rule is a professor is treated as hired to invent.

Copyrights are a very different matter. University statutes almost universally grant to the professor-author the copyright and royalties of his/her literary works.

> *Professors' intellectual property ownership is subject to university statutes.*

* * *

PART II

PATENTING

Chapter 1

Patents Overview

1. What is a patent?

A patent is a document issued to the inventor (or his/her assignee) by the federal government through the U.S. Patent and Trademark Office (USPTO) after performance of an examination by a Patent Examiner of a patent application formally submitted to the USPTO.

- The document grants a monopoly right to the patent owner to exclude others from making, using and selling the invention within the territorial jurisdiction of the United States.
- The monopoly right extends only to the definition of the invention recited in the claims of the patent and is limited to a term of years, whereupon it expires. It cannot be renewed.
- The patent application upon which the patent has issued must be in compliance with laws of the United States and rules of the USPTO, including:
    - a disclosure of the invention which enables a person of ordinary skill in the relevant art who reads the patent to make and use the invention without an undue amount of experimentation; and
    - the claimed subject matter of the invention is both novel and unobvious over the prior art.

No patent right is created by getting an idea, developing it into an invention, and making it into a prototype—a patent only comes about from the formal process of filing a patent application with the USPTO.

In contrast to patents, a copyright is created as soon as the artistic work is affixed (e.g., written down)—it is not necessary to file a copyright application with the Copyright Office, although valuable ancillary rights attend to doing so. With regard to trademarks, ownership comes from use. However, a filing with the USPTO or a state government, like with copyrights, creates valuable ancillary rights. As for trade secrets, they exist so long as they remain secret.

We've all heard of instances of monopolies being broken-up by the federal government because they unfairly restrain free trade in the marketplace. So you may justifiably ask, "Why does the federal government grant a monopoly when it issues a patent?" The rationale is encouragement to invent for the benefit of the people. Article I of the U.S. Constitution establishes the patent monopoly, and in so doing explicitly states, "To promote the Progress of Science and useful Arts." In essence, the monopoly right is a bargain between the federal government and the inventor: in exchange for publicly disclosing the invention, a right of monopoly is granted for a limited time by the federal government to the inventor.

The monopoly right granted under a patent is not absolute. A patent does not grant to the holder the right to make, use and sell the invention, only the right to exclude others from doing so. Laws, ordinances and other prohibitions are not overcome by possession of a patent. Also, if there is an already existing patent with claims covering your invention, e.g., there's an existing patent on chewing gum and your patent is for a new flavor of the chewing gum, then you'll need to wait for that "domineering patent" to expire or cut a deal with the patent owner. Another consideration is "misuse," in which unfair licensing practices could result in invalidation.

> *A patent is a document issued to the patent applicant by the federal government granting a monopolistic right, for a limited time, to exclude others from making, using and selling the claimed invention.*

2. Foreign Patents

As indicated above, the United States government can grant patent rights only to the extent of its territorial jurisdiction. However, there are several international treaties that expand certain rights during the patent application examination process to other territorial jurisdictions around the world.

In order to obtain patent rights in other territorial jurisdictions, a patent application must be filed in the desired territories. This can be done under the "Paris Convention" after filing first with the USPTO, or under the "Patent Cooperation Treaty" designating the USPTO as the receiving office. In any event, the patent laws require you to file first with the USPTO. If your invention has a market or manufacturing uniquely suited to a foreign country, your patent attorney will advise you whether it makes sense to foreign file or not.

> *Foreign filing of patent applications is necessary to get protection outside the USA.*

3. Economic Power of Patents

The overarching reason anyone would go through the effort and expense of obtaining a patent is to make money. Only half of the adage to do something for "fame and fortune" applies to inventing. Forget fame and keep your eyes focused on the almighty dollar.

A patent grants monopolistic rights to exclude others from making, using and selling the patented invention. The ability to stifle competition is the essential value of a patent, but that ability is restricted. It is limited to others making, using or selling variations of your invention within a scope recited in the patent by the claims. By scope is meant a definition of your invention that avoids over-stepping into the prior art realm of inventions, products and descriptions of others.

It is desirable to have the broadest possible scope of your invention recited in the claims. However, from the standpoint of market success, as long as a claim of your patent has a scope which covers the most commercially valuable aspect (embodiment), then you've got protection enough to make money. On the other hand, if all your claims fail to recite any scope covering the commercially valuable embodiments of your invention, then your patent may have very little value—even if it discloses an invention that has great value. See Chapter 4.

> *Be sure your claims recite the most commercially valuable aspect of your invention.*

4. Patent Ownership

The inventor is in exclusive command of his/her patent

application unless an entity, such as an employer, has superior rights.

In a typical scenario, an inventor engages a patent attorney to file his/her patent application, then receives the issued patent from the USPTO. In this case, the inventor is free to market the patent, which can include: selling products under the patent, assigning all monopoly rights (a sale), assigning a portion of the monopoly rights, or granting a limited right to use the monopoly rights (a license).

In a scenario in which an employer is involved, the employer will supervise the patent application process, during which the inventor is something of a mere bystander, with the patent issuing to the employer. The employer retains all patent rights of making, using and selling the invention, including assigning, licensing or selling the patent.

In situations where there are co-inventors, also referred to as joint inventors, the patent will issue jointly in the name of each, and each will have the right to exclude anyone other than a co-inventor from making, using and selling the invention.

In order to avoid future arguments/disagreements, co-inventors should enter into a mutual agreement regarding the rights conveyed to them jointly by the patent.

5. How to Read the Face of a Patent

At the top of the first page of an issued U.S. patent there is a lot of information. While it may look like hieroglyphics, below is your Rosetta Stone in the form of my Thawometer patent.

The numbers in parentheses are international codes for specific pieces of information pertaining to the patent. We don't need to concern ourselves with these, as the U.S. format of the information is standard.

The top most heading indicates on the left United States Patent above the inventor's last name (Keefe); on the right is the Patent Number (US 9,410,730 B1), where the country code precedes the number and a "kind code" follows the number, where "B1" refers to a patent issuing without a prior patent application publication, and below that is the date of issuance (August 9, 2016).

Below the top most heading, is the Title (Freezer Thaw Indicator); the Applicant (Keefe), this can be the inventor or the patent owner; the Inventor (Keefe), the Application Number (14/932,064), where each million starts a new series number, (14 was the then current series number); the Filing Date (November 4, 2015). This is followed by the CPC Symbols, discussed above.

US009410730B1

(12) **United States Patent**
Keefe

(10) **Patent No.:** **US 9,410,730 B1**
(45) **Date of Patent:** **Aug. 9, 2016**

(54) **FREEZER THAW INDICATOR**

(71) Applicant: **Peter David Keefe**, Roseville, MI (US)

(72) Inventor: **Peter David Keefe**, Roseville, MI (US)

(*) Notice: Subject to any disclaimer, the term of this patent is extended or adjusted under 35 U.S.C. 154(b) by 0 days.

(21) Appl. No.: **14/932,064**

(22) Filed: **Nov. 4, 2015**

(51) **Int. Cl.**
F25D 21/02 (2006.01)

(52) **U.S. Cl.**
CPC ***F25D 21/02*** (2013.01)

(58) **Field of Classification Search**
CPC ... F25D 21/02; F25D 2700/122; G01K 11/06; A23L 1/00
USPC 426/88
See application file for complete search history.

(56) **References Cited**

U.S. PATENT DOCUMENTS

3,063,235	A *	11/1962	Winchell	G01K 3/04	368/1
3,220,259	A *	11/1965	Beyer	G01K 3/04	116/217
3,414,415	A *	12/1968	Broad, Jr.	G01K 3/04	116/219
3,618,558	A *	11/1971	Tepfer	G01K 11/08	116/216
3,620,677	A *	11/1971	Morison	B01D 15/08	116/200
4,114,443	A *	9/1978	Clark	G01K 11/06	116/217
4,137,049	A *	1/1979	Couch	G01K 3/02	116/206
6,357,383	B1 *	3/2002	Al harshani	G01K 11/06	116/216
2008/0026110	A1 *	1/2008	Cooper	G01K 11/06	426/88
2011/0108551	A1 *	5/2011	Lee	B65D 45/325	220/212

OTHER PUBLICATIONS

RoadPro Freezer Alert Alarm Model RP2135 Fact Sheet of RoadPro, Palmyra, PA 17078. Copyright 2015.

Chaney Wireless Freezer Thermometer Instructions Sheet of Chaney Instrument Company, Lake Geneva, WI 53147. Date unknown.

VWR Freezer Thermometer Fact Sheet of VWR International, Radnor, PA 19087. Date unknown.

General Electric Refrigerator Diagnostic System Error, Fault and Function Codes Information Sheet of General Electric Company of Schenectady, NY, including Check frozen food, Code FF, and Power to refrigerator has been out, Code PF. Date believed Aug. 14, 2015.

Biosynergy StaFreez Irreversible Liquid Crystal Freeze-Thaw Indicator, Product Bulletin of Biosynergy, Inc., Elk Grove Village, IL 60007, dated 2014.

Biosynergy StaFreez Irreversible Liquid Crystal Freeze-Thaw Indicator, Fact Sheet of Biosynergy, Inc., Elk Grove Village, IL 60007, believed dated 2014.

Biosynergy StaFreez Irreversible Liquid Crystal Freeze-Thaw Indicator, Time/Temperature Solutions Fact Sheet of Biosynergy, Inc., Elk Grove Village, IL 60007, believed dated 2014.

* cited by examiner

Primary Examiner — Emmanuel Duke

(57) **ABSTRACT**

A container has a porous support member affixed thereinside defining upper and lower chambers and a liquid partly filling the container. The liquid is frozen in the upper chamber. The container is oriented so that the upper chamber is gravitationally above the lower chamber, wherein the frozen liquid remains in the upper chamber. The container is placed in a cold zone of a freezer. Thereafter, the presence of the liquid in the lower chamber is indicative that a thaw episode has occurred. The presence of the liquid frozen in the lower chamber is indicative that the thaw episode has been followed by a refreeze event.

3 Claims, 8 Drawing Sheets

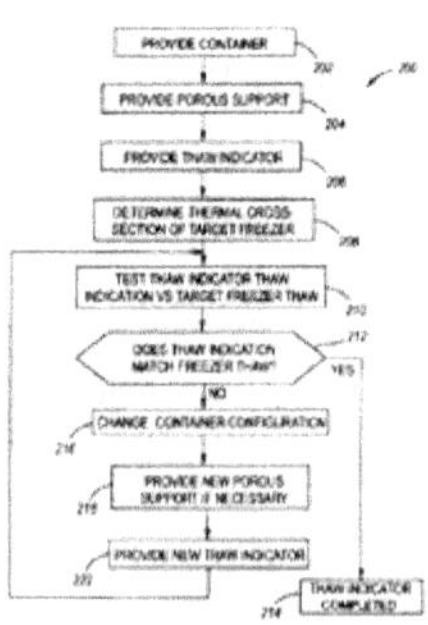

Image credit: USPTO.gov database.

Thereafter is a listing of all the references considered by the Examiner, where an asterisk indicates those cited by the Examiner, the others being cited by the Applicant in one or more Information Disclosure Statements.

Next is the name of the Examiner (Emmanuel Duke), where at a minimum the "Primary Examiner" who had signatory authority is provided; his/her "Assistant Examiner" is also provided, if involved in the examination.

The Abstract of the Disclosure is then presented, followed by the number of independent Claims and number of Drawing Sheets.

Lastly, a representative figure from the Drawing completes the face, or front page, of a patent.

* * *

Chapter 2

The Patent Office

Establishment

Article I of the U.S. Constitution provides Congress the power to grant to inventors, for a limited time, the exclusive right to their discoveries. Congressional implementing legislation created the U.S. Patent and Trademark Office (USPTO) under the patent laws codified in Title 35 of the United Sates Code (U.S.C.).

35 U.S.C. 1(a) gives us the details:

> *"The United States Patent and Trademark Office is established as an agency of the United States, within the Department of Commerce. In carrying out its functions, the United States Patent and Trademark Office shall be subject to the policy direction of the Secretary of Commerce, but otherwise shall retain responsibility for decisions regarding the management and administration of its operations ... in accordance with this title ..."*

Facilities

The USPTO headquarters is located in the Washington D.C. metropolitan area at 600 Dulany St., Alexandria, VA 22314. Besides housing the administration/examination facilities of the Patent Office, you can schedule a meeting with a USPTO specialist on any subject of intellectual property and visit the National Inventors Hall of Fame.

There are three ways to contact the USPTO: by postal mail addressed to Commissioner of Patents, P.O. Box 1450, Alexandria, VA 22314-1450 (once the principal portal to the Patent Office, it is now disfavored); by internet at https://uspto.gov (now the principal portal to the USPTO); and by calling 1-800-786-9199.

The USPTO operates several Regional Offices. See: https://www.uspto.gov/about-us/uspto-office-locations.

300 River Place Drive, Suite 2900, Detroit, MI 48207
MidwestRegion@uspto.gov
1-313-446-4800

207 South Houston St., Suite 159, Dallas, TX 75202
TexasRegionalOffice@uspto.gov
1-469-295-9000

1961 Stout St., 14th Floor, Denver, CO 80294
RockyMountain@uspto.gov
1-303-297-4600

26 South Fourth St., San Jose, CA 95112
SiliconValley@uspto.gov
1-408-918-9900

In addition, a Southeast Regional Office is located at the USPTO headquarters and a Community Outreach Office is located in Durham, NH. These offices are supplemented throughout the USA by local libraries designated as Patent and Trademark Resource Centers (PTRCs).

Organization

The USPTO is an organization within the Department of Commerce, subject to enacted laws, executive actions and directives of the Secretary of Commerce.

1. Administration

The head, who is appointed by the President, is the Under Secretary of Commerce and USPTO Director. Various positions, committees, boards and administrative units carry out specific aspects of the USPTO, such as public review, policy, government and international affairs, communication, finance, employment, and legal matters. Notable among these are: the Commissioner for Patents, the Commissioner for Trademarks, the Patent Trial and Appeal Board, and the Trademark Trial and Appeal Board.

2. Examination Corps

In order to efficiently and effectively examine patent applications for compliance with the patent laws and USPTO implementing rules of practice, the examining corps is arranged by types of technologies. These evolve as technology advances.

There are nine Patent Technology Centers, each led by an Assistant Commissioner:

TC 1600 Biotechnology and Organic Chemistry;

TC 1700 Chemical and Materials Engineering;

TC 2100 Computer Architecture Software, Information Security, and AI;

TC 2400 Computer Networks, Multiplexing, Cable, and Cryptography/Security;

TC 2600 Communications;

TC 2800 Semiconductors/Memory, Electrical Systems, Optics/ Photocopying, Printing/Measuring, and Testing;

TC 2900 Design;

TC 3600 Transportation, Construction, Electronic Commerce, Agriculture, Business Methods, Autonomous Vehicles, National Security, and Licensing Review; and

TC 3700 Mechanical Engineering, Manufacturing, Gaming, and Medical Devices/Processes.

Each of these Patent Technology Centers is further divided into sub-centers headed by a Director. For example, TC 1700 includes Patent Technology Center sub-center 1740: Tires, Adhesive Bonding, Glass/Paper Making, Plastics Shaping & Molding.

Each Patent Technology Center sub-center is further divided into Art Units, each headed by a Supervisory Patent Examiner. For example, sub-center 1740 is divided into Art Units 1741-1749 and 1754.

Each Art Unit has a staff of Patent Examiners who are assigned patent applications for examination. The Examiners are divided among

Primary Examiners, who have stand alone signatory authority, and Assistant Examiners, who examine under the wing of a Primary.

> *The USPTO is a responsive and efficient organization that has as its mission the encouragement of innovation through the issuance of examined patents.*

Operation

How the USPTO operates and conducts examination of patent applications is regulated by Title 35 of the United States Code (U.S.C.), Title 37 of the Code of Federal Regulations (CFR), and court rulings interpreting the laws and rules; all of which is summarized in the USPTO's Manual of Patent Examining Procedure (MPEP).

Title 35 U.S.C. codifies federal laws passed by acts of Congress. These laws constitute mandates that the USPTO must adhere to.

Title 37 CFR codifies rules of practice established by the USPTO in order to fairly and predictably carry out its mandates under Title 35 U.S.C.

Court rulings interpret the laws and rules under which the USPTO operates. These nearly always arise as a result of litigation and are issued by a federal district court, an appeals court or the Supreme Court, in order of primacy.

The MPEP is essentially a detailed guide for Patent Examiners and patent practitioners in the proper application of the laws and rules.

> *The MPEP provides a treasure-trove of information on everything patent related; it is essentially a bible of patent practice.*

* * *

Chapter 3

Patent Attorneys

The adage, "An attorney who represents himself has a fool for a client." applies with far greater seriousness to an inventor who represents himself/herself in the prosecution (processing) of his/her patent application at the USPTO. At least the attorney representing himself in the adage is an attorney; inventors, in particular novice inventors, are ill-equipped to assume the task of patent practitioner. As you'll see in the following chapters, patent application preparation and patent application prosecution are fraught with technical jargon, arcane rules of practice, and specialized language in the claims, all collectively serving up a mine field just waiting for you to make a misstep.

Patenting Yourself

The USPTO provides help for inventors prosecuting their own patent applications, what is referred to in *patentese* as "pro se." Indeed, a Patent Examiner is required to assist a pro se applicant. This assistance, however, is aimed at moving a patent application forward. An Examiner may propose a claim he/she will accept to issuance, but that claim may have little to no commercial value.

The thrust of this handbook is to protect your invention and yourself. You're not doing that by going it alone. The key to making serious money on your invention is not just getting a patent, it's getting an enforceable patent with claims that protect commercially valuable subject matter. Do you know how to do that? There are people who do.

Patent Practitioners

1. USPTO Registration

Traditionally, to become registered as a person authorized to practice at the USPTO, he/she must:

- have a degree in a technical discipline, most commonly engineering or science; and
- pass a rigorous examination administered by the USPTO.

The USPTO requires a technical degree because the subject matter of patents is necessarily anchored in technology. By way of example, my background in physics facilitated my understanding of a wide range of technical subject matter. The fringes of physics extend quite far in the technical arts, and the discipline, itself, is fundamental to all technologies.

I well remember, as Abraham Lincoln would say, "two score and two years ago," preparing for the USPTO practitioner examination, a requirement for admission to the "Patent Bar." I attended a review course in New York City, then studied carefully.

On my fateful day in downtown Detroit at the Federal Building, I answered the multitude of questions with confidence. Then came the make or break: the writing of a patent application claim. There was a choice between two inventions: a mechanical device and a chemical combination. Both had very close prior art. In fact, after carefully reading the prior art references, both inventions seemed to be unpatentable. I decided to go with the chemical combination invention. After taking a deep dive into the invention versus the prior art, I realized that there was a subtle aspect in the combination that got around the prior art. I wrote a claim reciting that novel aspect. A couple of months later, I opened my mail to find I had been assigned attorney practitioner number 31,114.

2. Types of Patent Bar Practitioners

There are three types:

- attorneys, who are licensed to practice law in at least one state, who can file utility, design and plant patents;
- agents, who can file utility, design and plant patents; and
- design practitioners, who can only file design patents.

Both attorneys and agents have the required technical knowledge and have passed the same practitioner examination. As far as patent application prosecution is concerned, both are equally capable to get you an enforceable patent with commercially valuable claims.

Patent attorneys have the advantage that, as a lawyer, they can perform legal services for you, such as advising on contracts, setting up a company and litigating.

Traditional patent practitioners are attorneys and agents.

The USPTO created "design practitioners" on January 2, 2024. They must have a college degree, a design background and pass a USPTO exam. See: MPEP 1502.02. I advise to use only traditional attorney/agent practitioners. See my discussion of this topic in Keefe's Korner of Reader Support at www.PatentApplication.com.

This handbook uses the term "patent attorney" interchangeably with "patent agent," except where legal services are involved.

For patent prosecution, patent attorneys and patent agents are equally able, but only attorneys can represent you in legal matters.

3. Finding a Patent Practitioner

The USPTO provides an online roster of registered patent practitioners; see the QR code on page 210. Even if you find a practitioner elsewhere, it is a good idea to check out the status of his/her registration at the USPTO.

Word of mouth is, by far, the best way to find a patent practitioner. Short of that, an online search of "patent attorneys" in your local area should turn up what you're looking for.

Your best option is to go for a small firm or a solo practitioner. The reason is that large law firms are geared to billing for whatever they legitimately can. I once had someone ask me to call his patent attorney at a large firm here in Detroit to see what the status of his patent application was. I asked him, "Why don't you call him yourself?" He replied, "Because he'll send me a bill!" Small law firms, solo attorneys and agents tend to be fee sympathetic—you won't (shouldn't) get billed for a simple inquiry on patent application status (and the bills for services should be more reasonable, too!).

So should you ever use a big law firm? Yes. If there are issues, as for example an employer asserting ownership, co-inventor difficulties, or chance of infringement, then a large firm can be very assistive to you. But if your invention has no inherent issues surrounding it, then go for the small firm or solo practitioner. Don't pay for what you don't need.

This story may assist you in making your decision. When I was ending my apprenticeship at a successful patent law firm, the head partner's wife stood at the entrance to my office shaking her head. I asked, "Can I help you?" She replied, "Peter, I don't think you're going to make it as a patent attorney." I responded, "Why's that?" She said, "Because you care too much about the clients; you'll never make any money."

Small firms and solo practitioners are usually an inventor's best choice.

4. Fee Structure

When an attorney says he/she works for $250/hour, what does that tell you about how much your patent application is going to cost? Not much. Is there a way to avoid getting nickel and dimed to death? Yes!

The best approach is to enter into a flat fee agreement with your patent attorney. That way, no matter how many hours he/she puts in or how many times you call, you'll only pay that flat fee. Large firms will almost never do this, but if they do, the flat fee will be high. Once again, your best bet is a small firm or a solo practitioner.

Another possibility is to enter into a contingency fee arrangement with your patent attorney. In a typical contingency fee arrangement, no fee is paid by you unless the patent application makes money. The patent attorney will receive a percentage of interest in the patent application via an assignment from you, typically 10 to 25%.

> *Flat and contingency fees save you from periodic billing, while contingency fees encourage your patent practitioner to work hard for you all the way through marketing.*

Is there a way to get free legal help? Yes! There are patent attorneys who donate their time, what in *patentese* is called "pro bono." If your income is less than three times the federal poverty level guidelines, you can turn to the USPTO Patent Pro Bono Program at https://www.uspto.gov/patents/basics/using-legal-services/pro-bono/patent-pro-bono-program.

5. Working with Your Patent Attorney

Your primary job is to develop your idea into a perfected invention. It is also a good idea to perform a preliminary patent search to get a view (even if vague) of where you stand in the patentability landscape. With that accomplished, it's a good time to have an initial consultation with a patent attorney.

Many patent attorneys do not charge for an initial consultation, so find one of these good guys and gals. Prepare a written "record of invention" that describes everything you can think of alongside a set of drawings. Bring it and any prototype with you. Be open and honest. The attorney is going to ask you probing questions aimed at getting to know you and your invention. One of the key aspects he/she will want to learn is if there is any impediment to your getting a patent. Besides employer and co-inventor issues, there is also the issue as to whether you've made any public disclosures.

Assuming you both hit it off, the next step is for the patent attorney to perform a professional novelty search. The attorney may subcontract the actual search to a professional searcher, but in any event your attorney will prepare a patentability report which includes copies of the relevant prior art. The report will conclude with a recommendation to proceed or not. A patent attorney is not always going to say, "Go ahead!" simply for the reason it's unethical. If that doesn't sound like reason enough, the business reason is that inventions with very little chance of becoming a patent are a nightmare to prosecute at the USPTO; and besides, every attorney wants to brag that his/her success rate is as near to perfect as possible.

The patent attorney will let you think it over, unless some critical time window to file the patent application applies. If it does, don't dally. When you decide to proceed, your patent attorney will discuss in detail the fee arrangement, likely asking you to sign an acknowledgement. If you both decide on a contingency fee, then you'll be asked to sign an assignment of rights in the patent application. Otherwise, your patent attorney will ask for a retainer. The retainer is a commitment to the project from you and a hedge for the attorney against you reneging in midstream of the project. Billing will then periodically happen according to the fee arrangement.

Your patent attorney will prepare a patent application that covers your disclosure (updated record of invention, office consultations, and your submitted materials), along with patent search results and his/her own knowledge base. Wherever possible, your patent attorney will expand your disclosure to areas you might not have thought about. In my experience, there were countless times the broad smile on an inventor's face as he/she read the application I had written told me all I needed to know.

It is essential that you assist your patent attorney all through the patent application preparation. In particular, be sure your attorney is aware of the basic and best embodiments, alternative embodiments, your activities at promoting/marketing and any prior art you're aware of. When completed, read over the patent application with great care to detail and accuracy. Pay particular attention to the claims. They may be written in *patentese*, but they're also written in English.

Also, as discussed in Chapter 4, be sure the USPTO filing forms are accurately filled out and the Information Disclosure Statement is accurate and complete.

About a year or so after your patent application has been filed, an "Office Action" from the USPTO will be received by your patent attorney. Assist your attorney in formulating an "Amendment" aimed at overcoming objections and rejections in the Office Action. While I've had my share of first Office Actions that were "Notice of Allowances," this is a rarity. The vast majority of first Office Actions contain issues that must be overcome. This is not the fault of your patent attorney; it's the fault of the difficulties of getting a patent and only emphasizes why you need to hire a patent attorney to represent you at the USPTO.

> *Your patent attorney will be worth his/her weight in gold when it comes time to respond to an Office Action.*

* * *

Chapter 4

Patent Applications

A patent application is a formal document conforming to the patent laws and the rules of practice, which collectively require that the disclosure enable a person of ordinary skill in the relevant art to make and use the inventor's invention, while clearly defining the scope of the subject matter of that invention for which a patent is sought. The filing of a patent application is the necessary and essential event that starts the examination process at the USPTO toward the hoped for grant of a patent.

What is Patentable?

35 U.S.C. 101 gives the answer:

> *"Whoever invents or discovers any new and useful process, machine, manufacture, or*

> *composition of matter, or any new and useful improvement thereof, may obtain a patent therefor, subject to the conditions and requirements of this title."*

Generally speaking, "invention" and "discovery" are interchangeable descriptions for the act of inventing.

A key element in Section 101 is the term "new and useful." New has a dual meaning, the invention must be both novel, as defined in Section 102, and unobvious, as defined in Section 103, to those of ordinary skill in the art. Useful is a hurdle pretty easily overcome, as there are but few inventions that could be said to be not useful; nonetheless these can arise, such as for example an invention that is inoperable, e.g., it requires pivoting but no pivot is disclosed.

Next, the inventive subject matter of the patent application must fall into at least one of the enumerated categories.

A process is a method for taking matter from one stage to another. This consists of a starting point and then, through a series of steps of manipulation, a new and useful ending point is achieved. A process, for example, can be a series of steps describing how chemicals can be combined to make a new chemical, or a series of steps to take materials and manipulate them during manufacture into a finished product.

A machine is characterizable as something with moving parts, such as an electric motor.

A manufacture relates to things without moving parts, such as a ball bearing used in an electric motor or to new and useful ornamental shapes of matter (designs).

A composition of matter refers to chemicals, such as the composition of a ball bearing, pharmaceuticals, biotech and plants.

A new and useful improvement in any of the categories can also be patented. Indeed, the vast majority of inventions are for improvements. Few are for pioneering inventions that transcend everything before them, as for example Charles Townes' maser.

Types of Patents

The U.S. patent laws provide for three types of patents:

- Utility;

- Design; and
- Plant.

An invention will fall into at least one of these types, and that will determine the formulation of the patent application. I say "at least one" because a frequent situation arises when an invention can appropriately fall into both the utility and design types. The vast majority of patents issue as utility patents, as they provide the broadest protection; any associated design patent merely protects the ornamental appearance of a product claimed by the utility patent.

Utility Patents

A short, but maybe a bit circuitous, definition of a utility patent is every patent that is not a design or plant patent, both of which are specifically defined in Title 35. As such, the thrust of this handbook is to give you an introduction to the patent process as it pertains to utility patents, with the view that your heightened understanding will assist you in your interactions with your patent attorney.

A utility patent defines an invention in terms of its functionality, structure, operation, manufacture and spectrum of embodiments. For example, a bracket invention, though an article of manufacture without moving parts, is disclosed in terms of one or more exemplary embodiments and description of use. A design patent of the bracket would protect the ornamental appearance of an embodiment of the bracket.

A utility patent application can be filed either as a "provisional" or as a "regular" application.

A. Provisional Patent Applications

A provisional patent application has few formal requirements, as it is not examined by the USPTO. What is all important is to disclose, as well as possible, how to make and use the invention aimed at a person of ordinary skill in the art to which the invention pertains.

A title can be easily formulated without much worry as to whether it's too folksy, and the Specification can be as informal as copied notes that were used for other purposes, or as formal as write-up aimed at a comprehensive utility patent disclosure. The Drawing, likewise, can be informally drawn figures, copied crude pencil/pen figures, and/or copies of photographs.

In order to simplify the submission, claims, which recite the legal scope of the inventive subject matter, are unnecessary. Claims can be included, however.

A provisional patent application must be accompanied by a cover sheet, and the filing fee, which is modest.

Take note: 35 U.S.C. 111 provides for the abandonment (termination) of provisional patent applications at twelve months from the date of filing unless a regular application referencing the provisional application is filed with the USPTO within that time.

Why file a provisional patent application?

- It is a fast, simple and inexpensive way to secure priority—the first inventor to file wins;
- it allows for multiple provisional applications to be filed as the invention is developed, thus asserting early claims to priority for the latest developments;
- it is the simplest way to achieve "patent pending" status; and
- it gives the better part of a year for an inventor to test the market to see if it is worth the effort and expense to file a regular patent application.

While this handbook stands firm in the concept that the only good patent application is one prepared and filed by a patent attorney, there can arise emergencies in which an inventor simply has no time to schedule an appointment. These eventualities should be extremely rare—in fact, they should never happen!

Nonetheless, if you find yourself in such an untoward spot, then you're going to have to wing it and file a provisional patent application on your own. To this end, an example of a provisional patent application is provided at Reader Support of PatentApplication.com.

Filing a provisional application on your own involves an extreme risk that you will make a mistake or otherwise mess-up, thereby losing the all important priority date you are seeking. Keep in mind you must present sufficiently detailed information and drawings that will enable a person of ordinary skill in the art to make and use your invention, show you are in possession of an invention and not a mere idea, and disclose the best mode for carrying out the invention.

B. Regular Patent Applications

Regular patent applications have a term of 20 years from the "priority date," the date of earliest filing. The requirements for regular patent applications, also referred to as non-provisional applications, are given in the following sections of 35 U.S.C.:

> 112 requires a Specification that is enabling to a person of ordinary skill in the relevant art, discloses the best mode, and recites the scope of the invention by one or more claims;
>
> 113 requires a Drawing where needed for understanding; and
>
> 115 requires each inventor to specify belief of original inventorship of the claimed invention.

Parts of a Regular Utility Patent Application

In order to carry out the mandates of the patent laws and achieve uniformity in the requirements for disclosure and layout of that disclosure, the USPTO has established rules for the format and content of regular patent applications under 37 CFR 1.71 through 1.84. Without going into the tedious and technical details of these provisions, it all boils down to a regular patent application (hereafter, simply "Application") having the following parts in the order listed:

- Application Transmittal Form;
- Filing Fee and Fee Transmittal Form;
- Power of Attorney;
- Application Data Sheet Form;
- Declaration;
- Information Disclosure Statement;
- Assignment (if applicable);
- Petition (if Applicable); and, most importantly,
- The Disclosure:
    - Specification (including Claims and Abstract); and
    - Drawing.

With respect to forms, go to USPTO.gov to download the most current, preferably form-fillable, forms. Note: forms change frequently; those shown below are for exemplary purposes only.

1. Application Transmittal Form

PTO/SB/21 (07-09)
Approved for use through 05/31/2024. OMB 0651-0031
U.S. Patent and Trademark Office; U.S. DEPARTMENT OF COMMERCE
Under the Paperwork Reduction Act of 1995, no persons are required to respond to a collection of information unless it displays a valid OMB control number.

TRANSMITTAL FORM *(to be used for all correspondence after initial filing)*	Application Number	
	Filing Date	
	First Named Inventor	
	Art Unit	
	Examiner Name	
Total Number of Pages in This Submission	Attorney Docket Number	

ENCLOSURES ***(Check all that apply)***

☐ Fee Transmittal Form	☐ Drawing(s)	☐ After Allowance Communication to TC
☐ Fee Attached	☐ Licensing-related Papers	☐ Appeal Communication to Board of Appeals and Interferences
☐ Amendment/Reply	☐ Petition	☐ Appeal Communication to TC **(Appeal Notice, Brief, Reply Brief)**
☐ After Final	☐ Petition to Convert to a Provisional Application	☐ Proprietary Information
☐ Affidavits/declaration(s)	☐ Power of Attorney, Revocation Change of Correspondence Address	☐ Status Letter
☐ Extension of Time Request	☐ Terminal Disclaimer	☐ Other Enclosure(s) (please Identify below):
☐ Express Abandonment Request	☐ Request for Refund	
☐ Information Disclosure Statement	☐ CD, Number of CD(s) ______	
	☐ Landscape Table on CD	
☐ Certified Copy of Priority Document(s)	Remarks	
☐ Reply to Missing Parts/ Incomplete Application		
☐ Reply to Missing Parts under 37 CFR 1.52 or 1.53		

SIGNATURE OF APPLICANT, ATTORNEY, OR AGENT

Firm Name			
Signature			
Printed name			
Date		Reg. No.	

CERTIFICATE OF TRANSMISSION/MAILING

I hereby certify that this correspondence is being facsimile transmitted to the USPTO or deposited with the United States Postal Service with sufficient postage as first class mail in an envelope addressed to: Commissioner for Patents, P.O. Box 1450, Alexandria, VA 22313-1450 on the date shown below.

Signature			
Typed or printed name		Date	

A Federal agency may not conduct or sponsor, and a person is not required to respond to, nor shall a person be subject to a penalty for failure to comply with an information collection subject to the requirements of the Paperwork Reduction Act of 1995, unless the information collection has a currently valid OMB Control Number. The OMB Control Number for this information collection is 0651-0031. Public burden for this form is estimated to average 2 hours per response including the time for reviewing instructions, searching existing data sources, gathering and maintaining the data needed, and completing and reviewing the information collection. Send comments regarding this burden estimate or any other aspect of this information collection, including suggestions for reducing this burden to the Chief Administrative Officer, United States Patent and Trademark Office, P.O. Box 1450, Alexandria, VA 22313-1450 or email InformationCollection@uspto.gov. **DO NOT SEND FEES OR COMPLETED FORMS TO THIS ADDRESS. If filing this completed form by mail, send to: Commissioner for Patents, P.O. Box 1450, Alexandria, VA 22313-1450.**

Image credit: USPTO.gov database.

The form is intended as a clerical tool for the USPTO and is basically self explanatory.

2. Filing Fee Transmittal Form

PTO/SB/17 (12-22)
Approved for use through 05/31/2024. OMB 0651-0032
U.S. Patent and Trademark Office; U.S. DEPARTMENT OF COMMERCE
Under the Paperwork Reduction Act of 1995 no persons are required to respond to a collection of information unless it displays a valid OMB control number

FEE TRANSMITTAL		Complete if known	
		Application Number	
		Filing Date	
☐ Applicant asserts small entity status. See 37 CFR 1.27.		First Named Inventor	
☐ Applicant certifies micro entity status. See 37 CFR 1.29. Form PTO/SB/15A or B or equivalent must either be enclosed or have been submitted previously.		Examiner Name	
		Art Unit	
TOTAL AMOUNT OF PAYMENT	($)	Practitioner Docket No.	

METHOD OF PAYMENT (check all that apply)

☐ Check ☐ Credit Card ☐ Money Order ☐ None ☐ Other (please identify): ____________

☐ Deposit Account Deposit Account Number: ____________ Deposit Account Name: ____________

For the above-identified deposit account, the Director is hereby authorized to (check all that apply):

☐ Charge fee(s) indicated below ☐ Charge fee(s) indicated below, **except for the filing fee**

☐ Charge any additional fee(s) or underpayment of fee(s) under 37 CFR 1.16 and 1.17 ☐ Credit any overpayment of fee(s)

WARNING: Information on this form may become public. Credit card information should not be included on this form. Provide credit card information and authorization on PTO-2038.

FEE CALCULATION

1. BASIC FILING, SEARCH, AND EXAMINATION FEES (U = undiscounted fee; S = small entity fee; M = micro entity fee)

	FILING FEES			SEARCH FEES			EXAMINATION FEES			
Application Type	**U ($)**	**S ($)**	**M ($)**	**U ($)**	**S ($)**	**M ($)**	**U ($)**	**S ($)**	**M ($)**	**Fees Paid ($)**
Utility	320	128*	64	700	280	140	800	320	160	
Design	220	88	44	160	64	32	640	256	128	
Plant	220	88	44	440	176	88	660	264	132	
Reissue	320	128	64	700	280	140	2,320	928	464	
Provisional	300	120	60	0	0	0	0	0	0	

* The $128 small entity filing fee for a utility application is further reduced to $64 for a small entity applicant who files the application via Patent Center or EFS-Web.

2. EXCESS CLAIM FEES

Fee Description	**Undiscounted Fee ($)**	**Small Entity Fee ($)**	**Micro Entity Fee ($)**
Each claim over 20 (including Reissues)	100	40	20
Each independent claim over 3 (including Reissues)	480	192	96
Multiple dependent claims	860	344	172

Total Claims ______ -20 or HP = **Extra Claims** ______ x **Fee ($)** ______ = **Fee Paid ($)** ______

HP = highest number of total claims paid for, if greater than 20.

Indep. Claims ______ -3 or HP = **Extra Claims** ______ x **Fee ($)** ______ = **Fee Paid ($)** ______

HP = highest number of independent claims paid for, if greater than 3.

Multiple Dependent Claims **Fee ($)** ______ **Fee Paid ($)** ______

3. APPLICATION SIZE FEE

If the specification and drawings exceed 100 sheets of paper (excluding electronically filed sequence or computer listings under 37 CFR 1.52(e)), the application size fee due is $420 ($168 for small entity) ($84 for micro entity) for each additional 50 sheets or fraction thereof. See 35 U.S.C. 41(a)(1)(G) and 37 CFR 1.16(s).

Total Sheets ______ - 100 = **Extra Sheets** ______ / 50 = **Number of each additional 50 or fraction thereof** ______ (round up to a whole number) x **Fee ($)** ______ = **Fee Paid ($)** ______

4. OTHER FEE(S) **Fees Paid ($)**

Non-English specification, $140 fee ($56 for small entity) ($28 for micro entity) ______

Non-electronic filing fee under 37 CFR 1.16(t) for a utility application, $400 fee ($200 small or micro entity) ______

Other (e.g., late filing surcharge): ____________ ______

SUBMITTED BY			
Signature		Registration No. (Attorney/Agent)	Telephone
Name (Print/Type)			Date

A Federal agency may not conduct or sponsor, and a person is not required to respond to, nor shall a person be subject to a penalty for failure to comply with an information collection subject to the requirements of the Paperwork Reduction Act of 1995, unless the information collection has a currently valid OMB Control Number. The OMB Control Number for this information collection is 0651-0032. Public burden for this form is estimated to average 30 minutes per response, including the time for reviewing instructions, searching existing data sources, gathering and maintaining the data needed, and completing and reviewing the information collection. Send comments regarding this burden estimate or any other aspect of this information collection, including suggestions for reducing this burden to the Chief Administrative Officer, United States Patent and Trademark Office, P.O. Box 1450, Alexandria, VA 22313-1450 or email InformationCollection@uspto.gov. **DO NOT SEND FEES OR COMPLETED FORMS TO THIS ADDRESS.** If filing this completed form by mail, send to: **Commissioner for Patents, P.O. Box 1450, Alexandria, VA 22313-1450.**

Image credit: USPTO.gov database.

The form requests "entity status." This was created by the USPTO to bring down the costs to independent inventors. Generally speaking, inventors who have not assigned to a company with more than 500 employees qualify for small entity status. Micro entity status is available to an inventor if he/she qualifies as a small entity and: 1) has not filed more than four patent applications, and 2) has a maximum income under three times the median household income, or if his/her income is from an institution of higher education, or if the invention is assigned to such an institution. Claiming micro/small entity status can be omitted even if it might apply.

3. Power of Attorney Form

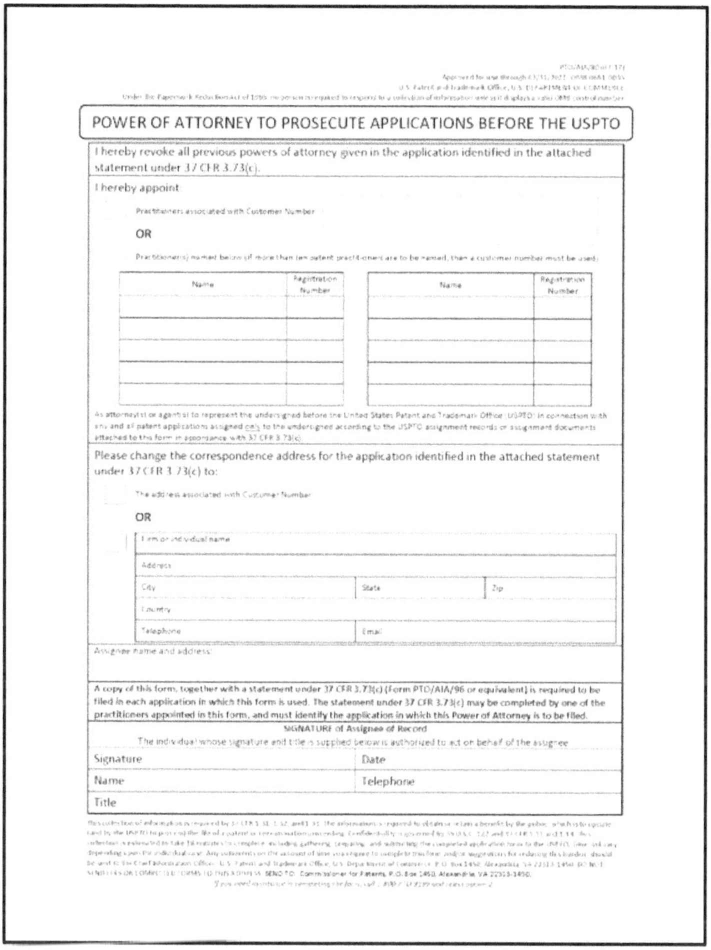

POWER OF ATTORNEY TO PROSECUTE APPLICATIONS BEFORE THE USPTO

I hereby revoke all previous powers of attorney given in the application identified in the attached statement under 37 CFR 3.73(c).

I hereby appoint:

Practitioners associated with Customer Number

OR

Practitioner(s) named below (if more than ten patent practitioners are to be named, then a customer number must be used):

Name	Registration Number	Name	Registration Number

As attorney(s) or agent(s) to represent the undersigned before the United States Patent and Trademark Office (USPTO) in connection with any and all patent applications assigned only to the undersigned according to the USPTO assignment records or assignment documents attached to this form in accordance with 37 CFR 3.73(c).

Please change the correspondence address for the application identified in the attached statement under 37 CFR 3.73(c) to:

The address associated with Customer Number

OR

Firm or individual name		
Address		
City	State	Zip
Country		
Telephone	Email	

Assignee name and address:

A copy of this form, together with a statement under 37 CFR 3.73(c) (Form PTO/AIA/96 or equivalent) is required to be filed in each application in which this form is used. The statement under 37 CFR 3.73(c) may be completed by one of the practitioners appointed in this form, and must identify the application in which this Power of Attorney is to be filed.

SIGNATURE of Assignee of Record

The individual whose signature and title is supplied below is authorized to act on behalf of the assignee

Signature	Date
Name	Telephone
Title	

SEND TO: Commissioner for Patents, P.O. Box 1450, Alexandria, VA 22313-1450.

Image credit: USPTO.gov database.

This form serves as proof of your appointment of a patent attorney as your representative to file and prosecute your patent application with the USPTO. In addition, the correspondence information will be used by the USPTO when communicating with you, always through your representative. No, you will not receive any communications from the USPTO. Your patent attorney will keep you informed.

I had a client who took it upon himself to visit the USPTO and seek out the Examiner handling his Application. He stepped into the Examiner's office, identifying himself as the inventor. The Examiner's reply was, "You have a representative, I don't think I'm allowed to talk to you."

4. Application Data Sheet Form

PTO/AIA/14 (01-22)
Approved for use through 05/31/2024. OMB 0651-0032
U.S. Patent and Trademark Office; U.S. DEPARTMENT OF COMMERCE
Under the Paperwork Reduction Act of 1995, no persons are required to respond to a collection of information unless it contains a valid OMB control number.

Application Data Sheet 37 CFR 1.76	Attorney Docket Number	
	Application Number	
Title of Invention		

The application data sheet is part of the provisional or nonprovisional application for which it is being submitted. The following form contains the bibliographic data arranged in a format specified by the United States Patent and Trademark Office as outlined in 37 CFR 1.76.
This document may be completed electronically and submitted to the Office in electronic format using the Electronic Filing System (EFS) or the document may be printed and included in a paper filed application.

Secrecy Order 37 CFR 5.2:

☐ Portions or all of the application associated with this Application Data Sheet may fall under a Secrecy Order pursuant to 37 CFR 5.2 (Paper filers only. Applications that fall under Secrecy Order may not be filed electronically.)

Inventor Information:

Inventor 1 [Remove]
Legal Name

Prefix	Given Name	Middle Name	Family Name	Suffix

Residence Information (Select One) ◉ US Residency ○ Non US Residency ○ Active US Military Service

City		State/Province		Country of Residence	

Mailing Address of Inventor:

Address 1			
Address 2			
City		State/Province	
Postal Code		Country	

All Inventors Must Be Listed - Additional Inventor Information blocks may be generated within this form by selecting the Add button. [Add]

Correspondence Information:

Enter either Customer Number or complete the Correspondence Information section below.
For further information see 37 CFR 1.33(a).

☐ An Address is being provided for the correspondence Information of this application.

Customer Number	
Email Address	[Add Email] [Remove Email]

Application Information:

Title of the Invention			
Attorney Docket Number		Small Entity Status Claimed ☐	
Application Type			
Subject Matter			
Total Number of Drawing Sheets (if any)		Suggested Figure for Publication (if any)	

Image credit: USPTO.gov database.

This multi-page form provides for identification of inventor(s) and assignee(s), correspondence information, prior application priority (provisional, regular and foreign), and other information. A relatively recent addition to the patent filing rules at the USPTO, over the years it has ballooned in complexity.

5. Declaration Form

PTO/AIA/01 (06-12)
Approved for use through 05/31/2024. OMB 0651-0032
U.S. Patent and Trademark Office; U.S. DEPARTMENT OF COMMERCE
Under the Paperwork Reduction Act of 1995, no persons are required to respond to a collection of information unless it displays a valid OMB control number.

DECLARATION (37 CFR 1.63) FOR UTILITY OR DESIGN APPLICATION USING AN APPLICATION DATA SHEET (37 CFR 1.76)

Title of Invention	

As the below named inventor, I hereby declare that:

This declaration is directed to:

☐ The attached application, or

☐ United States application or PCT international application number ____________________

filed on ____________________.

The above-identified application was made or authorized to be made by me.

I believe that I am the original inventor or an original joint inventor of a claimed invention in the application.

I hereby acknowledge that any willful false statement made in this declaration is punishable under 18 U.S.C. 1001 by fine or imprisonment of not more than five (5) years, or both.

WARNING:

Petitioner/applicant is cautioned to avoid submitting personal information in documents filed in a patent application that may contribute to identity theft. Personal information such as social security numbers, bank account numbers, or credit card numbers (other than a check or credit card authorization form PTO-2038 submitted for payment purposes) is never required by the USPTO to support a petition or an application. If this type of personal information is included in documents submitted to the USPTO, petitioners/applicants should consider redacting such personal information from the documents before submitting them to the USPTO. Petitioner/applicant is advised that the record of a patent application is available to the public after publication of the application (unless a non-publication request in compliance with 37 CFR 1.213(a) is made in the application) or issuance of a patent. Furthermore, the record from an abandoned application may also be available to the public if the application is referenced in a published application or an issued patent (see 37 CFR 1.14). Checks and credit card authorization forms PTO-2038 submitted for payment purposes are not retained in the application file and therefore are not publicly available.

LEGAL NAME OF INVENTOR

Inventor: ____________________ Date (Optional): ____________________

Signature: ____________________

Note: An application data sheet (PTO/SB/14 or equivalent), including naming the entire inventive entity, must accompany this form or must have been previously filed. Use an additional PTO/AIA/01 form for each additional inventor.

A Federal agency may not conduct or sponsor, and a person is not required to respond to, nor shall a person be subject to a penalty for failure to comply with an information collection subject to the requirements of the Paperwork Reduction Act of 1995, unless the information collection has a currently valid OMB Control Number. The OMB Control Number for this information collection is 0651-0032. Public burden for this form is estimated to average 1 minute per response, including the time for reviewing instructions, searching existing data sources, gathering and maintaining the data needed, and completing and reviewing the information collection. Send comments regarding this burden estimate or any other aspect of this information collection, including suggestions for reducing this burden to the Chief Administrative Officer, United States Patent and Trademark Office, P.O. Box 1450, Alexandria, VA 22313-1450 or email InformationCollection@uspto.gov. **DO NOT SEND FEES OR COMPLETED FORMS TO THIS ADDRESS.** If filing this completed form by mail, send to: **Commissioner for Patents, P.O. Box 1450, Alexandria, VA 22313-1450.**

If you need assistance in completing the form, call 1-800-PTO-9199 and select option 2.

Image credit: USPTO.gov database.

The Declaration (Oath) is signed by the inventor and carries legal consequences for a false statement. The inventor affirms he/she has authorized the Application to be made and, all importantly, is the original inventor of the claimed invention.

6. Information Disclosure Statement Form

Doc code: IDS
Doc description: Information Disclosure Statement (IDS) Filed

PTO/SB/08a (01-22)
Approved for use through 05/31/2024. OMB 0651-0031
U.S. Patent and Trademark Office; U.S. DEPARTMENT OF COMMERCE
Under the Paperwork Reduction Act of 1995, no persons are required to respond to a collection of information unless it contains a valid OMB control number.

INFORMATION DISCLOSURE STATEMENT BY APPLICANT (Not for submission under 37 CFR 1.99)		
	Application Number	
	Filing Date	
	First Named Inventor	
	Art Unit	
	Examiner Name	
	Attorney Docket Number	

U.S.PATENTS						
Examiner Initial*	Cite No	Patent Number	Kind Code[1]	Issue Date	Name of Patentee or Applicant of cited Document	Pages,Columns,Lines where Relevant Passages or Relevant Figures Appear
	1					
If you wish to add additional U.S. Patent citation information please click the Add button.						

U.S.PATENT APPLICATION PUBLICATIONS						
Examiner Initial*	Cite No	Publication Number	Kind Code[1]	Publication Date	Name of Patentee or Applicant of cited Document	Pages,Columns,Lines where Relevant Passages or Relevant Figures Appear
	1					
If you wish to add additional U.S. Published Application citation information please click the Add button.						

FOREIGN PATENT DOCUMENTS								
Examiner Initial*	Cite No	Foreign Document Number[3]	Country Code[2] i	Kind Code[4]	Publication Date	Name of Patentee or Applicant of cited Document	Pages,Columns,Lines where Relevant Passages or Relevant Figures Appear	T[5]
	1							☐
If you wish to add additional Foreign Patent Document citation information please click the Add button								

NON-PATENT LITERATURE DOCUMENTS			
Examiner Initials*	Cite No	Include name of the author (in CAPITAL LETTERS), title of the article (when appropriate), title of the item (book, magazine, journal, serial, symposium, catalog, etc), date, pages(s), volume-issue number(s), publisher, city and/or country where published.	T[5]

EFS Web 2.1.18

Image credit: USPTO.gov database.

To facilitate and standardize the disclosures made under the Duty of Disclosure, the USPTO has a multi-page form for filing an Information Disclosure Statement (IDS). The form provides for U.S. and foreign patent documents, as well as literature. A product on the market would be cited under literature. Accompanying such a citation would be copies of internet pages, product literature, photos, etc. If the QR code gives you an issue, just go directly to: https://www.uspto.gov/sites/default/files/documents/ids-autoload.pdf.

The USPTO is as serious as a heart attack when it comes to "The Duty of Disclosure." This onerous requirement has a brother, "The Duty of Reasonable Inquiry." Add to the mix the "Duty of Candor and Good Faith" in all dealings with the USPTO.

You may think you don't have to worry about these duties because you have a patent attorney shielding you. No, your attorney is ethically and legally obligated NOT to shield you. This is not some "attorney-client" privilege issue; these duties are owed by all persons, in particular, you, the inventor, *directly* to the USPTO. Keep in mind no patent can be granted to an inventor who has committed fraud, attempted fraud, or violated the Duty of Disclosure through bad faith or intentional misconduct on the USPTO.

What is the Duty of Disclosure? 37 CFR 1.56 requires the USPTO to be made aware of any information that is material to patentability. The MPEP further defines this duty in two parts: 1) *"The term 'information' is intended to be all encompassing"* and 2) *"Materiality is not limited to prior art but embraces any information that a reasonable examiner would be substantially likely to consider important in deciding whether to allow an application to issue as a patent."*

The Duty of Disclosure to the USPTO begins with the filing of the Application and continues until either the Application is abandoned or the patent is issued on the Application.

When you know something, say that something to your patent attorney. Do not hold back. If you do, it is at your peril. By something, I mean anything related to your invention. Besides publications, products and other evidences of prior art of others, you need to tell him/her of anything you've done, such as publicizing your invention, offering it for sale, placing it on the market, deriving it from something you've seen or heard about, and other acts of yours which render your invention known to others. There is a one year window for your acts, but don't assume you know the laws and rules so you can keep quiet. When you're in doubt whether something is worth mentioning, it is essential for you to mention it. Your patent attorney will take it from there.

> *The Duty of Disclosure applies to you, the inventor, and to anyone involved in the preparation of your Application.*

7. Assignment

An assignment is a transfer of an ownership interest in the Application, which follows through to and after the grant of the patent on the Application.

These are legal documents, and while there are forms available to use, each assignment has particular features which need to be recited. Your patent attorney will ensure the wording is correct before you sign and date it.

The USPTO records assignments in order to provide a publicly accessible recordation service to avoid any confusion over the ownership of an Application and its granted patent.

8. Petition

Situations can arise that go beyond the routine, requiring the USPTO to intervene. As such, the USPTO has an Office of Petitions for this very purpose. The reasons for petitioning the USPTO are quite diverse, but below are a few of the frequent ones.

- Petition to Make Special: An inventor 65 and over or with an infirmity that jeopardizes ability to assist during pendency of the Application, can petition to request the USPTO to take his/her application out of turn in order to hasten examination. I did this with the Thawometer.
- Petition Not to Publish: Usually an Application publishes 18 months after filing, but this can be prevented if the Application is not foreign filed. I also did this with the Thawometer.
- Petition for an Extension of Time: The USPTO routinely sets deadlines for responses to communications. Typically this is one month to correct informalities, or three months to respond to an Office Action. However, the patent laws give a six month response time. As such, Applicants can petition for month-long extensions of time inside of six months, with the payment of required, and progressively more onerous, fees.
- Petition to Revive: If for some reason an Application becomes abandoned for failure to respond timely to the USPTO, Applicants can petition to revive the Application under one of two categories, "unavoidable"

or "unintentional" for a fee. Unfortunately, an intentional abandonment can't be undone.

- Petition to Withdraw Attorney: Yes, your patent attorney can be changed mid-stream. Keep this in mind, as your choice of patent attorney is not written in stone. There is no fee.

9. The Disclosure

The Disclosure in a patent application consists of the Specification, which provides: a) information as to how to make and use the invention, b) the best mode and c) the scope of the invention; and the Drawing, which illustrates the invention.

Specification:

The Specification has the following parts:

- Title;
- Cross-Reference to Related Applications;
- Statement of Prior Disclosures by the Inventor;
- Technical Field;
- Background of the Invention;
- Brief Summary of the Invention;
- Brief Description of the Drawings;
- Detailed Description of the Invention;
- Claims; and
- Abstract of the Disclosure.

Drawing:

The terms "Drawing" and "Drawings" are interchangeable, with Drawing referring to the set of figures and Drawings referencing the figures, themselves. The Drawing is presented on separate sheets from the Specification. On these sheets is drawn one or more figures which exemplify one or more embodiments of the invention both structurally and operatively. Parts in the figures are numbered, and these numbers are used in the Specification to refer to the Drawing.

The preparation and filing of your Application requires your best efforts to work closely with your patent attorney. Use the information above as a guide for working with your patent attorney—not as a "DIY."

* * *

To bring the discussion of the Disclosure to life, I'll next reproduce my "Thawometer" patent application, entitled "FREEZER THAW INDICATOR," Serial No. 14/932,064, filed with the USPTO on November 4, 2015.

Note: the file history images of U.S. Patent 9,410,730 reproduced below in this handbook, including the Application, the Filing Receipt, the Office Action, the Amendment, the Notice of Allowance, and the Issue Notification are available to the public for viewing and downloading at https://patentcenter.uspto.gov/applications/14932064.

To access the Reader Support portal at PatentApplication.com, please enter the password:

Thawometer

https://PatentApplication.com

Keefe and Associates

1/8

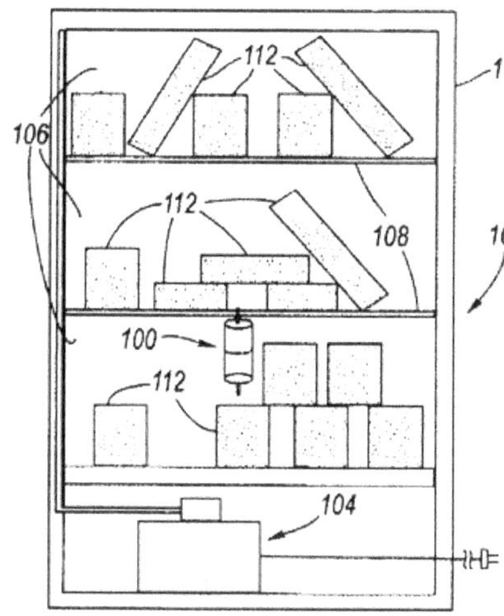

Fig. 1

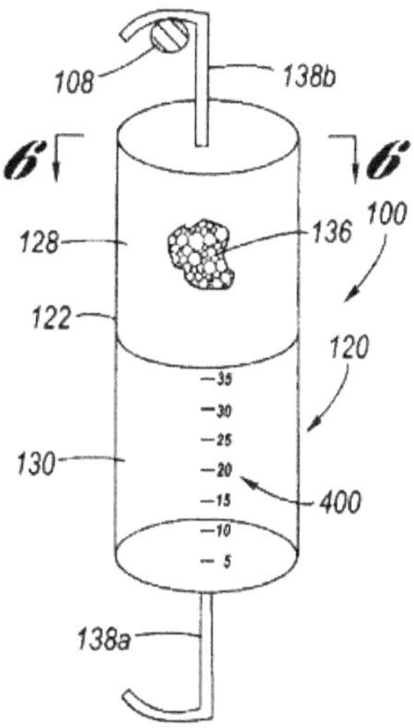

Fig. 2

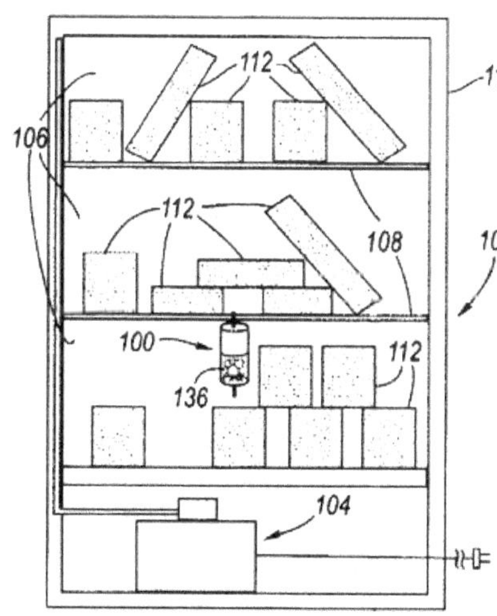

Fig. 3

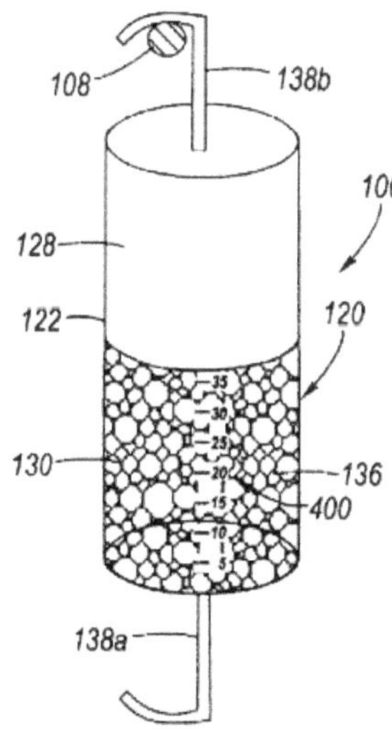

Fig. 4

Keefe and Associates

2/8

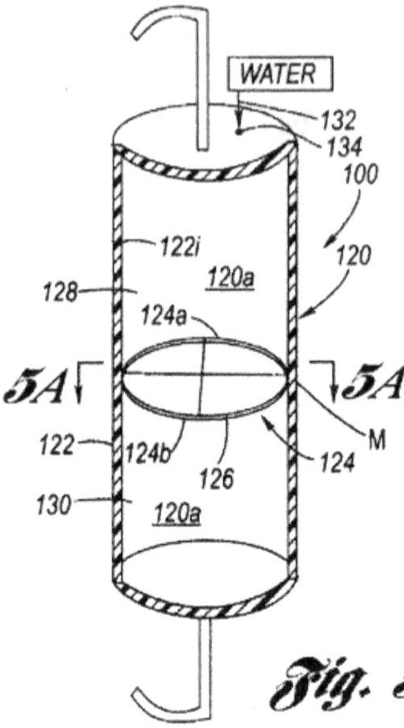

Fig. 5

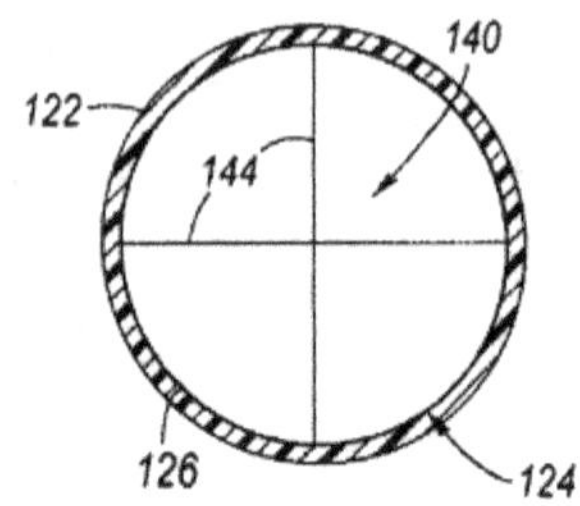

Fig. 5A

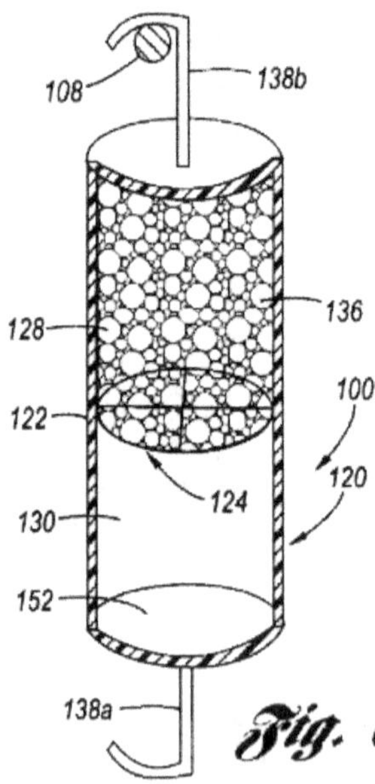

Fig. 6

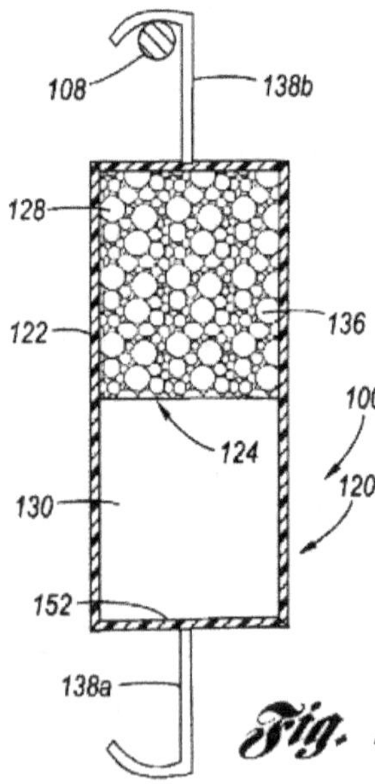

Fig. 7

Keefe and Associates

3/8

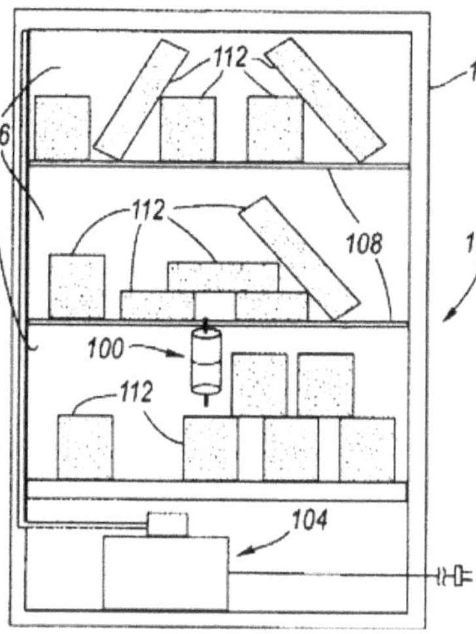

Fig. 8A

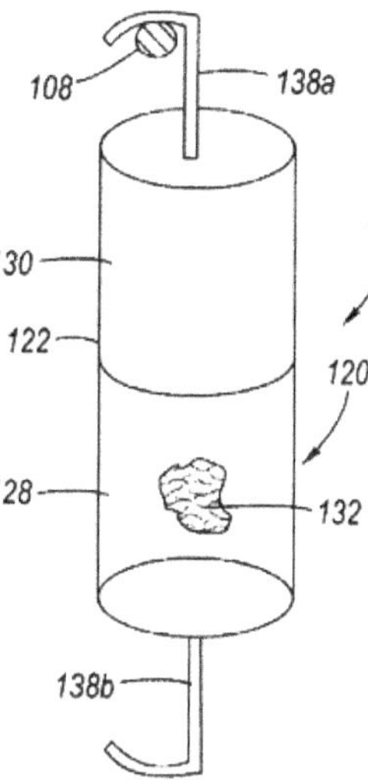

Fig. 8B

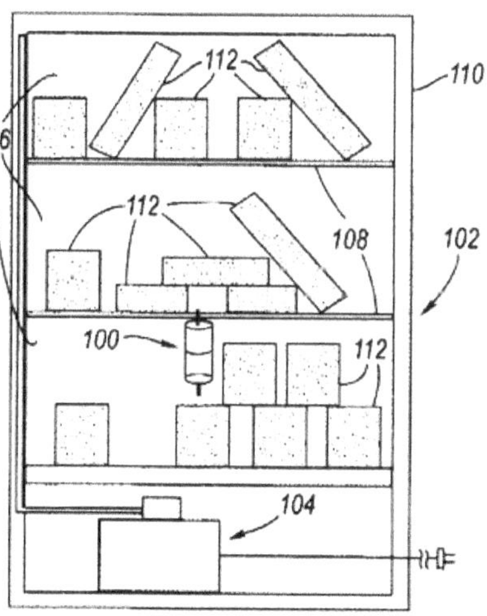

Fig. 8C

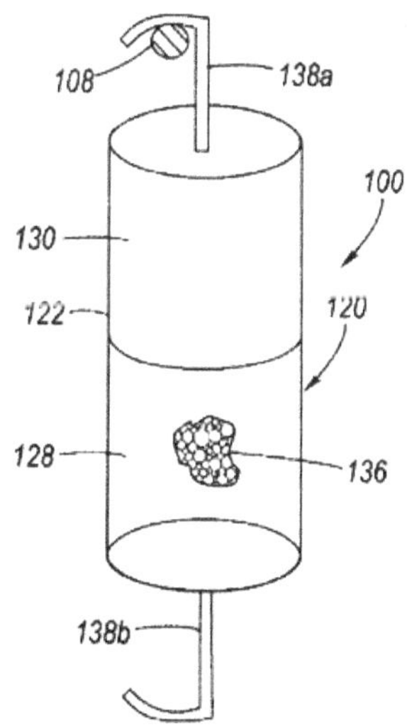

Fig. 8D

Keefe and Associates

4/8

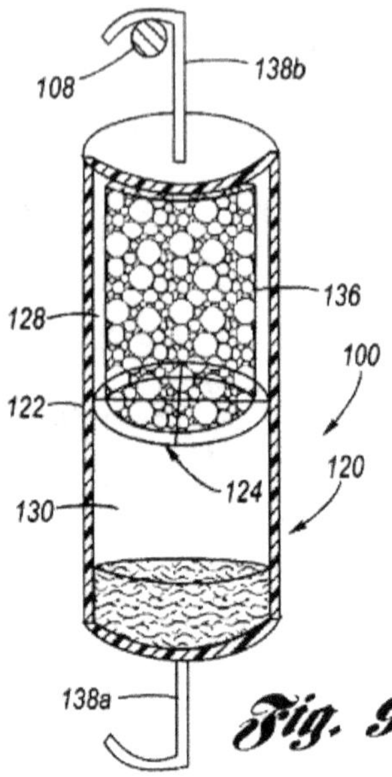

Fig. 9

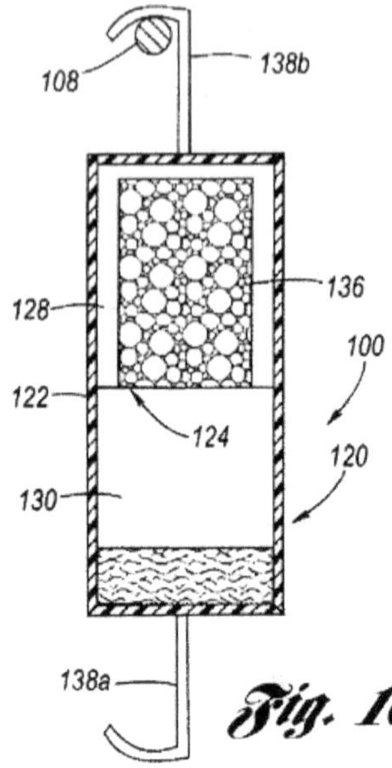

Fig. 10

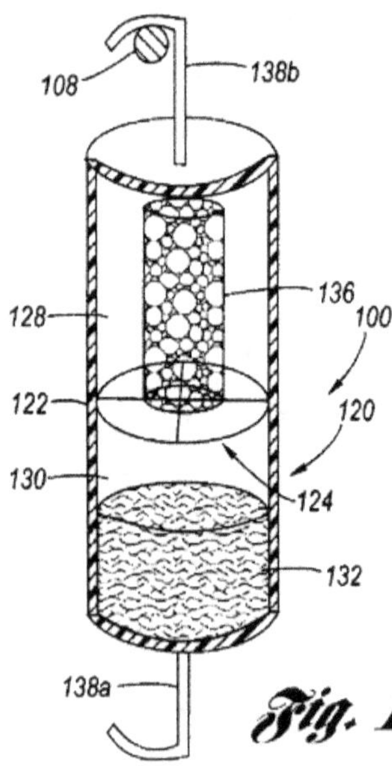

Fig. 11

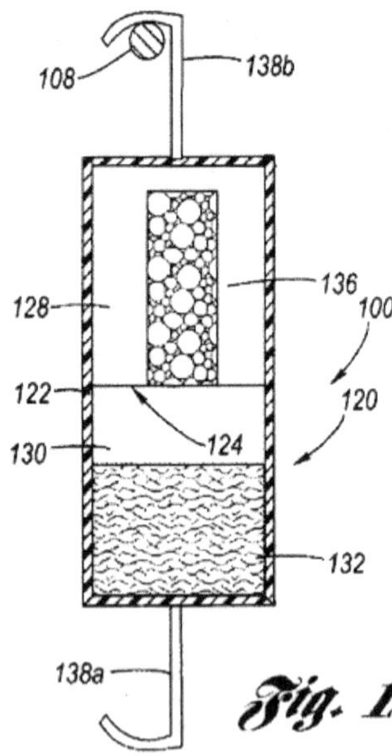

Fig. 12

Keefe and Associates

5/8

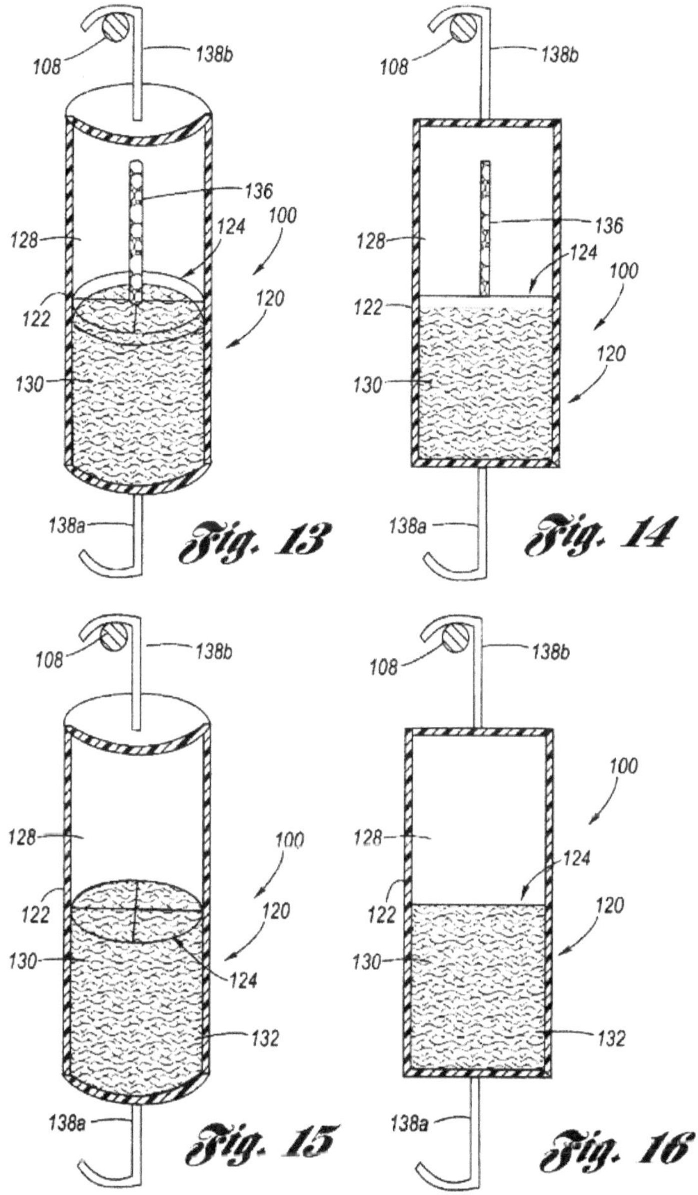

Keefe and Associates

6/8

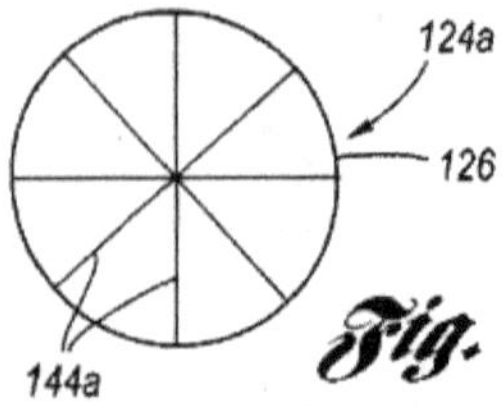

Fig. 17

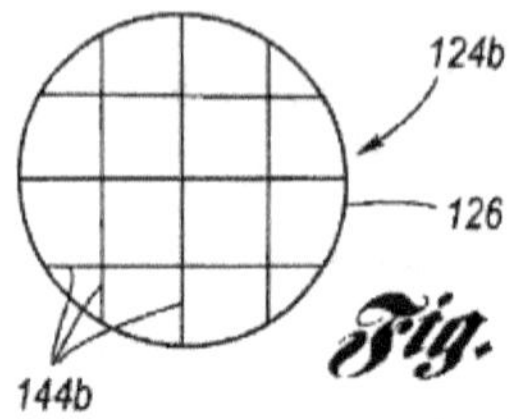

Fig. 18

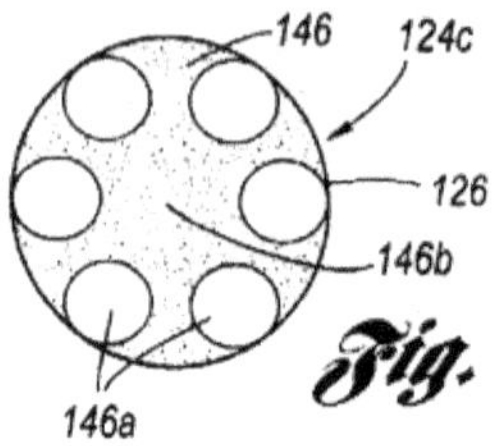

Fig. 19

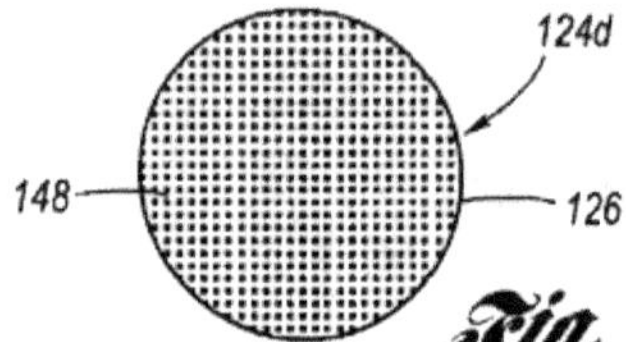

Fig. 20

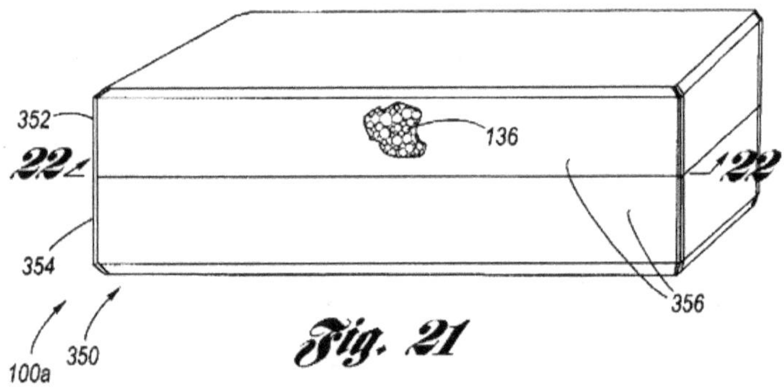

Fig. 21

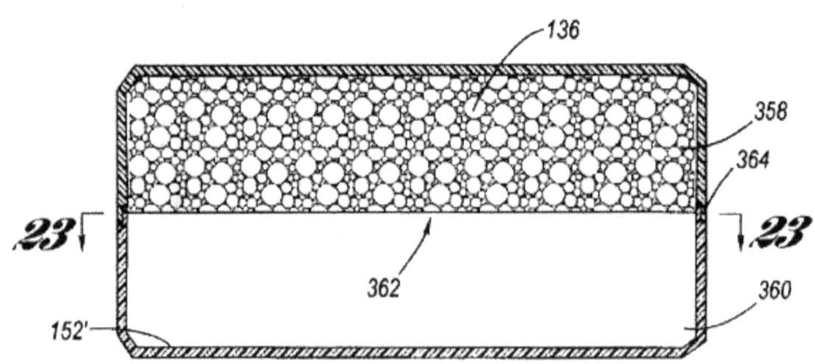

Fig. 22

Keefe and Associates

7/8

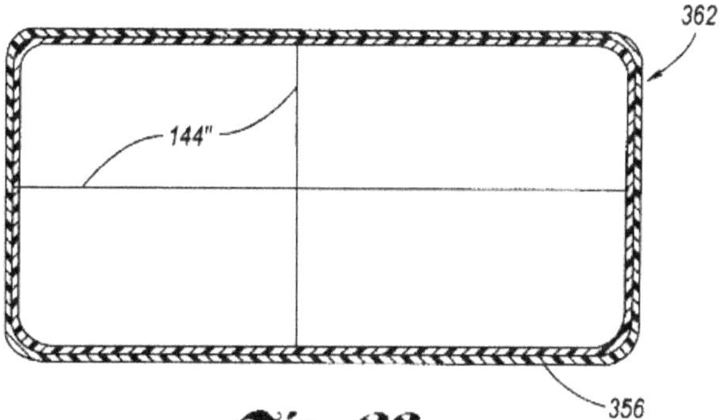

Fig. 23

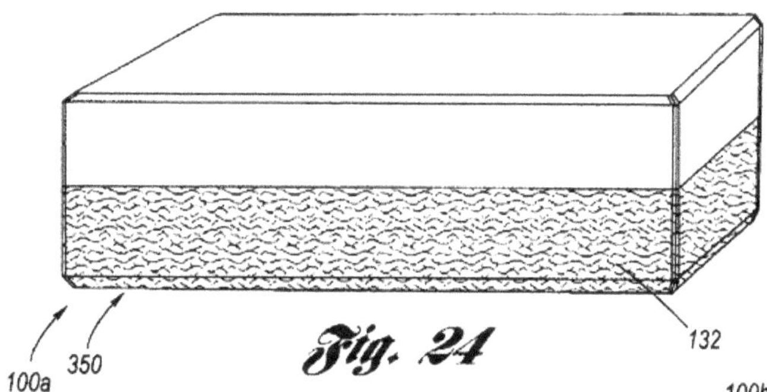

Fig. 24

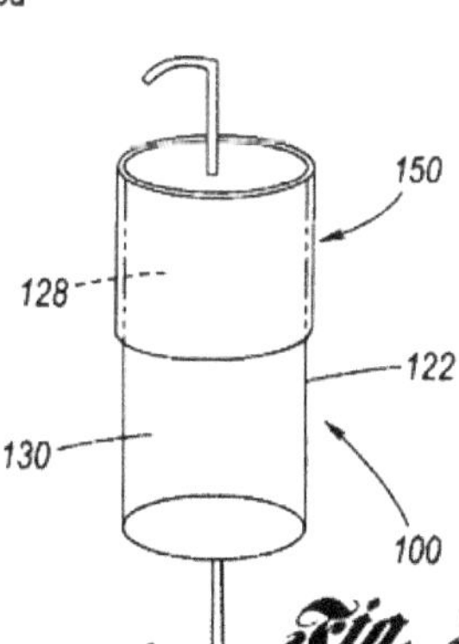

Fig. 25

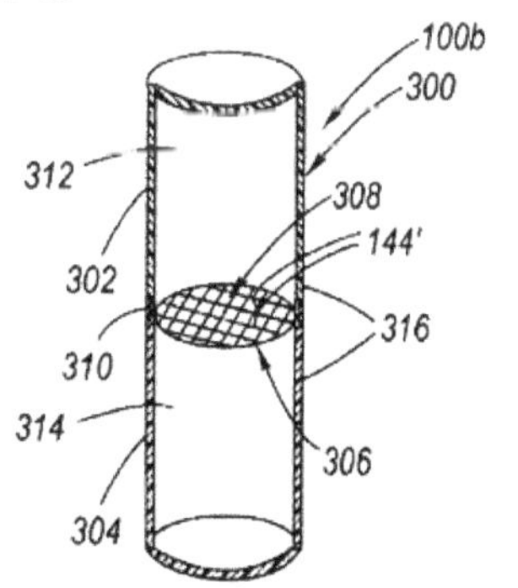

Fig. 26

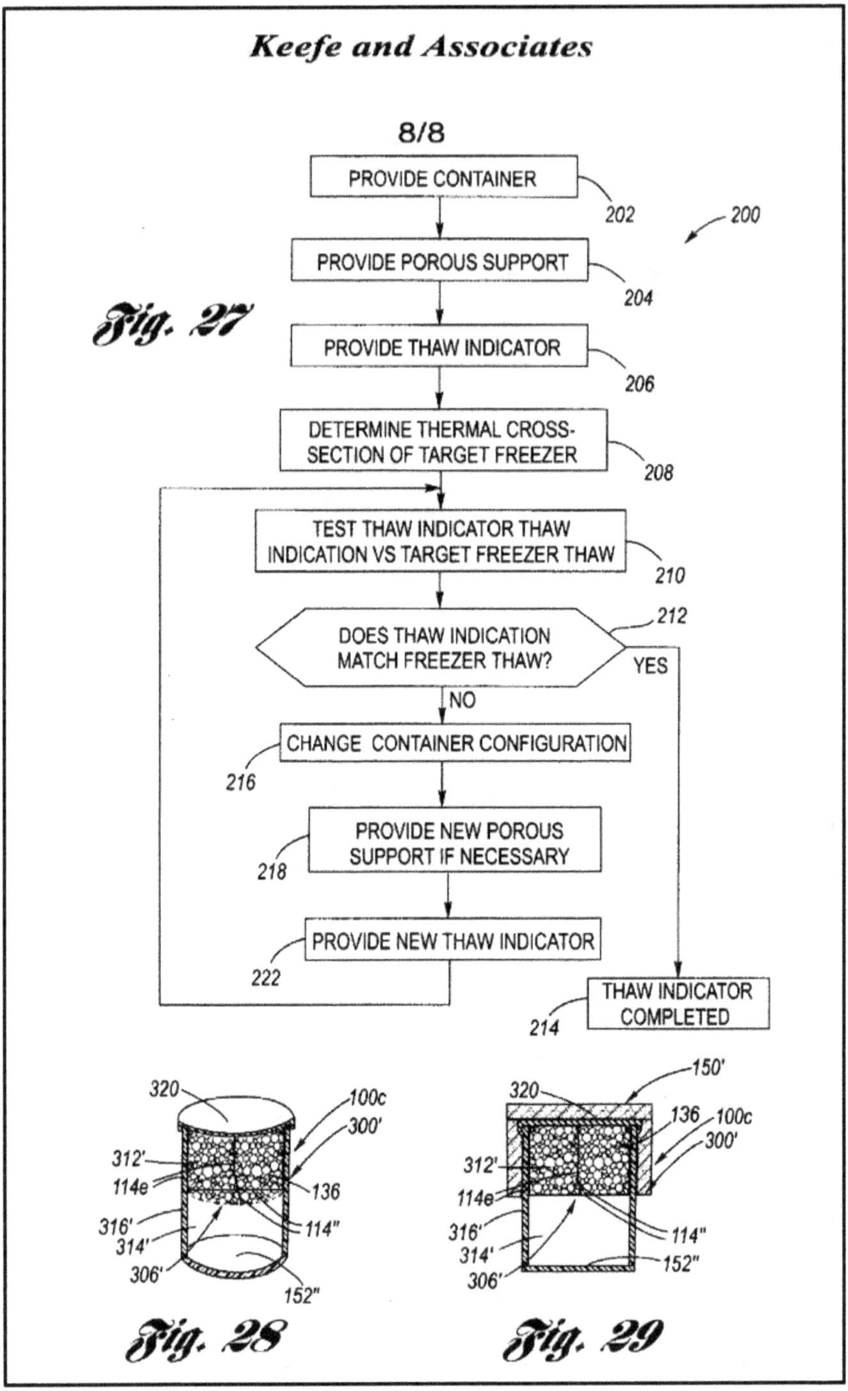
Keefe and Associates
8/8
PROVIDE CONTAINER
202
200
PROVIDE POROUS SUPPORT
204
Fig. 27
PROVIDE THAW INDICATOR
206
DETERMINE THERMAL CROSS-SECTION OF TARGET FREEZER
208
TEST THAW INDICATOR THAW INDICATION VS TARGET FREEZER THAW
210
212
DOES THAW INDICATION MATCH FREEZER THAW?
YES
NO
CHANGE CONTAINER CONFIGURATION
216
PROVIDE NEW POROUS SUPPORT IF NECESSARY
218
PROVIDE NEW THAW INDICATOR
222
THAW INDICATOR COMPLETED
214
320
100c
300'
312'
114e
136
316'
314'
114"
306'
152"
150'
Fig. 28
Fig. 29

1

FREEZER THAW INDICATOR

TECHNICAL FIELD

[0001] The present invention relates generally to refrigerated freezers which provide a cold zone of temperature below the freezing point of water at standard pressure.

[0002] More particularly, the present invention relates to an indicator device for indicating a thaw episode, wherein temperature above the freezing point of water has occurred in the cold zone.

[0003] Still more particularly, the present invention relates to an indicator device for indicating the thaw episode has been followed by a refreeze event.

BACKGROUND OF THE INVENTION

[0004] Refrigerated freezers (hereafter, simply freezers) are ubiquitous in household, commercial and industrial applications. Freezers provide a cold zone of temperature below the freezing point of water at standard pressure irrespective of the ambient temperature outside the freezer. Refrigeration is provided by a refrigeration apparatus, most commonly electrically powered, but other sources of power may be utilized, such as natural gas.

[0005] In the event the source of power is lost (a power outage), as for example the result of an interruption of service from a public utility, or even something so local as a child accidentally kicking out a power cord from its socket, the refrigeration apparatus of the freezer stops providing cooling of the cold zone. Heat from the ambient external environment is omnipresent and, assuming this is above the temperature of the cold zone, unremittingly transfers heat into the cold zone through the freezer walls (inclusive of door, seals, etc.). Without a regular extraction of heat by the refrigeration apparatus, heat transfer from the external environment will warm the cold zone, increasing the temperature thereof until the temperature of the cold zone and that of the external environment are equalized.

[0006] The rate at which the cold zone will warm depends upon the

2

difference in temperature between the cold zone and the external environment, the thermal conductivity of the freezer walls (inclusive of the door, seals, etc.), the specific heat of the materials of the freezer and the specific and latent heats of objects within the cold zone. The latent heat of the objects depends upon the mass of the objects and the inherent heat of fusion thereof. The combination of these physical properties shall be hereinbelow referred to as a "freezer thermal cross-section".

[0007] A freezer cold zone that is empty (filled with air) will warm much faster than one filled with objects. An example in everyday life of how latent heat retards heating is the duration for which an ice cube remains floating on a glass of tea in the summertime. Concomitant in this example, as long as the ice cube remains, the tea will stay cooler than the external environment of the glass.

[0008] While a power outage may be brief and the latent heat of the objects in the freezer able to absorb incoming heat so as to maintain substantially the below water freezing temperature of the cold zone of the freezer, an extended duration of power outage will eventually render a thaw of the objects in the freezer.

[0009] In the above nonlimiting scenarios, the power company will eventually restore power or a child may notice days later the plug had been kicked out of its socket and nonchalantly plug it back in. With power restored, the refrigeration apparatus of the freezer will re-establish the below water freezing temperature of the cold zone. A user of the freezer would likely be unable to know whether objects in the freezer stayed frozen or thawed and refroze. This is a worry for those who store frozen foods in a cold zone of a freezer and do not wish those foods to thaw and then refreeze.

[0010] Accordingly, what is needed in the art is a thaw indicator for indicating a thaw episode of a cold zone of a freezer has occurred, and further, indicating whether the thaw episode has been followed by a refreeze event.

SUMMARY OF THE INVENTION

[0011] The present invention is a freezer thaw indicator, or

3

“Thawometer”, for indicating a thaw episode of a cold zone of a freezer, and further indicating whether or not the thaw episode has been followed by a refreeze event.

[0012] The freezer thaw indicator according to the present invention is composed of a container providing a closed inner space composed of an upper chamber and a lower chamber. Between and demarcating the upper and lower chambers is a porous support member. Water, or another selected liquid, hereinafter simply ‘water’, partly fills the closed inner space of the container, preferably filling the upper chamber. At least a portion of the lower chamber is preferably transparent, most preferably clear. It is also preferred for the inside surface of the container walls to be hydrophobic (e.g., non-stick) so that the water does not wet the surface.

[0013] In operation, a user places the freezer thaw indicator into a cold zone of a freezer in an inverted attitude; that is, the upper chamber is vertically below the lower chamber with respect to gravity. After a period of time, the water freezes in the upper chamber.

[0014] The user then attitudinally rights the freezer thaw indicator so that the upper chamber is vertically above the lower chamber with respect to gravity, whereupon the ice remains in the upper chamber. No ice or water is present at the floor of the lower chamber, neglecting surface wetting as described in further detail hereinbelow.

[0015] In the event of occurrence of a thaw episode within the cold zone of the freezer, the ice in the upper chamber will melt, passing through the porous support member and collecting in the lower chamber. The severity of the thaw episode is recorded by the depth of water accumulation in the lower chamber.

[0016] In the event the refrigeration apparatus of the freezer re-establishes a frozen condition in the cold zone of the freezer, the water in the lower chamber will freeze into ice. The presence of ice in the lower chamber is indicative that the thaw episode, the severity of which being indicated by the depth of the ice, was followed by a refreeze event in the cold zone.

[0017] Accordingly, it is an object of the present invention to provide a

4

freezer thaw indicator for indicating occurrence of a thaw episode within the cold zone of a freezer.

[0018] It is a further object of the present invention to provide a freezer thaw indicator for indicating that a refreeze event of the cold zone of a freezer has transpired following the thaw episode.

[0019] It is yet another object of the present invention to provide a freezer thaw indicator of a simple, yet dependable mechanical construction that is not reliant on electronics.

[0020] This and additional objects, features and advantages of the present invention will become clearer from the following specification of a preferred embodiment.

BRIEF DESCRIPTION OF THE DRAWINGS

[0021] Figure 1 is a schematic diagram of a freezer in which the door and lower trim have been removed for clarity of the view, the view showing a refrigeration apparatus, a cold zone having therein objects, and insulated walls. The freezer thaw indicator according to the present invention is shown ready to indicate thaw.

[0022] Figure 2 is an enlarged view of the freezer thaw indicator of Figure 1.

[0023] Figure 3 is a schematic diagram as in Figure 1, wherein now the freezer thaw indicator indicates a thaw episode has occurred in the cold zone of the freezer, and further, that a refreeze event has thereafter transpired.

[0024] Figure 4 is an enlarged view of the freezer thaw indicator of Figure 3.

[0025] Figure 5 is a three dimensional cross-sectional view of the closed container and porous support member of the freezer thaw indicator of Figures 1 through 4, wherein the water has been removed for clarity.

[0026] Figure 5A is a cross-sectional view, seen along line 5A-5A of Figure 5.

[0027] Figure 6 is a three dimensional cross-sectional view, seen along line 6-6 of Figure 2.

5

[0028] Figure 7 is a two dimensional cross-sectional view, seen along line 6-6 of Figure 2.

[0029] Figures 8A and 8B show a first set-up step of installation of the freezer thaw indicator according to the present invention.

[0030] Figures 8C and 8D show a second set-up step of installation of the freezer thaw indicator according to the present invention.

[0031] Figures 9, 11, 13 and 15 are three dimensional cross-sectional views as in Figure 7, now showing progressive severity of thaw within the cold zone of the freezer of Figures 1 and 3.

[0032] Figures 10, 12, 14 and 16 are two dimensional cross-sectional views as in Figure 8, now showing progressive severity of thaw within the cold zone of the freezer of Figures 1 and 3.

[0033] Figures 17 through 20 are cross-sectional views as in Figure 5A, showing various structures of the porous support member.

[0034] Figure 21 depicts a squat cuboid configuration of the freezer thaw indicator according to the present invention, shown ready to indicate thaw.

[0035] Figure 22 is a sectional view, seen along line 22-22 of Figure 21.

[0036] Figure 23 is a sectional view, seen along line 23-23 of Figure 22.

[0037] Figure 24 is a view as in Figure 21, wherein now the freezer thaw indicator indicates a thaw episode has occurred in the cold zone of a freezer.

[0038] Figure 25 is a view of a freezer thaw indicator according to the present invention provided with a selective heat transfer rate sleeve.

[0039] Figure 26 is a cross-sectional view of a freezer thaw indicator similar to Figure 5, wherein now the porous support member is a window screen and the upper and lower hooks are absent.

[0040] Figure 27 is an algorithm for selectively adjusting the thaw sensitivity of the freezer thaw indicator according to the present invention with respect to a predetermined thermal cross-section of a freezer.

[0041] Figure 28 is a three dimensional cross-sectional view of a freezer thaw indicator according to the present invention described in Examples IV and VI.

[0042] Figure 29 is a two dimensional cross-sectional view of a freezer

6

thaw indicator according to the present invention described in Example V.

DESCRIPTION OF THE PREFERRED EMBODIMENT

[0043] Referring now to the Drawings, Figures 1 through 4 depict aspects for implementing a freezer thaw indicator 100 according to the present invention. Throughout the views and description below, water is referenced; however, another selected liquid can be substituted for water.

[0044] The freezer thaw indicator 100 can be implemented with any freezer 102, irrespective of its mode of refrigeration. Merely by way of example, the freezer 102 utilizes an electrically operated refrigeration apparatus 104, but natural gas refrigeration or other modalities of refrigeration may be utilized by the freezer to provide a cold zone 106 thereinside.

[0045] The cold zone 106 is a region within the freezer 102 which provides a volume at a selected cold temperature, T_c, below the freezing temperature of water at ambient atmospheric pressure. For example, at sea level, the freezing temperature of water is 32 degrees Fahrenheit (zero degrees Celsius). A cold zone 106 for the preservation of frozen food, by way of example, may have a cold temperature, T_c, of between zero and 10 degrees Fahrenheit. The cold zone 106 is shielded from the heat of the (typically) warmer external environment by insulated walls 110, wherein the term "walls" includes the door, seals, etc. Of course, in applications where the freezer is subjected to external cold, such as an application in which the freezer is disposed in an unheated garage in winter of a northern state, the temperature of the external environment can fall below the cold zone temperature, in which case the refrigeration apparatus is idle.

[0046] The cold zone 106 may have compartments and/or shelving 108 for the placement of objects 112 therein. The objects 112 may be foods, medications, chemicals, etc. The objects 112 may be pre-frozen or freeze after placement into the cold zone 106.

[0047] As depicted at Figures 1 and 3, the freezer thaw indicator 100 dependingly hangs from a shelf 108 of the freezer 102. As will be discussed hereinbelow, this mode of operation is not required, as the freezer thaw

7

indicator according to the present invention may simply rest upon any surface in the cold zone 106 (see Examples I through VI).

[0048] Turning attention now additionally to Figures 5 and 5A, the freezer thaw indicator 100 is composed of a container 120.

[0049] The container walls 122 may be, for nonlimiting example, composed of plastic, glass, or another material suitable for the purpose of the present invention. The container 120 is closed in the sense that a liquid thereinside cannot leak out.

[0050] A porous support member 124 is disposed cross-sectionally at a predetermined location within the container walls 122, preferably at the mid-point M thereof. By way of example, the porous support member 124 is glued, heat or sonic welded, over-molded, snap-fit, anchored or otherwise fixed in relation to the container walls 122. For example as shown at Figure 5A, a ring 126 supporting filaments 144 may attach to the inside surface 122i of the container walls 122. The selected location of the porous support member 124 provides a demarcation at which the interior space 120a of the container 120 is divided into an upper chamber 128 on one side 124a of the porous support member and a lower chamber 130 on the other side 124b of the porous support member.

[0051] It should be noted that the presence of a ring could cause melt water retention between the ice and the container wall during the initial stage of a thaw event. If the thaw event abruptly ceases and the melt refreezes, there could be no indication of thaw in the lower chamber. To prevent this, the ring should be very thin (i.e., the diameter of a filament), as shown at Figure 5A, set into a recess of the container walls, or otherwise configured to prevent any ice melt retention.

[0052] Water 132 is placed into the closed inner space 120a, preferably filling the upper chamber 128. For example as shown at Figure 5, water is injected into the container through an opening 134, after which the opening is sealed. Other examples of water filling techniques include removing a cap at one end of the container, filling the water, then replacing the cap as shown at Figures 28 and 29 (preferably a one time removable cap modality), or having

8

the container assemble from two or more component parts, wherein water is filled prior to assembly of the parts as shown at Figures 22 and 26. Other water filling techniques may be used.

[0053] Preferably, the container has equal volumes of the upper and lower chambers 128, 130, although this is not requisite. The lower chamber 130 is preferably transparent, most preferably transparently clear, which may be for example realized by a vertically transparent sight provided in the wall 122 for observing the liquid level in the lower chamber. The upper chamber 128 may be likewise transparent, or may be otherwise, as for example opaque.

[0054] The water 132 is preferred to be visually altered by addition of a visual marker. The visual marker may be for example coloration, as for example by the addition of dye, ink or food/water coloring, or may be for example luminescence, as for example by the addition of a luminescent pigment or dye, wherein the visual marker makes notable to an onlooker the presence of water in the lower chamber 130. It is also preferred for the inside surface 122i of the container walls 122 to be hydrophobic (e.g., non-stick) so that the water does not wet the surface.

[0055] Referring now additionally to Figures 6 through 16, operation of the freezer thaw indicator 100 will be detailed.

[0056] As shown at Figures 8A through 8D, a user places the freezer thaw indicator 100 into the cold zone 106 of a freezer 102 in an inverted attitude, that is, the upper chamber 128 is vertically below the lower chamber 130 with respect to gravity. This may be accomplished, for example, by a first hook 138a hooked onto a shelf 108. In this orientation, the water 132 is present in the upper chamber 128, by way of example shown at Figure 8B. After a period of time, the water 132 freezes into ice 136 in the upper chamber 128, by way of example shown at Figure 8D.

[0057] As shown at Figures 1, 2, 6 and 7, the user then attitudinally rights the freezer thaw indicator 100, whereupon the upper chamber 128 is vertically above the lower chamber 130 with respect to gravity. For example, this may be accomplished by a second hook 138b hooked onto the shelf 108. The ice 136 in the upper chamber 128 is held in place by surface interaction with the

9

inside surface 122i and/or by resting upon the porous support member 124 and no ice or water is present at the floor 152 of the lower chamber 130, ignoring any water present due to surface wetting.

[0058] As progressively depicted in Figures 9 through 16, in the event of occurrence of a thaw episode within the cold zone of the freezer, the ice 136 in the upper chamber 128 will melt, whereupon water 132 of the melt will pass through the porous support member 124 and collect in the lower chamber 130. The severity of the thaw episode is recorded by the depth of water 132 accumulated in the lower chamber 130. During melting, ice 136 in the upper chamber 128 will be supported by the porous support member 124.

[0059] In the event the refrigeration apparatus 104 of the freezer 102 re-operates and re-establishes a freezing temperature, as for example the cold temperature, T_c, in the cold zone 106 of the freezer 102, the water 132 in the lower chamber 130 will refreeze into ice (the liquid frozen) 136, as depicted at Figures 3 and 4.

[0060] The presence of either water 132 or ice 136 in the lower chamber 130 is indicative that a thaw episode has occurred, the severity of which being indicated by the depth of the water or ice. The presence of ice 136 in the lower chamber 130 is indicative that after the thaw episode a refreeze event transpired. This means the objects in the refrigerator have been subjected to a thaw and refreeze cycle. Of course, this may include several thaw/refreeze cycles in the final result observed in the lower chamber 130.

[0061] In the prior art, if after a thaw episode the refrigeration apparatus has re-frozen the objects 112 in the cold zone 106, an unsuspecting user would not know of the thaw episode. However in accordance with the present invention, the presence of ice 136 in the lower chamber 130 of the freezer thaw indicator 100 reliably reveals information regarding the thaw and refreeze cycle to the user.

[0062] The freezer thaw indicator is usable over and over again. To reset the freezer thaw indicator 100 for another usage, if ice is present in the lower chamber, preferably but not necessarily, it is allowed to thaw, as for example by placement in a room temperature kitchen area. Then the steps above are repeated: an inverted attitude freeze, as per Figures 8A through 8D is followed by a righted attitude operability, as per Figures 1, 2, 6 and 7.

[0063] In Figures 1 through 16, the porous support member 124 consists of a cross-hairs 140 attached to a ring 126 (see Figure 5A). The cross-hairs 140 are mutually orthogonal and may be composed of aluminum wire, fiberglass thread or other filaments or rods 144. By way of example, a filament may be on the order of 0.01 inch diameter. The ring 126, preferably thin, recessed or otherwise configure as discussed hereinabove, provides a periphery of the porous support member 124 for abutting relation to the inside surface 122i of the container walls 122, whereat the ring is attached, as mentioned above. In this regard, filaments are preferably stretched taut across the ring 126, whereas stiff rods may connect with the ring or obviate the ring by direct interface with the container walls 122.

[0064] Figures 17 through 20 show examples of variations of configuration of the porous support member 124. In Figure 17, the porous support member 124a is composed of a plurality of filaments 144a arranged in a mutually radial configuration. In Figure 18, the porous support member 124b is composed of a plurality of filaments 144b arranged in a mutually rectilinear configuration. In Figure 19, the porous support member 124c is composed of a disc 146 having formed therein a plurality of openings 146a. Note that the central region 146b of the disc 146 has no hole, as the ice melt will likely result in an ice shard (see for example Figures 13 and 14) which would undesirably otherwise fall through a central hole if it was to be provided. In Figure 20, the porous support member 124d is composed of a stiff mesh 148, as for example a stiff polyether foam. Other configurations can be implemented, as for example described in Examples IV through VI.

[0065] While the freezer thaw indicator according to the present invention may have an elongated cylinder configuration with first and second hooks as shown generally at Figures 1 through 16, the freezer thaw indicator can have other shapes. By way of example, Figures 21 through 24 depict a squat cuboid shaped freezer thaw indicator 100a suitable for resting upon a shelf 108 of the freezer 102. An example of the freezer thaw indicator 100a is

11

discussed in detail in Example III.

[0066] It is to be understood that any shape and/or size of freezer thaw indicator is contemplated by the present invention.

[0067] Figure 25 depicts a variation of the freezer thaw indicator 100 in which a sheath 150 is slid over the container walls 122. While the sheath 150 may be disposed over the upper chamber 128, as shown, it can also cover the lower chamber 130 if it is cooperatively transparent thereat. The purpose of the sheath 150 is to adjust the thermal sensitivity of the upper chamber 128 during a thaw episode to coincide with a thermal cross-section of the freezer 102 such that the melt rate of the ice 136 coincides with the thaw rate of the objects 112 in the cold zone 106. The sheath may be used for any configuration freezer thaw indicator, as for example including that shown in Figures 21 through 24; see also Figure 29.

[0068] In summation, the method according to the present invention includes: providing a freezer thaw indicator having container walls defining a closed inner space, a porous support member disposed in the closed inner space and fixed in positional relation to the container walls such that on one side of the porous support member is an upper chamber of the closed inner space and on the other side of the porous support member is a lower chamber of the closed inner space, wherein a liquid partly fills the closed inner space; orienting the container to a first orientation such that the lower chamber is vertically above the upper chamber with respect to gravity, wherein the liquid is disposed in the upper chamber; freezing the liquid, as for example by cold of the cold zone of the freezer; orienting the container to a second orientation such that the upper chamber is vertically above the lower chamber with respect to gravity, wherein the frozen liquid remains in the upper chamber; placing the container in the cold zone; and indicating occurrence of a thaw episode of the cold zone of the freezer by presence of the liquid in the lower chamber.

[0069] Further according to the method of the present invention, indicating occurrence of the thaw episode and occurrence of a refreeze event thereafter by presence of the liquid frozen in the lower chamber.

12

[0070] Still further according to the method of the present invention, reusing the freezer thaw indicator. The reuse including: preferably but not necessarily, melting any frozen liquid in the lower chamber; reorienting the container to the first orientation, wherein the liquid is disposed in the upper chamber; refreezing the liquid, as for example by cold of the cold zone of the freezer; reorienting the container to the second orientation, wherein the frozen liquid remains in the upper chamber; placing the container in the cold zone; and re-indicating occurrence of a thaw episode of the cold zone of the freezer by presence of the liquid in the lower chamber.

[0071] Figure 27 is an algorithm 200 for adjusting the thermal sensitivity of a freezer thaw indicator according to the present invention, wherein the ice melt in the upper chamber thereof during a thaw episode coincides with a thermal cross-section of the freezer.

[0072] The algorithm begins at Block 202, whereat container walls are configured.

[0073] At Block 204, a porous support member is provided.

[0074] At Block 206, the porous support member is fixed in positional relation to the inside surface of the container walls, establishing demarcation between upper and lower chambers of the container walls. For example, the container walls may be constructed of two components, allowing placement of the porous support member, whereupon the two components are then sealingly attached to each other. For a second example, the container walls may be molded over the porous support member. Water is introduced into the container walls. This may be carried out as a shown at Figure 5 with the opening 134 therefor sealed thereafter. The water introduction step can be separate or performed in conjunction with the two component attachment operation.

[0075] At Block 208, a thermal cross-section for a cold zone of a freezer is determined. For example, a freezer is provided (or simulated) which has a predetermined thermal transfer rate and includes an estimate of specific and latent heat capacities of a likely collection of objects in the cold zone together with the thermal heat transfer rate from an external environment into the cold

13

zone based upon selected initial thaw episode starting temperatures of the external environment (considered a constant) and the cold zone (continually rising until the temperature of the external environment is reached). For example, the objects may equivocate to the specific and latent heat capacities of 6 gallons of frozen water and the heat transfer is from room temperature (72 degrees Fahrenheit) of the external environment to progressively increasing cold zone temperature starting at 3 degrees Fahrenheit. A freezer thermal cross-section time for heat from the external environment to raise the temperature in the cold zone to above 32 degrees Fahrenheit (whereupon thawing occurs at sea level) is determined empirically or by standard and well known equations of physics for heat transfer processes. A freezer thermal heat cross-section time may, for example, be 36 hours. A food safety factor may be included which reduces the freezer thermal heat cross-section time.

[0076] At Block 210, the freezer thaw indicator is tested in the cold zone of a freezer with the determined thermal cross-section by inducing a thaw episode. In this regard, the test empirically examines whether ice melt in the freezer thaw indicator matches with thaw of the objects in the cold zone.

[0077] At Decision Block 212, inquiry is made whether the freezer thaw indicator properly indicated the severity of the thaw episode. For example, if the lower chamber is filled with water at about the same time the objects thawed, then agreement is made. If, however, there is yet ice in the upper chamber and the objects are thawed, then the freezer thaw indicator is not sensitive enough. If, however, the lower chamber is filled with water and the objects are still generally frozen, then the freezer thaw indicator is too sensitive.

[0078] If the answer to the inquiry at Decision Block 212 is yes, then the algorithm proceeds to Block 214 and ends with a completed freezer thaw indicator for a range of freezers generally having the freezer thermal cross-section.

[0079] If the answer to the inquiry at Decision Block 212 is no, then the algorithm proceeds to Blocks 216 through 220, and then to Block 210. In this regard, the process can proceed as in Blocks 202 through 206, and/or a sheath, as for example shown in Figure 25, may be installed or adjusted for thermal transfer therethrough. More particularly by way of example, if there was yet ice in the upper chamber as a result of the inquiry of Decision Block 212, then the freezer thaw indicator needs to be provided with a higher heat conductivity through the upper chamber. On the other hand more particularly by way of example, if the lower chamber was prematurely filled with water as a result of the inquiry of Decision Block 212, then the freezer thaw indicator needs to be provided with a lower heat conductivity through the upper chamber. These heat transfer adjustments may be made, for example, by adjusting the thickness and/or material of the container walls and/or of the sheath.

[0080] It is to be noted the above steps may be carried out empirically or by electronic computer simulation.

[0081] Advantageously, a graduated scale 400 may be placed visibly onto the container wall 122 at the lower chamber 130. The graduation of the graduated scale may indicate, for example, depth of melt water during a thaw event, percent of thaw of the ice in the upper chamber, and/or the graduation may be calibrated with respect to the freezer thermal cross-section so as to indicate duration of the thaw, as for example in hours (or selected multiples thereof), as for example shown at Figures 2 and 4.

[0082] It is to be noted that some regions of the cold zone of the freezer may be more susceptible to thaw than others. For example, objects in shelves of the door will be more susceptible to thaw than objects in the center of the freezer cold zone. In this regard, a user could utilize two or more freezer thaw indicators, preferably with differing thermal sensitivities. For example, one placed on a door shelf and another centrally disposed in the cold zone.

[0083] Further, the sheath may have user application. For example, the freezer thaw indicator can be supplied with a preset sensitivity to thaw, suitable for central placement in a cold zone sparsely populated by objects, or for a freezer door shelf. In which case, if the freezer is densely populated with objects, the user would slip the sheath over the upper chamber to reduce thermal sensitivity of the freezer thaw indicator when placed centrally in the

15

cold zone.

EXAMPLE I

[0084] A freezer thaw indicator 100b according to the present invention was fashioned as schematically shown at Figure 26. The container 300 was composed of two commercially available translucent cylindrical plastic components 302 and 304, each about 4 inches long and about one inch in diameter, which provided thin container walls 316 and upper and lower chambers 312, 314. An air hole at the end of each component was sealed by hot melt glue. The porous support member 306 was fashioned from a piece of common aluminum window screen 308 composed of a plurality of aluminum wire filaments 114' in a rectilinear pattern glued to the upper component adjacent the opening thereof. Water, not shown, was added so as to fill the upper component, and the components were thereupon pressed together at a stair-step interconnection 310.

[0085] The test freezer was the freezer unit of a Whirlpool "side-by-side" refrigerator. The cold temperature of the cold zone thereof was about 3 degrees Fahrenheit. The assembled freezer thaw indicator was inverted, the upper chamber 312 being vertically below the upper chamber 314 with respect to gravity, and placed into the cold zone and the water was allowed to freeze overnight.

[0086] The freezer thaw indicator was then removed from the cold zone of the freezer. The freezer thaw indicator was turned right side up, wherein the upper chamber 312 having ice thereinside (the ice not being shown in Figure 26), was vertically above the lower chamber 314 and the ice supported on the window screen. The freezer thaw indicator was then placed into a room temperature location of a kitchen in the right side up orientation.

[0087] Simultaneously, several frozen dinners were placed side-by-side with each other in proximal spatial relation to the freezer thaw indicator in order to provide a simulated objects thaw in a freezer with a determined thermal cross-section undergoing a thaw episode.

16

[0088] In approximately 3 hours the ice in the upper chamber melted and collected as water in mostly the bottom chamber. The frozen dinners were on the verge of thaw, but could be considered still frozen enough for safe re-freezing, although this is subjective.

[0089] It was noted that because of surface tension at the window screen, melt water tended to accumulate in the upper chamber until the weight of the water exceed the force of the surface tension.

[0090] It was concluded the performance of the freezer thaw indicator was dissatisfactory for its intended purpose due to melt water retention in the upper chamber caused by the surface tension of the window screen.

EXAMPLE II

[0091] A freezer thaw indicator according to the present invention was fashioned as schematically shown at Figure 26, but now with the cross-hairs porous support member of Figure 5A. The container 300 was composed of the previously described translucent, thin walled, cylindrical plastic components 302 and 304 forming the upper and lower chambers 312, 314 of Example I. The porous support member was fashioned from a cross-hair of two aluminum wire window screen filaments, see 144 in Figure 5A, oriented orthogonal to each other, and secured by an overage portion of the filaments held to the outside of the wall by adhesive tape. Water was added as described above, and the components ere pressed together at the stair-step interconnection.

[0092] The test freezer was the Whirlpool "side-by-side" refrigerator of Example I. The assembled freezer thaw indicator was inverted, as per Example I, and placed into the cold zone and allowed to freeze overnight.

[0093] The freezer thaw indicator was then removed from the cold zone of the freezer, turned right side up (as per Example I), and placed into a room temperature location of a kitchen, wherein the ice was supported on the cross-hairs.

17

[0094] In approximately just over 2.5 hours the ice in the upper chamber melted and collected as water in the bottom chamber. The observed melt process went forward substantially as depicted in Figures 9 through 16.

[0095] It was noted that the ice remained supported on the cross-hairs due to a small amount of melt grooving, which essentially secured the ice to the cross-hairs as the ice melted. There was a total absence of melt water retention in the upper chamber due to surface tension.

[0096] It was concluded the performance of the freezer thaw indicator was satisfactory for its intended purpose of indicating a thaw episode.

EXAMPLE III

[0097] A freezer thaw indicator 100a according to the present invention was fashioned as schematically shown at Figures 21 through 24, having a squat cuboid shape and a cross-hairs porous support member.

[0098] The container 350 was composed of two commercially available translucent cuboid plastic components 352 and 354 having thin walls 356. Each component was about 0.75 inch deep, about 4 inches long and about 2.75 inches wide, providing upper and lower chambers 358, 360 (see Figure 22).

[0099] The porous support member 362 was fashioned from a cross-hair of two aluminum window screen filaments 144'' oriented orthogonal to each other, as shown at Figure 23. In this regard, the filaments were secured by an overage portion thereof being held to the outside of the wall by adhesive tape. Water was added so as to fill the upper component 358, and the components then pressed together at a stair-step interconnection 364.

[00100] The test freezer was the Whirlpool "side-by-side" refrigerator as described in Example I. The assembled freezer thaw indicator was inverted (as described in Example I) and then placed into the cold zone and allowed to freeze overnight.

[00101] The freezer thaw indicator was then removed from the cold zone of the freezer and then turned right side up (as described in Example I).

18

No discernable ice or water was present on the floor 152'. The freezer thaw indicator was thereupon placed into a room temperature location of a kitchen, wherein the ice was supported on the cross-hairs.

[00102] In approximately 3 hours the ice in the upper chamber melted and collected as water in the bottom chamber. The observed melt process went forward analogous to that depicted in Figures 9 through 16, wherein now the ice was configured as a block, rather than as a cylinder.

[00103] It was noted that the ice remained supported on the cross-hairs due to a small amount of melt grooving, which essentially secured the ice to the cross-hairs as the ice melted. There was a total absence of melt water retention in the upper chamber due to surface tension.

[00104] It was concluded the performance of the freezer thaw indicator was satisfactory for its intended purpose of indicating a thaw episode.

EXAMPLE IV

[00105] A freezer thaw indicator 100c according to the present invention was fashioned as schematically shown at Figure 28. The container 300' was composed of a commercially available clear, thin walled, cylindrical plastic cylinder with an open mouth top with an outwardly facing rim bulb. A resilient cap 320 press-fit onto the mouth to provide a sealed inner space of the container. The cap and the plastic cylinder constituted the container walls 316'. The container 300' had a height of about 1.5 inches and a diameter of about 1.12 inches. A commercial car finish wax was applied to the inside surfaces of the container and the cap in an effort to provide a hydrophobic property.

[00106] The porous support member 306' was fashioned from a cross-hair of two aluminum wire window screen filaments 114'' oriented orthogonal to each other, and secured by a vertical leg 114e anchored at the seal of the cap with the mouth.

19

[00107] A commercial food coloring (red 3) was added to water and stirred to provide water with a visual marker. The water with visual marker was added with the cap removed, wherein the lower chamber 314' was filled and wherein the upper chamber 312' was about the same volume. The cap was then snapped onto the mouth.

[00108] The test freezer was the Whirlpool "side-by-side" refrigerator of Example I. The freezer thaw indicator was inverted, as per Example I, and placed into the cold zone and allowed to freeze for several hours.

[00109] The freezer thaw indicator was then removed from the cold zone of the freezer, turned right side up, and placed into a room temperature location of a kitchen, wherein the ice 136 was supported on the cross-hairs.

[00110] In approximately 1.5 hours the ice in the upper chamber melted and collected as water in the bottom chamber. The observed melt process went forward substantially as depicted in Figures 9 through 16.

[00111] It was noted that the ice remained supported on the cross-hairs due to a small amount of melt grooving, which essentially secured the ice to the cross-hairs as the ice melted. There was a total absence of melt water retention in the upper chamber due to surface tension. However, the wax did not provide the desired level of hydrophobic property, as some wetting occurred in the 90 degree corner of the periphery of the floor 152''. In this regard, it was surmised the rounded corners of the container walls of Example III reduced observance of surface wetting, and conjectured that the plastic may have been natively hydrophobic.

[00112] It was concluded the performance of the freezer thaw indicator was moderately satisfactory for its intended purpose of indicating a thaw episode.

EXAMPLE V

[00113] A freezer thaw indicator 100c according to the present invention was fashioned as schematically shown at Figure 29 (containers 300' and porous support members 306' are identical in both Figures 28 and 29).

20

The container 300' was composed of a commercially available clear, thin walled, cylindrical plastic cylinder with an open mouth top with an outwardly facing rim bulb. A resilient cap 320 press-fit onto the mouth to provide a sealed inner space of the container. The cap and the plastic cylinder constituted the container walls 316'. The container 300' had a height of about 1.5 inches and a diameter of about 1.12 inches. A commercial car finish wax was applied to the inside surfaces of the container and the cap in an effort to provide a hydrophobic property.

[00114] The porous support member 306' was fashioned from a cross-hair of two aluminum wire window screen filaments 114'' oriented orthogonal to each other, and secured by a vertical leg 114e anchored at the seal of the cap with the mouth.

[00115] A commercial food coloring (red 3) was added to water and stirred to provide water with a visual marker. The water with visual marker was added with the cap removed, wherein the lower chamber 314' was filled and wherein the upper chamber 312' was about the same volume. The cap was then snapped onto the mouth.

[00116] A commercial 0.375 inch thick foam weather strip with an adhesive backing was applied to the container walls at the upper chamber 312' to provide a sheath 150'.

[00117] The test freezer was the Whirlpool "side-by-side" refrigerator of Example I. The freezer thaw indicator was inverted, as per Example I, and placed into the cold zone and allowed to freeze overnight. After application of the sheath 150', the freezer thaw indicator was placed into the cold zone for another two hours to achieve thermal equilibrium to the temperature of the cold zone.

[00118] The freezer thaw indicator was then removed from the cold zone of the freezer, turned right side up, and placed into a room temperature location of a kitchen, wherein the ice 136 was supported on the cross-hairs.

[00119] In approximately just under 2.5 hours the ice in the upper chamber melted and collected as water in the bottom chamber. The observed melt process went forward substantially as depicted in Figures 9 through 16.

21

[00120] It was noted that the ice remained supported on the cross-hairs due to a small amount of melt grooving, which essentially secured the ice to the cross-hairs as the ice melted. There was a total absence of melt water retention in the upper chamber due to surface tension.

[00121] It was concluded the performance of the freezer thaw indicator was moderately satisfactory for its intended purpose of indicating a thaw episode due to the aforementioned peripheral wetting at the floor 152''.

EXAMPLE VI

[00122] A freezer thaw indicator 100c according to the present invention was fashioned as schematically shown at Figure 28. The container 300' was composed of a commercially available clear, thin walled, cylindrical plastic cylinder with an open mouth top with an outwardly facing rim bulb. A resilient cap 320 press-fit onto the mouth to provide a sealed inner space of the container. The cap and the plastic cylinder constituted the container walls 316'. The container 300' had a height of about 1.5 inches and a diameter of about 1.12 inches. A hydrophobic silicone polymer, commercially known as "Rain-X", a registered trademark product distributed by Sopus Products of Houston, TX, was applied to the inside surfaces of the container and the cap to provide a hydrophobic property.

[00123] The porous support member 306' was fashioned from a cross-hair of two aluminum wire window screen filaments 114'' oriented orthogonal to each other, and secured by a vertical leg 114e anchored at the seal of the cap with the mouth.

[00124] Rolling ball pen liquid ink (red) was added to water and stirred to provide water with a visual marker. The water with visual marker was added with the cap removed, wherein the lower chamber 314' was filled and wherein the upper chamber 312' was about the same volume. The cap was then snapped onto the mouth.

22

[00125] The test freezer was the Whirlpool "side-by-side" refrigerator of Example I. The freezer thaw indicator was inverted, as per Example I, and placed into the cold zone and allowed to freeze for several hours.

[00126] The freezer thaw indicator was then removed from the cold zone of the freezer, turned right side up, and placed into a room temperature location of a kitchen, wherein the ice 136 was supported on the cross-hairs.

[00127] In approximately 1.75 hours the ice in the upper chamber melted and collected as water in the bottom chamber. The observed melt process went forward substantially as depicted in Figures 9 through 16.

[00128] It was noted that the ice remained supported on the cross-hairs due to a small amount of melt grooving, which essentially secured the ice to the cross-hairs as the ice melted. There was a total absence of melt water retention in the upper chamber due to surface tension. Additionally, the hydrophobic silicone polymer provided the desired level of hydrophobic property, as there was no wetting in the 90 degree corner of the periphery of the floor 152''.

[00129] It was concluded the performance of the freezer thaw indicator was satisfactory for its intended purpose of indicating a thaw episode.

[00130] To those skilled in the art to which this invention appertains, the above described preferred embodiment may be subject to change or modification. For example, the freezer thaw indicator according to the present invention could serve as a thaw/refreeze indicator in other applications, such as a frozen carbon dioxide cooled ice chest. Such change or modification can be carried out without departing from the scope of the invention, which is intended to be limited only by the scope of the appended claims.

23

CLAIMS

1. A freezer thaw indicator, comprising:

a container comprising container walls defining a closed inner space;

a porous support member disposed in said closed inner space of said container, said porous support member being affixed in positional relation to said container walls, said porous support member dividing said closed inner space into an upper chamber on one side of said porous support member and a lower chamber on the other side of said support member; and

a liquid disposed in said closed inner space, wherein said liquid partly fills said closed inner space;

wherein said porous support member is porous with respect to said liquid;

wherein if said liquid freezes into a frozen liquid in said upper chamber and said container is oriented such that said upper chamber is vertically above said lower chamber in relation to gravity, then said frozen liquid remains in said upper chamber; and

wherein if said frozen liquid melts in said upper chamber and said container is oriented such that said upper chamber is vertically above said lower chamber in relation to gravity, then said porous support member supports said frozen liquid and said liquid passes through said porous support member and collects in said lower chamber.

2. The freezer thaw indicator of Claim 1, further comprising:

a first hook connected to said container walls adjacent said lower chamber; and

a second hook connected to said container walls adjacent said upper chamber.

3. The freezer thaw indicator of Claim 1, wherein said container walls are hydrophobic.

24

4. The freezer thaw indicator of Claim 1, wherein said container walls at said lower chamber are transparent.

5. The freezer thaw indicator of Claim 1, further comprising a graduated scale on said wall of said lower chamber.

6. The freezer thaw indicator of Claim 1, wherein said liquid contains a visual marker.

7. The freezer thaw indicator of Claim 1, further comprising a sheath at least partly covering said sidewalls adjoining said upper chamber.

8. The freezer thaw indicator of Claim 1, wherein said upper and lower chambers have substantially equal volumes.

9. The freezer thaw indicator of Claim 1, wherein:
said container walls at said lower chamber are transparent;
said container walls are hydrophobic;
said liquid contains a visual marker.

10. The freezer thaw indicator of Claim 9, further comprising:
a first hook connected to said container walls adjacent said lower chamber; and
a second hook connected to said container walls adjacent said upper chamber.

11. The freezer thaw indicator of Claim 9, further comprising a sheath at least partly covering said sidewalls adjoining said upper chamber.

12. The freezer thaw indicator of Claim 9, wherein said liquid comprises water and said frozen liquid comprises ice.

25

13. The freezer thaw indicator of Claim 9, wherein said upper and lower chambers have substantially equal volumes.

14. The freezer thaw indicator of Claim 9, further comprising a graduated scale on said wall of said lower chamber.

15. A method for indicating occurrence of a thaw episode of a cold zone of a freezer, said method comprising the steps of:

providing a freezer thaw indicator having container walls defining a closed inner space, a porous support member disposed in the closed inner space and fixed in positional relation to the container walls such that on one side of said porous support member is an upper chamber of said closed inner space and on the other side of said porous support member is a lower chamber of said closed inner space, wherein a liquid partly fills the closed inner space;

orienting the container to a first orientation such that the lower chamber is vertically above the upper chamber with respect to gravity, wherein the liquid is disposed in the upper chamber;

freezing the liquid in the first orientation;

orienting the container to a second orientation such that the upper chamber is vertically above the lower chamber with respect to gravity, wherein the frozen liquid remains in the upper chamber;

placing the container in the cold zone; and

indicating occurrence of a thaw episode of the cold zone of the freezer by presence of the liquid in the lower chamber.

16. The method of Claim 15, further comprising indicating occurrence of the thaw episode and occurrence of refreeze event thereafter by presence of the liquid frozen in the lower chamber.

17. The method of Claim 15, further comprising reusing the freezer thaw indicator after said step of indicating, comprising the steps of:

26

reorienting the container to the first orientation, wherein the liquid is disposed in the upper chamber;

refreezing the liquid in the first orientation;

reorienting the container to the second orientation, wherein the frozen liquid remains in the upper chamber;

placing the container in the cold zone; and

re-indicating occurrence of a thaw episode of the cold zone of the freezer by presence of the liquid in the lower chamber.

18. A method for adjusting thermal sensitivity of a freezer thaw indicator to match a thermal cross-section of a freezer, said method comprising the steps of:

providing container walls defining a closed inner space;

providing a porous support member disposed in the closed inner space and fixed in positional relation to the container walls such that on one side of the porous support member is an upper chamber of the closed inner space and on the other side of the porous support member is a lower chamber of the closed inner space;

providing a freezer thaw indicator by introduction of a liquid into the closed inner space, wherein the liquid partly fills the inner space;

providing a cold zone of a freezer having a thermal cross-section, the thermal cross-section including at least one frozen object;

orienting the container to a first orientation such that the lower chamber is vertically above the upper chamber with respect to gravity, wherein the liquid is disposed in the upper chamber;

freezing the liquid in the first orientation;

orienting the container to a second orientation such that the upper chamber is vertically above the lower chamber with respect to gravity, wherein the frozen liquid remains in the upper chamber;

inducing a thaw episode of the cold zone;

indicating occurrence of the thaw episode of the cold zone of the freezer by presence of the liquid in the lower chamber; and

27

determining whether the indication of occurrence matches thaw of the at least one frozen object;

wherein if said step of determining determines a match, then the freezer thaw indicator has a correct sensitivity; and

wherein if said step of determining determines a mismatch, then the freezer thaw indicator has an incorrect sensitivity and said step of providing container walls is repeated until said step of determining determines a match.

19. The method of Claim 18, wherein said steps are carried out electronically by a computer based simulation.

20. The method of Claim 18, wherein the repeating of said step of providing container walls further comprises adjusting a sheath, wherein the sheath at least partly covers the container walls adjoining the upper chamber.

28

FREEZER THAW INDICATOR

ABSTRACT OF THE DISCLOSURE

A container has a porous support member affixed thereinside defining upper and lower chambers and a liquid partly filling the container. The liquid is frozen in the upper chamber. The container is oriented so that the upper chamber is gravitationally above the lower chamber, wherein the frozen liquid remains in the upper chamber. The container is placed in a cold zone of a freezer. Thereafter, the presence of the liquid in the lower chamber is indicative that a thaw episode has occurred. The presence of the liquid frozen in the lower chamber is indicative that the thaw episode has been followed by a refreeze event.

Note: Submissions that accompanied the Thawometer Application are not included for the sake of brevity: Application Data Sheet, Declaration, Information Disclosure Statements, Non-Publication Request, and Petition to Make Special.

Disclosure: Specification and Drawing

Each of these parts of an Application will now be discussed with reference to the Thawometer Application. In view the Drawing is integral to the writing and reading of the Specification, these will be discussed collectively.

<u>1. Title</u>

The title must be concise and technically descriptive. Of course, an inventor can call his/her invention anything he/she wants, and usually this is a name that has a "ring" to it for commercializing purposes. However, the USPTO requires fanciful names to take a flight of fancy out of the patent application.

By way of example, I coined the name for my invention, "Thawometer" as a play on the term, "thermometer." This is a fanciful name that no Examiner would accept for a title. As such, I gave it the technically descriptive term of "Freezer Thaw Indicator."

You see why patent application titles rarely serve as product names.

<u>2. Cross-Reference to Related Applications</u>

A patent application's priority date (the date by which you can overcome prior art) is its filing date, unless there is an earlier filed application to which priority can be claimed. In that case, the earlier filed "related" application can provide an earlier priority date.

If you have a prior patent application, provisional, regular or foreign (applicable to foreign inventors), then right up front in the patent application this information is made known and priority claimed.

For example, let's say you filed a provisional application on March 3, 2023, then filed your regular application on September 20, the Cross-Reference would be worded, "The present application claims the benefit of priority of corresponding co-pending provisional application, Serial Number 62-999999, filed on March 3, 2023, the disclosure of which is hereby incorporated herein by reference."

<u>3. Statement of Prior Disclosures by the Inventor</u>

This is a bit of a sticky wicket for the reason that admitting a prior disclosure is against one's own interest (in particular if the inventor misspeaks the facts) and for another because the Information Disclosure

Statement has traditionally taken care of this. I say that because this requirement came about recently as part of the USPTO's response to the latest revamp of the patent laws.

What the USPTO wants to know is your entitlement to a patent under 35 U.S.C. 102: whether you, or someone deriving from you, publicly disclosed your invention more than one year before the earliest priority date you are entitled to. If so, you need to tell the USPTO what you disclosed.

While you can expect the Examiner to do a thorough prior art search, you can never expect that he/she will ferret out what part of your invention you disclosed to the public over a year before your priority date.

Your patent attorney will handle this sticky wicket for you. Just tell him/her exactly the what, when and where of any public disclosures of your invention. He/she will then make sure the USPTO is aware of any necessary information, not necessarily in this part of the patent application, but in an Information Disclosure Statement.

4. Technical Field

This part lets the Examiner (and anyone subsequently reading the patent) to zero-in on the technology that the invention relates to.

For the Thawometer, I used a step approach, each step narrowing the field. The first step is to freezers, the next step to an indicator of thaw episodes, and the last step to an indicator that a thaw episode has been followed by a refreeze event.

5. Background of the Invention

This portion of the Specification identifies the state of the art related to the invention and how it suffers from one or more deficiencies, setting the stage for the invention providing a most welcome solution. This is also a place where prior patents and other references can be discussed with a respectful eye on why they are not so great. Some patent attorneys like to discuss prior art, others omit it.

In my Thawometer Application, I first discussed freezers, then the problem of their warming up during a power outage, resulting in the contents thawing. Mention is given to how freezers warm differently when there is present inside more or less heat capacity of the freezer contents.

In most patent applications I've written, I elected to discuss prior art because I had to distinguish it from the invention. For the Thawometer, I didn't need to distinguish over any of the electronic-based prior art that I had found online; I would only muddy the waters. Instead, I elected to cite these in Information Disclosure Statements.

6. Brief Summary of the Invention

This part of the Specification is extremely important for the simple reason it is intended to get to the heart of the invention in as concise and direct a manner as possible so that the reader can get in his/her mind just what the invention is all about. It serves as a boon to Patent Examiners, who have little time to struggle to understand the invention from the long winded, circuitous blah, blah, blah of the Detailed Description.

Generally speaking, the structural aspects of the invention are first described. This is then followed by an operational description of how the invention works. Usually, but not always, this part concludes with one or more "objects," intended to focus in on advantageous aspects of the invention.

In writing the Application for the Thawometer, I first described the cylinder, the medial porous support member and the half filling fluid. Then, with the words, "In operation," I revealed how to use this structure to provide a freezer thaw indication and a refreeze indication. I then concluded with a series of objects of the invention.

7. Brief Description of the Drawings

Without this part of the Specification, the various figures of the Drawing would be mysterious, if not down-right impossible to interpret. Being no more than a brief description, the reader is able to quickly understand what he/she is looking at, figure to figure.

In writing the Brief Description for the Thawometer Application, I described each drawing first by its view aspect, such as a schematic view, then provided a concise description of what the figure shows.

8. Detailed Description of the Invention/Drawings

This is where the gold vein of information on how to make and use the invention is presented. Here, the structure and function of the basic embodiment and the preferred embodiment (the best mode for carrying out the invention) are rigorously described, as are any alternative embodiments of the invention.

The details of the invention are described in combination with the figures of the Drawing. To facilitate this, numbers are placed in the figures, each with a leader line, or leadline, to particular features, while in the Detailed Description these numbers are correspondingly referenced when explaining the embodiments shown in the figures. Often in this regard, a large round number is used to point to an embodiment, such as 100, 200, 300 or 1000, 2000, 3000, etc., with the leadline ending in an arrowhead. For each embodiment, the Drawing cooperates with its corresponding portion of the Specification to reveal the structural and operational features of that embodiment.

The traditional heading for this section of an Application is, "Description of the Preferred Embodiment," and that was the heading I used in writing the Thawometer Application.

Before writing the Detailed Description of the Thawometer Application, I completed my testing and laid out the various figures in my mind. In view I had used CorelDraw 11 in association with my most excellent patent draftsman, Mark Thornton,[1] I drew the figures myself. Figures 1 to 4 show the invention in operation, while Figures 5 and 5A show the structural configuration of the preferred embodiment. With these figures provided, it was rather easy for me to write the Detailed Description of this preferred embodiment. Operational views of how the ice would melt in a freezer thaw event are shown at Figures 6 through 16. Once again, these figures made writing the Detailed Description a straightforward task. Figures 17 though 26, 28 and 29 show alternative embodiments, with Figure 28 being arguably the most basic. Figure 27 is a flow chart for carrying out a process to adapt a Thawometer to properly operate in various freezer settings.

The USPTO requires a Drawing if some aspect of the invention can be shown in order to aid understanding of the invention—but a nice set of figures makes for a well written Detailed Description, as well.

9. Claims

The Detailed Description in combination with the Drawing

[1] Before the use of computer aided drawing, all drafting was done by hand using black India ink on a drafting paper called "Bristol board." My many thanks to the incomparable artwork of Walter Braem and his assistant, Wayne Tabor.

usually lay out a very broad scope of the invention. Unless the scope of the invention is clearly defined in the Application, an Examiner can't determine patentability. This is where the claims come in. They serve a vital, indeed fateful, role in defining what is and is not your invention.

A. Scope

The larger the scope of the claims, the better? In a word, no! If the claims encompass all kinds of possible stuff they risk stepping on prior art, rendering your invention unpatentable. What is essential is for the claims to recite the embodiments of the invention that have the best chances of making money. It's the job of your patent attorney, with your help, to get you patentable claims which are also commercially valuable.

The elusive solution to the problem of how to write a "good" set of claims that are both patentable and commercially valuable requires the use of the clearest of crystal balls. My mom actually gave me one (a small one because she said they are so expensive). It did not come with instructions, but I didn't need to use it because there is a form of patent conjuring that serves quite nicely: writing claims with differing scopes and subject matter to snag that commercially valuable sweet spot even if your patent attorney and you are guessing at the commercial future of your invention.

B. What Are Claims?

Claims define the scope of the subject matter of an invention. Claims are formulated typically as either a mutually linked list of elements in structural or compositional terms, or as a series of mutually linked method steps for making and/or carrying out the invention.

Claims are a single sentence laid out in multi-paragraph format composed of three parts:

- Preamble;
- Transition; and
- Body.

The preamble serves as an introductory clause describing what the subject matter being claimed is. An example of a structural preamble is, "A widget;" while a method preamble is, "A method for making a widget."

The transition is a word or phrase of utmost legal significance. For example, the word "comprising" means the invention is, at minimum, those parts enumerated below it, but if anything else is added, that's okay. Whereas the phrase, "consisting of" restricts the enumeration to just those mentioned.

The body enumerates each element or step of the invention being claimed, a separate paragraph being provided for each enumerated element or step. Each recited element or step must interrelate to the other recited elements or steps. The body may, and frequently does, end with a statement of functionality in the form of one or more "whereas clauses," each of which tying the recited elements or steps together into a correlated whole.

C. Claim Strategy

A stand alone claim is referred to as an "independent" or "base" claim. You immediately know a base claim by its preamble, "A [structure, composition or method] ..." Claims which further define a base claim are referred to as "dependent" claims. You immediately know a dependent claim by its preamble, "The [structure, composition or method] of Claim 1 ..."

The USPTO has long allowed Applicants to file a set of claims with up to 3 base claims and 20 total claims without paying additional fees. While this may seem an unreasonable limitation on claim writing, almost always it's not.

Another type of claim is referred to as "multiply dependent." You know it when you see, "The [structure, composition or method] of Claims 1, 2 or 3 ..." These are very unusual in U.S. practice, being more often seen in foreign practice. That the USPTO charges a separate fee for them is one of the reasons they are rare.

In formulating the claims for the Thawometer Application, I wrote Claim 1 as an independent claim, having the broadest possible structural scope. Claims 2 through 14 were written as dependent claims referencing to Claim 1. In each of these dependent claims, the elements recited add elements to the minimum elements recited in Claim 1, thereby narrowing the scope that defines the Thawometer. Base Claim 15 recites the broadest scope of the Thawometer in terms of method steps for carrying out the invention. Claims 16 and 17 depend from base Claim 15, with additional method steps. The third base claim, Claim 18, defines the broadest scope of the Thawometer in terms of a method for thermal sensitivity adjustment to a thermal cross-section of a freezer to which it will be used. Claims 19 and 20 are dependent on base Claim 18, where Claim 20 mentions adjusting a sheath (as per Claims 7 and 11).

One of the claim strategy tools used by patent attorneys is known as the "claim tree." Below are the claim trees for each of the independent claims of the Thawometer Application.

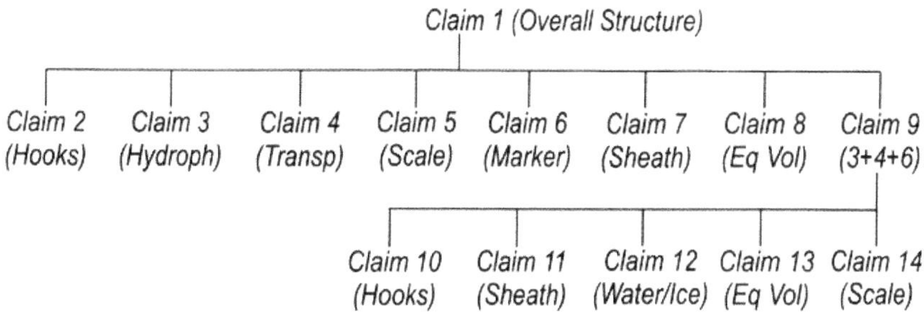

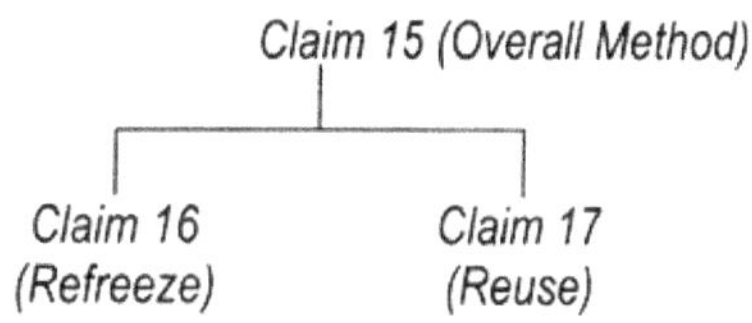

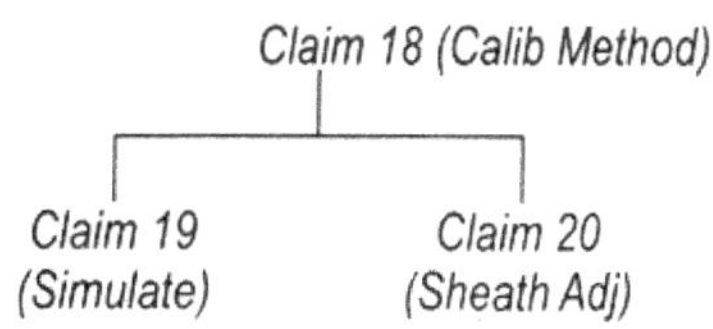

There are three trees (the trees are usually written upside-down), each with a trunk in the form of an independent claim. By showing the branching of claims off from the trunk, it is easy to see and understand the dependency of the claims and the relation of each to the other. The label beside each claim allows for a quick reference to what that claim defines.

D. How Claims Work

When you're buying a piece of property, you have it surveyed for the property lines. Once you own the property, you can keep people out, while people on adjoining property can go wherever they want so long as they stay out of yours. How do you manage to do that? Simple. You put up a fence on the property line. In a nutshell, claims are fences you use to protect your intellectual property from infringers (trespassers), while at the same time telling the world what property you own.

Let's now see how claims form fences, using the Thawometer Application as an example.

The realm of subject matter of the Freezer Thaw Indicator idea is pretty broad. It can be done electronically or mechanically. However, the subject matter of the Thawometer invention was a simple mechanical device.

I had two sweet spots in mind for commercialization. The first, Sweet Spot 1, was the basic embodiment composed of a container half filled with water with a porous member at mid-container. The other, Sweet Spot 2 (a subset of SP 1), was a method to calibrate the structure of the Thawometer to match the contents of a freezer so that the rate of melt in the calibrated Thawometer would reliably match the rate of melt in the freezer. For example, a single frozen chicken breast will thaw far faster in a freezer having an interruption to its power, as compared to a freezer stuffed full of frozen chicken breasts. The reason is the heat capacity of all the frozen chicken collectively keeps one another in a frozen state for a longer time.

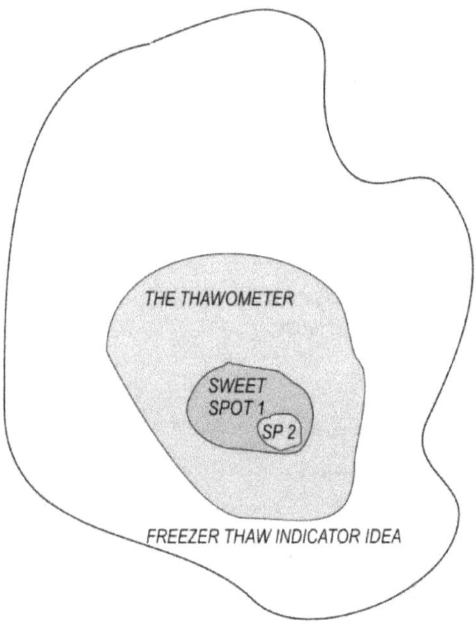

As a result of my online searching, I had uncovered several electronic devices that in one way or another indicated a freeze thaw episode. These are shown on the next page as Prior Art 1, 2 and 3, with 2 and 3 overlapping 1. None of these touched upon the purely mechanical subject matter of the Thawometer. While I cited these in several information disclosure statements, I didn't need to worry about them as long as I kept the claimed subject matter restricted to the Thawometer.

Base Claims 1 and 15 formed fences at the boundary of the scope of the intellectual property of the Thawometer. The fences (dashed lines) did not run into the intellectual property represented by Prior Art 1, 2 and 3. Claim 18 was written as an insurance policy, providing a fence protecting the scope of the calibration method of SP 2.

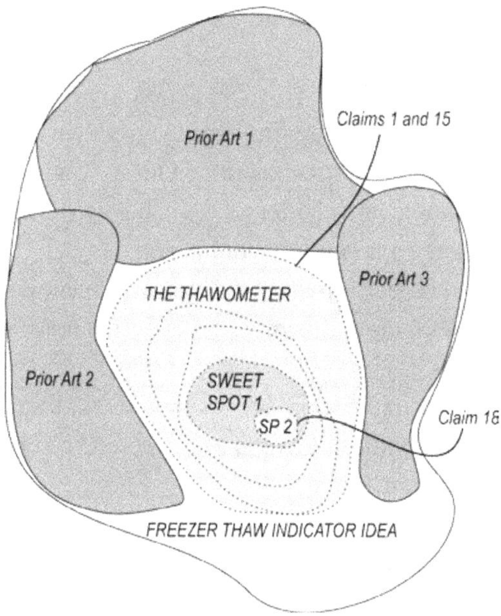

The claims were written to encompass variously sized portions of the intellectual property being claimed. The reason for this is that there may be other undiscovered prior art lurking and quite often the USPTO will find one or more of these, resulting in rejection of claims that fence into them—with the loss of intellectual property.

You can expect any claims that do not fence into prior art to be allowable, but there is a caveat: the claims must be supported by the Specification and the Drawing. If the fencing goes outside the boundary of the Disclosure, it is said to be "unsupported." This is fatal because the USPTO Examiner will reject a claim for lack of support ("over claiming").

The most important claims are those that form inner fences encircling the Sweet Spots. In theory, if you were to lose all your intellectual property except that portion inside those inner fences, you would still enjoy commercial success.

10. Abstract of the Disclosure

The abstract is placed on a separate sheet following the claims. It is written in the form of a short, single paragraph that succinctly describes the invention to which the Application is directed. The abstract is a tool for searching, intended to allow a searcher to quickly identify what the patent is about.

Final Thoughts

The mechanical arts are predictable, while the chemical arts are not.

Why is that important? Because if your invention lies in an unpredictable art area, you can't say with certainty that you are in full possession of how to make and use without experimentation. Without experimental examples, an Examiner can challenge you, but if he/she doesn't, an infringer might later seek to invalidate your patent.

Indeed, whatever the subject matter of your invention, experimentation is useful, but in the unpredictable arts, experimentation is essential.

In the Specification of an Application in an unpredictable art area, examples need to be disclosed so that the scope of the claims can be identified and operability clearly demonstrated.

Even though my Thawometer was within the mechanical arts, I provided several examples in the Application.

> *Examples of carrying out your invention are necessary to include in your Application if the subject matter is in an unpredictable art area. But even in predictable art areas, examples not only aid teaching how to make and use, they enhance confirmation of your command of the inventive subject matter.*

* * *

Design Patents

35 U.S.C. 171 defines what designs are patentable:

> *"Whoever invents any new, original, and ornamental design for an article of manufacture may obtain a patent therefor, subject to the conditions and requirements of this title."*

A design patent pertains to the ornamental appearance of an inventively configured article of matter. Ordinarily, this applies to manufactures, but most products have some ornamental shape (design) which can often be patented even if it otherwise has moving parts. An example is the design of a computer mouse.

Design patents protect only ornamental appearance, not function, operation, composition or method of making or using. The appearance is defined by the Drawing. While a design patent prevents others from mimicking the appearance of his/her invention, it can be easily gotten around by an alternative design.

Returning to the computer mouse example, the inventor's design patent does not protect the button functions, wheel operation, battery and LED electronics and other functionalities. It only prevents a competitor from making a mouse looking like the inventor's mouse design.

A patent application for a design will include a title describing the invention in terms of its technical form, but not a fanciful form. For example, a combined fork and spoon could be titled, "The Ornamental Design for a Spoon and Fork Combination," not "The Ornamental Design for a Dandy Spork."

The Drawing must show the design in its various viewpoints so that the invention is fully disclosed. Shading is used to depict surface aspects, such as curvatures, and standardized graphic symbols to show features. These drawings are best left to a professional patent draftsman.

A single claim defines the subject matter of the invention. As the Drawing is all important and there is no written description other than to identify the various figures, the claim recites the Drawing as its subject matter. Returning to the fork/spoon combo, the single claim would recite, "The ornamental design for the spoon and fork combination, as shown."

A design patent application must be a regular application (provisionals are not allowed) and include: Title, Claim, Description, Drawing, Declaration, in which the inventor asserts his/her inventorship of the design, and Filing Fee. Design patents have a term of 15 years from the date of issuance. They cannot be renewed.

Below is an example of a design patent, D319,952.

United States Patent [19]
Harvey, Sr.

[11] **Patent Number: Des. 319,952**
[45] **Date of Patent: ** Sep. 17, 1991**

[54] **TROWELING AND WEEDING GARDEN TOOL BLADE**

[76] Inventor: **Louis Harvey, Sr.,** 15107 Ilene, Detroit, Mich. 48238

[**] Term: **14 Years**

[21] Appl. No.: **513,155**

[22] Filed: **Apr. 20, 1990**

[52] **U.S. Cl.** **D8/9;** D8/10

[58] **Field of Search** D8/10, 1, 9, 45; 172/375, 378; 294/7, 51; 7/116

[56] **References Cited**

U.S. PATENT DOCUMENTS

D. 29,443	10/1898	Pearson	D8/9
D. 32,854	6/1900	McClintock	D8/10 X
D. 102,957	1/1937	Renner	D8/10
D. 254,705	4/1980	Whiteside .	
D. 256,979	9/1980	Nadle .	
D. 270,611	9/1983	Check et al. .	
D. 278,966	5/1985	Anaya .	
D. 283,196	4/1986	Hasse .	
D. 292,865	11/1987	Scott .	
D. 294,555	3/1988	Tremaine	D8/10
D. 295,942	5/1988	Featherman et al. .	
982,575	1/1911	Carpenter	7/114 X
2,137,458	11/1938	Phelps	294/7 X
2,261,063	10/1941	Joyce	D8/45

FOREIGN PATENT DOCUMENTS

29419 11/1908 Fed. Rep. of Germany 294/51

OTHER PUBLICATIONS

A. M. Leonard p. 16, Fall 1986, Trowel, Items 9821 and 9822 located on left side of page.

Primary Examiner—Wallace R. Burke
Assistant Examiner—Holly H. Baynham
Attorney, Agent, or Firm—Peter D. Keefe

[57] **CLAIM**

The ornamental design for a troweling and weeding garden tool blade, as shown.

DESCRIPTION

FIG. 1 is a perspective view of a troweling and weeding garden tool blade showing my new design;
FIG. 2 is a top plan view thereof;
FIG. 3 is a right side elevational view thereof;
FIG. 4 is a front elevational view thereof;
FIG. 5 is a rear elevational view thereof;
FIG. 6 is a bottom plan view thereof; and
FIG. 7 is a left side elevational view thereof.
The broken line showing of a garden tool handle is for illustrative purposes only and forms no part of the claimed design.

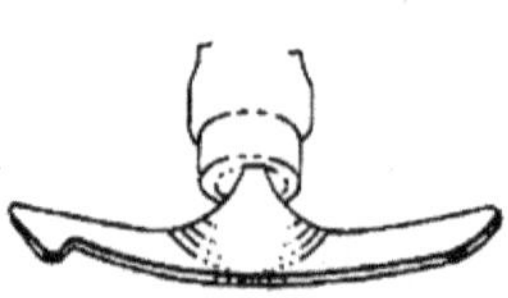

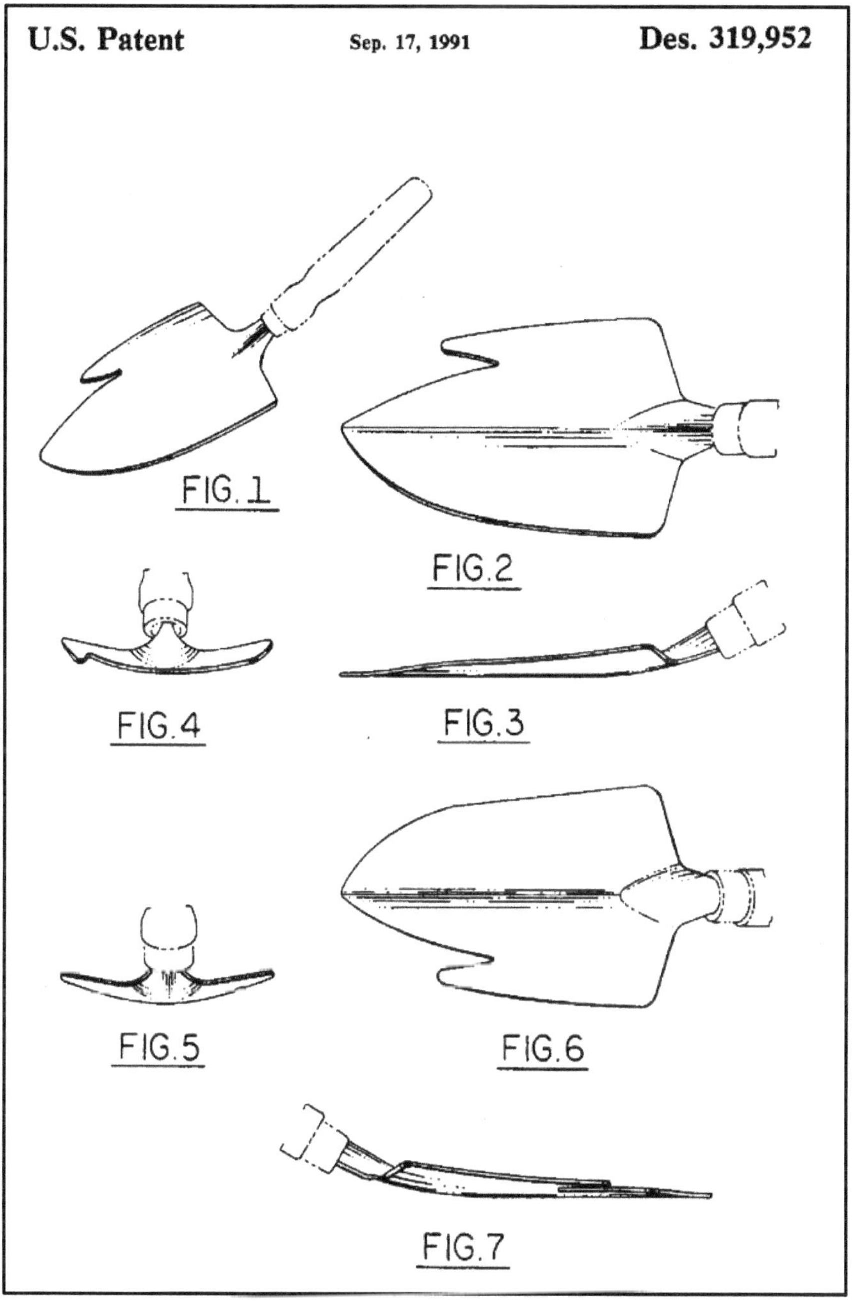

Images credit: USPTO.gov database.

Entitled "Troweling and Weeding Garden Tool Blade," disclosed is a static article of manufacture. Novelty and unobviousness reside in the shown slot feature, which suggests where weeds are cut through or otherwise unearthed.[2]

The single claim defines the patentable subject matter: "The ornamental design for a troweling and weeding garden tool blade, as shown." This claim is defined by the Drawing and the brief descriptions of the seven figures of the Drawing, where each figure shows the design in various orientations. Interestingly, following the figures description, is a statement specifying what part of the Drawing constitutes the claimed design. The statement reads, "The broken line showing of a garden tool handle is for illustrative purposes only and forms no part of the claimed design." The rationale for this is that the inventor invented a design for the trowel blade, and he recognized any handle shape would do. This greatly magnified protection for the claimed subject matter of the design.

It is rare for a design patent to convey the subject matter of a utility patent, but this design patent comes as close as any, with the Drawing in combination with the title conveying its utility. This is because a design patent protects only the appearance of an article. But a design disclosure can implicitly suggest utility, preventing others from obtaining a utility patent on modifications of the design, unless more than ordinary skill was used in the modification.

This is not a panacea. The inventor has the right to exclude others from making, using and selling his/her claimed design, but since he/she has no claim to utility or alternative embodiments, a modification of the design by another could get around the design patent claim. The standard for design infringement is tricky to apply, but in essence, if a competitor's design is confusingly similar to the claimed design, then the competitor's design infringes. And who makes that evaluation? That would be an ordinary person, often referred to as the "reasonable man standard." It's likely an ordinary person would consider a longer slot or a slot placed on the left edge of the blade to be confusingly similar. What of a slot at the leading point? A trier of fact would need to make that decision. But it's moot, as a slot there would render the design a poor trowel tool.

Why file a design patent for subject matter that is best claimed by a utility patent? Usually, that answer boils down to the inventor's vision for his/her invention and how much time, effort and investment he/she is willing to spend to make a go of it.

---

[2] Many thanks to my patent draftsman extraordinaire, Walter Bream, for the renderings.

Plant Patents

35 U.S.C. 161 succinctly defines what a patent for a plant is:

> *"Whoever invents or discovers and asexually reproduces any distinct and new variety of plant, including cultivated sports, mutants, hybrids, and newly found seedlings, other than a tuber propagated plant or a plant found in an uncultivated state, may obtain a patent therefor, subject to the conditions and requirements of this title.*
>
> *The provisions of this title relating to patents for inventions shall apply to patents for plants, except as otherwise provided.*
>
> *Asexually propagated plants are those that are reproduced by means other than from seeds, such as by the rooting of cuttings, by layering, budding, grafting, inarching, etc. Plants capable of sexual reproduction are not excluded from consideration if they have also been asexually reproduced. ..."*

Plant patent applications are relatively rare, and very few patent attorneys have ever filed one. Nonetheless, those who specialize in the horticultural arts have frequent contact with them.

A plant patent requires: Title, Abstract, Specification, Drawing, Declaration and Filing Fee. However, unique to plant patent applications, the Specification must include: the Latin name of the genus and species of the plant, variety denomination and a detailed botanical description. The Specification must particularly point out where and in what manner the plant variety was asexually reproduced. Only a single claim is permitted. If color is a distinctive feature of the plant, the color must be specified, and shown in the Drawing. Typically, the Drawing constitutes color photographs.

The examination process includes searching prior art with respect to novelty and unobviousness of the claimed plant. The USPTO may require the inventor to submit specimens of the claimed plant for study and inspection. Such a submission is to be made only if the

Examiner requires it.

Plant patents, like regular utility patents, can be originally filed as a provisional and have a term of 20 years from the priority date.

Below is an example of a plant patent, PP30,346.

US00PP30346P2

(12) **United States Plant Patent**
Hansen

(10) **Patent No.: US PP30,346 P2**
(45) **Date of Patent: Apr. 2, 2019**

(54) ***KNIPHOFIA* PLANT NAMED 'POKER FACE'**

(50) Latin Name: ***Kniphofia hybrida***
Varietal Denomination: **Poker Face**

(71) Applicant: **Hans A Hansen**, Zeeland, MI (US)

(72) Inventor: **Hans A Hansen**, Zeeland, MI (US)

(73) Assignee: **Walters Gardens Inc**, Zeeland, MI (US)

(*) Notice: Subject to any disclaimer, the term of this patent is extended or adjusted under 35 U.S.C. 154(b) by 0 days.

(21) Appl. No.: **15/932,530**

(22) Filed: **Mar. 12, 2018**

(51) **Int. Cl.**
A01H 5/02 (2018.01)

(52) **U.S. Cl.**
USPC **Plt./443**

(58) **Field of Classification Search**
USPC Plt./443
See application file for complete search history.

Primary Examiner — Annette H Para

(57) **ABSTRACT**

A new and distinct cultivar of Red Hot Poker plant named *Kniphofia* 'Poker Face' with gracefully-arching, strap-like, keeled, glaucous, gray-green foliage and numerous scapes beginning in early summer and repeating though early fall. Flowers are bright orange, densely arranged on scapes up to 82 cm tall. The new plant is useful for landscaping as a specimen, en masse, as a container plant, or as a long-lasting cut flower.

2 Drawing Sheets

1

Botanical classification: *Kniphofia hybrida*.
Variety denomination: 'Poker Face'.

BACKGROUND AND ORIGIN OF THE PLANT

The present invention relates to the new and distinct Red Hot Poker, *Kniphofia* 'Poker Face' hybridized under the direction of the inventor at a wholesale perennial nursery in Zeeland, Mich., USA. The new plant was the result of a single seedling selection from a cross of 'Echo Rojo' U.S. Plant Pat. No. 22,791 as the female parent as the female parent and 'Papaya Popsicle' U.S. Plant Pat. No. 22,915 as the male parent as the male parent in 2012. The plant passed initial evaluation in the summer of 2014 and was subsequently given the breeder code KNIF-12-5. *Kniphofia* 'Poker Face' has been successfully asexually propagated by garden rhizome division method since 2014 at the same wholesale perennial nursery in Zeeland, Mich. and subsequently by shoot tip tissue culture, and both methods have been found to be stable and produce identical plants that maintain the unique characteristics of the original plant through multiple generations.

No plants of *Kniphofia* 'Poker Face' have been sold, in this country or anywhere in the world, with this name or any other name, prior to the filing of this application, nor has any disclosure of the new plant been made prior to the filing of this application except that which was disclosed within one year of the filing of this application and was either derived directly or indirectly from the inventor.

SUMMARY OF THE PLANT

Kniphofia 'Poker Face' differs from its parents as well as all other *Kniphofia* known to the applicant. The most similar known *Kniphofia* cultivars are the female parent 'Echo Rojo', 'Mango Popsicle' U.S. Plant Pat. No. 22,968, the male parent 'Papaya Popsicle' and 'Poco Orange' U.S. Plant patent application Ser. No. 14/545,806. 'Echo Rojo' is slightly taller in scape height but more reddish in flower

2

color and the new plant is more persistent in the Michigan landscape. 'Mango Popsicle' is shorter in scape and foliage height with more yellow-orange flower color. 'Papaya Popsicle' is shorter in scape and foliage height with deeper orange flower color. 'Poco Orange' is smaller in scape height, foliage height and overall habit and has a lighter orange flower color.

Kniphofia 'Poker Face' differs from these above cultivars and all cultivars known to the inventor in that it has:

1. Gracefully arching, strap-like, keeled, gray-green foliage.
2. Rapidly growing, dense habit, winter-hardy, heat and low moisture tolerant, rabbit and deer tolerant, large-sized clumps.
3. Numerous spikes of medium orange flowers on tall stems lightening in maturity;
4. Flowering beginning the first week of summer and repeating into early October in Michigan.

BRIEF DESCRIPTION OF THE DRAWINGS

The photographs of the new plant demonstrate the overall appearance of the plant, including the unique traits. The colors are as accurate as reasonably possible with color reproductions. Ambient light spectrum, source and direction may cause the appearance of minor variation in color.

FIG. **1** shows the side-view habit of a three-year-old plant in midseason.

FIG. **2** shows a close-up of the flowers and buds.

DETAILED BOTANICAL DESCRIPTION

The following descriptions and color references are based on the 2015 edition of The Royal Horticultural Society Colour Chart except where common dictionary terms are used. The new plant, *Kniphofia* 'Poker Face', has not been observed under all possible environments. The phenotype may vary slightly with different environmental conditions, such as temperature, light, fertility, moisture and maturity

US PP30,346 P2

3 4

levels, but without any change in the genotype. The following observations and size descriptions are of a four-year-old plant in a trial garden of a wholesale perennial nursery in Zeeland, Mich. under full sun with supplemental water and fertilizer as needed.

Botanical classification: *Kniphofia* hybrid;

Parentage: Proprietary unreleased selection of *Kniphofia* (not patented) as the female or seed parent and the male or pollen parent is unknown;

Propagation method: By garden division of the rhizome;

Growth rate: Vigorous, flowering in 3.5 liter containers in about 10 to 12 weeks from a 25 mm plug liner in late winter to spring and from a one-year-old bare root plant to flowering in 6 to 8 weeks in a 4.0 liter container;

Rooting habit: Fibrous from base of rhizomes, lightly branching; color nearest RHS 158C;

Plant description: Dense, rhizomatous, acaulescent, perennial clump with long thin foliage to about 100.0 cm across and about 68.0 cm tall; flowering to about 82.0 cm tall;

Leaves: Linear; keeled; arranged about 10 leaves per basal division; apex narrowly acute; base truncate, clasping; margin entire; no fragrance observed;

Leaf size: To about 70.5 cm long and 17.0 mm across at base, average about 67.0 cm long and 16.0 mm across at base;

Leaf color: Mature and expanding leaves same; both surfaces nearest RHS 137A;

Leaf venation: Parallel; color same as leaf abaxial and adaxial;

Stem: Acaulescent; rhizome about 28.0 mm across at base;

Inflorescence: In spike-like raceme; about 150 to 180 flowers per stem; about 60 to 80 peduncles per plant; flowering portion about 14.0 cm tall and about 5.4 cm across; lasting about three weeks; flower spacing less than 1.0 mm apart on raceme;

Peduncle: Terete; glabrous; glaucous; to about 82.0 cm long and 14.0 mm diameter;

Peduncle color: Nearest RHS 139D proximally and blushed with nearest RHS 167D distally;

Buds one day prior to opening: Ellipsoidal to tubular with swollen apex; glabrous; lustrous; about 20.0 mm long and about 3.0 mm diameter at base and 6.0 mm diameter at widest point near apex; apex subacute; base rounded;

Bud attitude: Beginning outwardly and drooping as maturing toward anthesis;

Bud color: Nearest RHS N34B becoming nearest RHS 24B in main portion with midrib nearest RHS 33A and secondary veins nearest RHS N25B;

Flowers: Cylindrical forming tubular corolla; perfect; actinomorphic; individually open and effective about three to four days;

Corolla size: To about 21.0 mm long, fused in basal 18.0 mm; face to about 12.0 mm tall and about 8.0 mm wide; tube about 4.0 mm diameter near base and 8.0 mm near throat;

Flower attitude: Drooping;

Flower fragrance: None detected;

Flowering period: Individual racemes effective for about 3 weeks; beginning early summer Michigan for about six week, then continuing with repeat racemes until early fall with a short two week break in the heat of the summer;

Tepals: Six, in two sets of three; both sets with acute apices and fused in basal 18.0 mm forming tube; margin entire; glabrous and lustrous abaxial and adaxial; about 21.0 mm long and about 5.1 mm across just above fusion point;

Tepal color (young abaxial): Distal 3.0 mm of outer tepal set nearest RHS 33A; inner set with 1.0 mm margin of RHS 11D; both sets with midrib nearest RHS 33A and main portion nearest RHS 21D toward base and distally nearest RHS 33B;

Tepal color (young adaxial): Distal 3.0 mm of outer tepal set nearest RHS 34B; inner set with 1.0 mm margin nearest RHS NN155; both sets with midrib nearest RHS 28B and main portion proximally nearest RHS 19B and distally between RHS 32 C and RHS 32D;

Tepal color (mature abaxial): Inner tepal with 1.0 mm lighter margin of nearest RHS 4D; veins nearest RHS 151D and main portion nearest RHS 13C proximally and nearest RHS 21C distally;

Tepal color (mature adaxial): Inner tepals with 1.0 mm lighter margin of nearest RHS 4D; veins nearest RHS 151D proximally and RHS 17C distally; main portion nearest RHS 11 A proximally and RHS 17C distally;

Androecium: Six, different lengths;

Filaments.—Six; terete; glabrous; lustrous; from about 28.0 to 32.0 mm long and about 0.8 mm diameter; color nearest RHS 2C proximally and nearest RHS 1B distally.

Anther.—Ellipsoidal, flattened ventrally to dorsally; about 2.0 mm long and 1.5 mm across and 1.0 mm thick; color nearest RHS 9A.

Pollen.—Abundant: color nearest RHS 13A.

Gynoecium: Single; about 30.0 mm long;

Style.—Terete; glabrous; lustrous; about 25.0 mm long and 0.8 mm diameter: color nearest RHS 1B.

Pedicel: Terete; glabrous; stiff; drooping; about 2.0 mm long and about 0.5 mm diameter;

Pedicel color: Nearest RHS 174A;

Bracts: Lanceolate; subtending individual flowers; with acute apices and truncate base; to about 10.0 mm long and 5.0 mm across at base; average about 5.0 mm long and 2.5 mm across; color blushed with nearest RHS 167B;

Fruit: Tri-valved loculicidal capsule; ovoid-globose; about 8.0 mm long and 8.0 mm across; glabrous; with rounded apex and rounded base; typically four to eight seeded; color upon maturity nearest RHS 199C;

Seed: Irregular with angular sides, acute apex and base; about 4.0 mm and 2.5 mm across; color nearest RHS 200A;

Disease and pest resistance: Resistance beyond that of other *Kniphofia* has not been observed. The plant grows best with good drainage and is able to tolerate some heat when established. Hardiness at least from USDA zone 5b through 9.

I claim:

1. A new and distinct cultivar of Red Hot Poker plant named *Kniphofia* 'Poker Face' as herein described and illustrated.

* * * * *

U.S. Patent Apr. 2, 2019 Sheet 1 of 2 US PP30,346 P2

FIG. 1

U.S. Patent Apr. 2, 2019 Sheet 2 of 2 US PP30,346 P2

FIG. 2

Images credit. USPTO.gov database

The color plates may be viewed at University of Maryland: https://digital.lib.umd.edu/plantpatents/search?query=PP30347. Note: PP30346 is mislabeled PP30347 at the Maryland site. ☺

* * *

Chapter 5

Patent Prosecution

"Patent prosecution" is *patentese* for the process of interaction by an Applicant with the USPTO in pursuit of his/her patent—there is no "prosecution" in the criminal sense of the term. While referring to USPTO interactions during the time of pendency of the patent application (the time between filing and issuance of a patent or abandonment), it also includes appeals, petitions and post issuance interactions.

Preliminary Review

Initially, a patent application is reviewed to determine completeness. This check includes quite a number of things by clerical staff: missing parts, completeness of inventor identification, correctness of submitted forms/petitions, issues of superficial conformity with the patent laws and the rules of practice, whether the correct fee has been paid, etc. In addition, specially designated personnel determine whether or not the subject matter may be licensed for filing in foreign patent offices, whether or not the patent application is subject to a secrecy order for national security reasons and assignment of the CPC symbol most appropriate to the application's technology.

These days, the clerical function has been delegated to contractors outside the USPTO, whose responsiveness to queries is less than perfect. At any rate, if there are any deficiencies found, the Applicant is notified and given time to make corrections, usually one month.

The Application is then assigned to a best technology fit with a Patent Technology Center based upon its CPC symbol. There, it is assigned to a most technologically relevant sub-center and then its most relevant Art Unit. The assigned Examiner is the most qualified based on the CPC symbol.

A Filing Receipt will be issued which gives a summary of information, including acknowledgement of the filing date, assignment of an Application Serial Number and an indication of the Group Art Unit to which the Application has been assigned. The Patent Examiner is not identified in the Filing Receipt.

Below is an abridged copy the Thawometer Official Filing Receipt, dated November 18, 2015.

UNITED STATES PATENT AND TRADEMARK OFFICE

UNITED STATES DEPARTMENT OF COMMERCE
United States Patent and Trademark Office
Address: COMMISSIONER FOR PATENTS
P.O. Box 1450
Alexandria, Virginia 22313-1450
www.uspto.gov

APPLICATION NUMBER	FILING or 371(c) DATE	GRP ART UNIT	FIL FEE REC'D	ATTY DOCKET NO	TOT CLAIMS	IND CLAIMS
14/932,064	11/04/2015	3744	730	PDK-775	20	3

CONFIRMATION NO. 6261

FILING RECEIPT

23592
PETER D KEEFE
KEEFE AND ASSOCIATES
24405 GRATIOT AVENUE
EASTPOINTE, MI 48021

Date Mailed: 11/18/2015

Receipt is acknowledged of this non-provisional patent application. The application will be taken up for examination in due course. Applicant will be notified as to the results of the examination. Any correspondence concerning the application must include the following identification information: the U.S. APPLICATION NUMBER, FILING DATE, NAME OF APPLICANT, and TITLE OF INVENTION. Fees transmitted by check or draft are subject to collection. Please verify the accuracy of the data presented on this receipt. **If an error is noted on this Filing Receipt, please submit a written request for a Filing Receipt Correction. Please provide a copy of this Filing Receipt with the changes noted thereon. If you received a "Notice to File Missing Parts" for this application, please submit any corrections to this Filing Receipt with your reply to the Notice. When the USPTO processes the reply to the Notice, the USPTO will generate another Filing Receipt incorporating the requested corrections**

Inventor(s)

Peter David Keefe, Roseville, MI;

Applicant(s)

Peter David Keefe, Roseville, MI;

Power of Attorney: None

Domestic Applications for which benefit is claimed - None.
A proper domestic benefit claim must be provided in an Application Data Sheet in order to constitute a claim for domestic benefit. See 37 CFR 1.76 and 1.78.

Foreign Applications for which priority is claimed (You may be eligible to benefit from the **Patent Prosecution Highway** program at the USPTO. Please see http://www.uspto.gov for more information.) - None.
Foreign application information must be provided in an Application Data Sheet in order to constitute a claim to foreign priority. See 37 CFR 1.55 and 1.76.

If Required, Foreign Filing License Granted: 11/17/2015

The country code and number of your priority application, to be used for filing abroad under the Paris Convention, is **US 14/932,064**

Projected Publication Date: Request for Non-Publication Acknowledged

Non-Publication Request: Yes

Early Publication Request: No
**** SMALL ENTITY ****

page 1 of 3

Title

Freezer Thaw Indicator

Preliminary Class

062

Examination

The decision as to which Examiner is assigned to examine the patent application is done without consideration to anything other than non-partisan internal processing, which is equally applied to all incoming patent applications.

The assigned Examiner has a strong background in the technology of his/her Art Unit, being trained and periodically retrained to properly apply the patent laws and rules of practice to patent applications in his/her Art Unit.

The Examiner will read the patent application to assess:

1. whether the claims are adequately supported by the Disclosure (that is, the Specification and the Drawing);
2. whether the Disclosure complies with the patent laws; and
3. whether the Disclosure conforms with the USPTO rules of practice.

The Examiner will then prepare a communication summarizing and explaining his/her findings, referred to as an "Office Action." The Office Action must specify which of the patent laws and rules of practice are referenced and explain how the Application is affected, either in terms of an "objection" or a "rejection." The Applicant is then permitted to respond in what is called an "Amendment." This term is a bit of a misnomer, in that amending the Application is not always necessary; mere argument can carry the day. In the Amendment, all grounds of objection/rejection must be responded to. The Amendment includes argument ("Remarks") detailing why the claims (and the whole of the Application) are now placed into allowable condition, overcoming the grounds of objection/rejection.

The Examiner, who is identified in the Office Action, will almost always set a "shortened" time for response of three months. However, the patent laws allow for six months. Requesting an extension of time of up to an additional three months (not to go over the six month "statutory time") involves the payment of unpleasant fees. But what is more ominous is the likely elimination of added days of patent term extension to the patent because of "Office delay" if the Applicant was also a cause of the delay.

The process can go back and forth, as shown in the flow chart on page 7. Ultimately, one of the following happens:

- the Examiner allows the Application; or
- the Applicant abandons the Application.

Along the way, it may be necessary to refile the Application, known as a "Request for Continued Examination" (RCE) in view the second Office Action is almost always marked "Final." If the Examiner cannot be persuaded to allow the Application (including by telephone or personal interview), then appeal can be made to the Patent Trial and Appeal Board, a three member panel within the USPTO. The Board will review the file history of the Application in order to fully analyze the complained of rejection by the Examiner. The Board is composed of administrative law judges who have a deep understanding of the patent laws and rules of practice. You can expect the Board to be fair.

<u>Objections/Rejections</u>

Objections involve nonconformities/informalities. If present, they will result in the Examiner raising objections to any of the Specification and the Drawing. Objections are almost always easily correctable. Examples are a fanciful title, misnumbered claims, spelling errors, and the like. An objection is typically clerical in nature and can be overcome by the Applicant or by the Examiner in an "Examiner's Amendment," which usually happens at the time he/she issues a Notice of Allowance.

A rejection is a serious impediment to an Application maturing into a patent due to nonconformity with the patent laws. A rejection is a fatal failure that must be corrected to the Examiner's satisfaction.

The most common statutory grounds under Title 35 for rejection are:

- Section 101, which defines what is patentable;
- Section 102, which defines novelty;
- Section 103, which defines obviousness;
- Section 111, which defines the content and arrangement of patent applications;
- Section 112, which specifies requirements for the Specification (in particular the claims); and
- Section 113, which defines requirements for the Drawing.

Rejections under Sections 101, 111, 112 and 113 are inherent to the Application, itself, and are not based upon prior art.

Rejections under Sections 102 and 103 are based upon prior art. This necessitates the Examiner to consider any references the inventor has submitted in his/her IDS, as well as any references the Examiner has found in a search. A seasoned Examiner will be aware of relevant references pertinent to his/her Art Unit and will utilize the search facilities of the USPTO to perform a comprehensive search of U.S. patent documents, international patent documents and published literature. The references the Examiner finds in combination with any references cited in an IDS will then be applied to the claims of the Application to determine whether the subject matter is both novel and unobvious. In this regard, the patent laws, the rules of practice and decisions of the courts guide the Examiner in his/her analysis.

Rejections under Section 101

Rejections for non-patentable subject matter under Section 101 are deadly. It makes no difference how perfectly prepared the Application is, nor the fact that there is no prior art; if the invention is non-statutory subject matter, it is not patentable. Period.

Section 101 specifies that to be patentable an invention be both new and useful, and be one of the following:

- a process;
- a machine;
- a manufacture; or
- a composition of matter.

While these may appear to be clear, are they? Is a process for doing business one of them? Is a lab manufactured life form one of them?

A serious rejection arises when an Examiner determines an Application contains two or more inventions, known as "double patenting," in that Section 101 specifies "a patent" for each invention. A "restriction requirement" in an Office Action means an Applicant has to decide which invention to proceed with; the filing of a "divisional" application on the other(s) keeps it/them alive.

Rejections under Section 111

I'm unaware of a patent attorney experiencing such a rejection. It is rare, to say the least. It is probably the realm of novice inventors who foolishly file their own patent applications.

Rejections under Section 112

Section 112 specifies requirements of the Specification (particularly the claims) under two paragraphs, a and b.

Section 112a specifies three crucial requirements for the written description:

- A written description of the invention:

  This entails a description understandable to a person of ordinary skill in the art area of the invention sufficient to indicate that the inventor is in possession of an understanding of the invention as defined by the claims.

- How to make and use the invention:

  The Specification must enable a person ordinarily skilled in the art area of the invention to make and use the invention as claimed. The Supreme Court test is whether the Specification enables an artisan of ordinary skill to make/use *without an undue amount of experimentation*.

- Description of the inventor's best mode for carrying out the invention:

  This is a bit of a grey area, in that ferreting out whether an inventor has disclosed what he/she considers the best mode at the time the Application was filed is subjective. There may be clues from the Disclosure. More objectively, marketing efforts the inventor has engaged in before filing are telling.

Section 112b specifies two crucial requirements for the claims:

- The subject matter the inventor regards as the invention:

  This is another grey area, as it gets to what the inventor was thinking of when the Application was filed. Once again, clues from the Disclosure or acts of the inventor can shed light.

- Particularly point out and distinctly define the scope of the subject matter of the invention:

  This requires that the scope of the invention

being claimed is rendered clear to a person of ordinary skill in the relevant art.

It is somewhat rare to get a rejection based upon 112a, simply because it needs the inventor to have missed the mark of describing what his/her invention is. Section 112b, on the other hand, is a very frequent ground for rejection.

Rejections under Section 113

The Drawing must have one of more figures where necessary for the understanding of the invention. This translates to the Specification in combination with the Drawing providing an enabling disclosure of the invention.

Objections are common, but rejections are rare. A rejection example would be if a component is required to pivot with respect to another component, but no pivot is shown. Such a failure of the Drawing can be remedied by amendment only if the pivot is disclosed, or unambiguously implied, in the Specification. If not, the failure of the Drawing is fatal, requiring the Application to be refiled with a corrected Drawing. Indeed, this could also be a rejection under Section 101, as an inoperable device is not "useful."

Rejections under Section 102

Section 102 specifies that a patent will be granted unless the claimed invention was:

- patented;
- described in a printed publication; or
- in public use, on sale, or otherwise available to the public before the earliest priority date of the Application.

These three "granted unless" elements constitute the "prior art" that Examiners cite in rejections. An exception is provided for disclosures made one year or less before the priority date of the Application if the disclosures were made by the inventor or someone else who got the information from the inventor. This is referred to as the "one year grace period."

Rejections under Section 102 are known as "novelty" rejections. Novel means new, as in never done before. When a single prior art reference discloses all the subject matter of a claim, it is said to "anticipate the claim." A single reference either anticipates a claim or it doesn't. If other references are cited under a Section 102 rejection, each reference must independently anticipate.

Rejections under Section 103

Section 103 specifies that even though no single reference anticipates, if the differences between the claimed invention and the prior art render the claimed invention obvious to a person of ordinary skill in the art, then the claimed invention is not patentable. The prior art can be one reference or a combination of references. It can also include "official notice" of well known information, like water expands when it freezes. By far, rejections under Section 103 are the most common.

The sixty-four thousand dollar question is: "What exactly is the meaning of obvious?" This has long remained a matter of subjective opinion.

The question has gone to the Supreme Court a number of times.

In a definitive case, Graham v. John Deere, 148 U.S.P.Q. 459, 466 (1966), the Court held:

> *"Under section 103, the scope and content of the prior art is to be determined; the differences between the prior art and the claims at issue are to be ascertained; and the level of ordinary skill in the pertinent art resolved; against this background, obviousness of subject matter is determined."*

It would take a subsequent trip to the Supreme Court to flesh out the meaning of obviousness in the Graham case. This was KSR International Co. v. Teleflex Inc., 127 S. Ct. 1727, 1740 (2007), where the Court held,

> *"[R]ejections on obviousness cannot be sustained by mere conclusory statements; instead, there must be articulated reasoning with some rational underpinning to support the legal conclusion of obviousness."*

In response to KSR, the USPTO published examination guidelines for determining obviousness under the factual inquiries of

Graham in the form of a set of rationales, summarized in MPEP Section 2141, as follows:

> *"(A) Combining prior art elements according to known methods to yield predictable results;*
>
> *(B) Simple substitution of one known element for another to obtain predictable results;*
>
> *(C) Use of known technique to improve similar devices (methods, or products) in the same way;*
>
> *(D) Applying a known technique to a known device (method, or product) ready for improvement to yield predictable results;*
>
> *(E) "Obvious to try"-choosing from a finite number of identified, predictable solutions, with a reasonable expectation of success;*
>
> *(F) Known work in one field of endeavor may prompt variations of it for use in either the same field or a different one based on design incentives or other market forces if the variations would have been predictable to one of ordinary skill in the art; and*
>
> *(G) Some teaching, suggestion, or motivation in the prior art that would have led one of ordinary skill to modify the prior art reference or to combine prior art reference teachings to arrive at the claimed invention."*

These guidelines are there not only for Examiners, they are there for patent attorneys to formulate rationale for arguing nonobviousness.

Below is the Examiner's first Office Action for the Thawometer Application from the USPTO file history of U.S. Patent 9,410,730.

The First Office Action of January 28, 2016:

UNITED STATES PATENT AND TRADEMARK OFFICE

UNITED STATES DEPARTMENT OF COMMERCE
United States Patent and Trademark Office
Address: COMMISSIONER FOR PATENTS
P.O. Box 1450
Alexandria, Virginia 22313-1450
www.uspto.gov

APPLICATION NO.	FILING DATE	FIRST NAMED INVENTOR	ATTORNEY DOCKET NO.	CONFIRMATION NO.
14/932,064	11/04/2015	Peter David Keefe	PDK-775	6261

23592 7590 01/28/2016
PETER D KEEFE
KEEFE AND ASSOCIATES
24405 GRATIOT AVENUE
EASTPOINTE, MI 48021

EXAMINER
DUKE, EMMANUEL E

ART UNIT	PAPER NUMBER
3744	

MAIL DATE	DELIVERY MODE
01/28/2016	PAPER

Please find below and/or attached an Office communication concerning this application or proceeding.

The time period for reply, if any, is set in the attached communication.

PTOL-90A (Rev. 04/07)

Office Action Summary	Application No. 14/932,064	Applicant(s) KEEFE, PETER DAVID	
	Examiner EMMANUEL DUKE	Art Unit 3744	AIA (First Inventor to File) Status Yes

– The MAILING DATE of this communication appears on the cover sheet with the correspondence address –

Period for Reply

A SHORTENED STATUTORY PERIOD FOR REPLY IS SET TO EXPIRE 3 MONTHS FROM THE MAILING DATE OF THIS COMMUNICATION.

- Extensions of time may be available under the provisions of 37 CFR 1.136(a). In no event, however, may a reply be timely filed after SIX (6) MONTHS from the mailing date of this communication.
- If NO period for reply is specified above, the maximum statutory period will apply and will expire SIX (6) MONTHS from the mailing date of this communication.
- Failure to reply within the set or extended period for reply will, by statute, cause the application to become ABANDONED (35 U.S.C. § 133). Any reply received by the Office later than three months after the mailing date of this communication, even if timely filed, may reduce any earned patent term adjustment. See 37 CFR 1.704(b).

Status

1)☒ Responsive to communication(s) filed on *11/04/2015*.
☐ A declaration(s)/affidavit(s) under **37 CFR 1.130(b)** was/were filed on ______.

2a)☐ This action is **FINAL**. 2b)☒ This action is non-final.

3)☐ An election was made by the applicant in response to a restriction requirement set forth during the interview on ______; the restriction requirement and election have been incorporated into this action.

4)☐ Since this application is in condition for allowance except for formal matters, prosecution as to the merits is closed in accordance with the practice under *Ex parte Quayle*, 1935 C.D. 11, 453 O.G. 213.

Disposition of Claims*

5)☒ Claim(s) *1-20* is/are pending in the application.
5a) Of the above claim(s) ______ is/are withdrawn from consideration.
6)☐ Claim(s) ______ is/are allowed.
7)☒ Claim(s) *1-17* is/are rejected.
8)☒ Claim(s) *18-20* is/are objected to.
9)☐ Claim(s) ______ are subject to restriction and/or election requirement.

* If any claims have been determined allowable, you may be eligible to benefit from the **Patent Prosecution Highway** program at a participating intellectual property office for the corresponding application. For more information, please see http://www.uspto.gov/patents/init_events/pph/index.jsp or send an inquiry to PPHfeedback@uspto.gov.

Application Papers

10)☐ The specification is objected to by the Examiner.
11)☒ The drawing(s) filed on *11/04/2015* is/are: a)☒ accepted or b)☐ objected to by the Examiner.
Applicant may not request that any objection to the drawing(s) be held in abeyance. See 37 CFR 1.85(a).
Replacement drawing sheet(s) including the correction is required if the drawing(s) is objected to. See 37 CFR 1.121(d).

Priority under 35 U.S.C. § 119

12)☐ Acknowledgment is made of a claim for foreign priority under 35 U.S.C. § 119(a)-(d) or (f).
Certified copies:
a)☐ All b)☐ Some** c)☐ None of the:
1.☐ Certified copies of the priority documents have been received.
2.☐ Certified copies of the priority documents have been received in Application No. ______.
3.☐ Copies of the certified copies of the priority documents have been received in this National Stage application from the International Bureau (PCT Rule 17.2(a)).

** See the attached detailed Office action for a list of the certified copies not received.

Attachment(s)

1) ☒ Notice of References Cited (PTO-892)
2) ☒ Information Disclosure Statement(s) (PTO/SB/08a and/or PTO/SB/08b) Paper No(s)/Mail Date ______.
3) ☐ Interview Summary (PTO-413) Paper No(s)/Mail Date. ______.
4) ☐ Other: ______.

U.S. Patent and Trademark Office
PTOL-326 (Rev. 11-13) **Office Action Summary** Part of Paper No./Mail Date 20160122

Application/Control Number: 14/932,064 Page 2
Art Unit: 3744

DETAILED ACTION

Notice of Pre-AIA or AIA Status

The present application, filed on or after March 16, 2013, is being examined under the first inventor to file provisions of the AIA.

In the event the determination of the status of the application as subject to AIA 35 U.S.C. 102 and 103 (or as subject to pre-AIA 35 U.S.C. 102 and 103) is incorrect, any correction of the statutory basis for the rejection will not be considered a new ground of rejection if the prior art relied upon, and the rationale supporting the rejection, would be the same under either status.

Claim Rejections - 35 USC § 112

1. The following is a quotation of 35 U.S.C. 112(b):

> (b) CONCLUSION.—The specification shall conclude with one or more claims particularly pointing out and distinctly claiming the subject matter which the inventor or a joint inventor regards as the invention.

> The following is a quotation of 35 U.S.C. 112 (pre-AIA), second paragraph:
> The specification shall conclude with one or more claims particularly pointing out and distinctly claiming the subject matter which the applicant regards as his invention.

Claims 18-20 are rejected under 35 U.S.C. 112(b) or 35 U.S.C. 112 (pre-AIA), second paragraph, as being indefinite for failing to particularly point out and distinctly claim the subject matter which the inventor or a joint inventor, or for pre-AIA the applicant regards as the invention. *In re Venezia,* 530 F.2d 956, 189 USPQ 149 (CCPA 1976).

Claim 18, fails to interrelate essential element, i.e., the "computer based simulation" of the invention as defined by Applicant in the specification.

Application/Control Number: 14/932,064 Page 3
Art Unit: 3744

Appropriate correction is required.

Claim Rejections - 35 USC § 102

2. The following is a quotation of the appropriate paragraphs of 35 U.S.C. 102 that form the basis for the rejections under this section made in this Office action:

A person shall be entitled to a patent unless –

(a)(1) the claimed invention was patented, described in a printed publication, or in public use, on sale or otherwise available to the public before the effective filing date of the claimed invention.

Claims 1, 4, 5, 8 and 12-17 *are rejected under 35 U.S.C. 102(a)(1) as being anticipated by Winchell (**U.S. Patent No.: 3,063,235**), hereinafter referred to as Winchell '235.*

Regarding claims 1, 4, 5, 8 and 12-17, Winchell '235 discloses a freezer thaw indicator and method, comprising: a container (10) comprising container walls (12, 14, 16) defining a closed inner space (18) (as shown in Figs. 1-3: Col 1, lines 58-72 and Col 2, lines 64 through Col 3, lines 1-6); a porous support member (20) disposed in said closed inner space of said container, said porous support member being affixed in positional relation to said container walls, said porous support member dividing said closed inner space into an upper chamber (12a) on one side of said porous support member and a lower chamber (12b) on the other side of said support member (see annotated Figs. 1-2: Col 1, lines 58-72); and a liquid (22) disposed in said closed inner space, wherein said liquid partly fills said closed inner space; wherein said porous support member is porous with respect to said liquid (see annotated Figs. 1-2: Col 1, lines 64-66); wherein if said liquid freezes into a frozen liquid (25) in said upper chamber and said container is oriented such that said upper chamber is vertically above said lower chamber in relation to gravity, then said frozen liquid remains in said upper chamber (as shown in Fig 2: Col 2, lines 4-27); and wherein if said frozen liquid melts in said upper chamber and said container is oriented such that said upper chamber is vertically above said lower chamber in relation to gravity, then

Application/Control Number: 14/932,064 Page 4
Art Unit: 3744

said porous support member supports said frozen liquid and said liquid passes through said porous support member and collects in said lower chamber (as shown in Fig 2: Col 2, lines 4-27).

Applicant is reminded that, under the principals of inherency, if a prior art device, in its normal and usual operation, would necessarily perform the method claimed, then the method claimed will be considered to be anticipated by the prior art device. When the prior art device is the same as a device described in the specification for carrying out the claimed method, it can be assumed the device will inherently perform the claimed process. See MPEP § 2112.02.

Regarding claim 4, Winchell '235 discloses the freezer thaw indicator of Claim 1, wherein said container walls at said lower chamber are transparent (as shown in Fig. 1: Col 1, lines 29-33 and lines 64-65 and Col 2, lines 66-67).

Regarding claim 5, Winchell '235 discloses the freezer thaw indicator of Claim 1, further comprising a graduated scale (23) on said wall of said lower chamber (as shown in Fig. 1: Col 1, lines 71-72 through Col 2, line 1 and lines 71-72).

Regarding claim 8, Winchell '235 discloses the freezer thaw indicator of Claim 1, wherein said upper and lower chambers have substantially equal volumes (as shown in Figs. 1-2: Col 2, lines 66-69).

Regarding claim 12, Winchell '235 discloses the freezer thaw indicator of Claim 9, wherein said liquid comprises water (22) and said frozen liquid comprises ice (25) (see Col 1, lines 65-66 and Col 2, lines 4-9).

Regarding claim 13, Winchell '235 discloses the freezer thaw indicator of Claim 9, wherein said upper and lower chambers have substantially equal volumes (as shown in Figs. 1-2: Col 2, lines 66-69).

Application/Control Number: 14/932,064 Page 5
Art Unit: 3744

Regarding claim 14, Winchell '235 discloses the freezer thaw indicator of Claim 9, further comprising a graduated scale (23) on said wall of said lower chamber (as shown in Fig. 1: Col 1, lines 71-72 through Col 2, line 1 and lines 71-72).

Claim Rejections - 35 USC § 103

3. The following is a quotation of 35 U.S.C. 103 which forms the basis for all obviousness rejections set forth in this Office action:

> A patent for a claimed invention may not be obtained, notwithstanding that the claimed invention is not identically disclosed as set forth in section 102 of this title, if the differences between the claimed invention and the prior art are such that the claimed invention as a whole would have been obvious before the effective filing date of the claimed invention to a person having ordinary skill in the art to which the claimed invention pertains. Patentability shall not be negated by the manner in which the invention was made.

This application currently names joint inventors. In considering patentability of the claims the examiner presumes that the subject matter of the various claims was commonly owned as of the effective filing date of the claimed invention(s) absent any evidence to the contrary. Applicant is advised of the obligation under 37 CFR 1.56 to point out the inventor and effective filing dates of each claim that was not commonly owned as of the effective filing date of the later invention in order for the examiner to consider the applicability of 35 U.S.C. 102(b)(2)(C) for any potential 35 U.S.C. 102(a)(2) prior art against the later invention.

Claim 2 is rejected under 35 U.S.C. 103 as being unpatentable over *Winchell '235, in view of Tepfer* ***(U.S. Patent No.: 3,618,558)****, hereinafter referred to as Tepfer '558.*

Application/Control Number: 14/932,064 Page 6
Art Unit: 3744

Regarding claim 2, Winchell '235 discloses the freezer thaw indicator of Claim 1, except the limitation of further comprising: a first hook connected to said container walls adjacent said lower chamber; and a second hook connected to said container walls adjacent said upper chamber.

Tepfer '558 teaches: the concept of a first hook (20) connected to container walls (12) adjacent said lower chamber (as shown in Fig. 2: Col 2, lines 10-16); and a second hook (19) connected to said container walls (12) adjacent said upper chamber (as shown in Fig. 2: Col 2, lines 10-16).

Since all claimed elements were known in the art at the time of the invention, it would have been obvious to one having ordinary skill in the art before the effective filing date of the claimed invention was made to modify the Winchell '235 to include the use of a first hook connected to said container walls adjacent said lower chamber; and a second hook connected to said container walls adjacent said upper chamber as taught by Tepfer '558, in order to facilitate mounting of the device to desire object or surface (Tepfer '558 – Col 2, lines 13-15).

Therefore, it would have been obvious to one having ordinary skill in the art before the effective filing date of the claimed invention was made to modify the Winchell '235 in view of Tepfer '558 to obtain the invention as specified in claim 2.

Claim 3 is rejected under 35 U.S.C. 103 as being unpatentable over *Winchell '235, in view of LEE et al.* ***(U.S. PG Pub No.: 2011/0108551 A1)***, *hereinafter referred to as LEE et al. '551.*

Regarding claim 3, Winchell '235 discloses the freezer thaw indicator of Claim 1, except the limitation of wherein said container walls are hydrophobic.

LEE et al. '551 teach: the concept of wherein said container walls are hydrophobic (31, 32, and 33) (as shown in Figs. 2-3: [0038-0041]).

Since all claimed elements were known in the art at the time of the invention, it would have been obvious to one having ordinary skill in the art before the effective filing date of the

Application/Control Number: 14/932,064 Page 7
Art Unit: 3744

claimed invention was made to modify the container of Winchell '235 in view of LEE et al. '551 such that the container walls are hydrophobic, in order to prevent liquid from adhering to the inner surface of the container (LEE et al. '551 – [0040]).

Therefore, it would have been obvious to one having ordinary skill in the art before the effective filing date of the claimed invention was made to modify the Winchell '235 in view of LEE et al. '551 to obtain the invention as specified in claim 3.

Claims **6 and 7** are rejected under 35 U.S.C. 103 as being unpatentable over *Winchell '235, in view of Morison (**U.S. Patent No.: 3,620,677**), hereinafter referred to as Morison '677.*

Regarding claim 6, Winchell '235 discloses the freezer thaw indicator of Claim 1, except the limitation of wherein said liquid contains a visual marker.

Morison '677 teaches: the concept of liquid containing a visual marker (see Col 1, lines 2-12 and Col 18, lines 48-63, wherein soluble dye constitutes a visual marker).

Since all claimed elements were known in the art at the time of the invention, it would have been obvious to one having ordinary skill in the art before the effective filing date of the claimed invention was made to modify the liquid of Winchell '235 in view of Morison '677 such that the liquid containing a visual marker, in order to enable accurate and inexpensive means for furnishing information on melted liquid (Morison '677 – Col 1, lines 13-26).

Therefore, it would have been obvious to one having ordinary skill in the art before the effective filing date of the claimed invention was made to modify the Winchell '235 in view of Morison '677 to obtain the invention as specified in claim 6.

Regarding claim 7, Winchell '235 discloses the freezer thaw indicator of Claim 1, except the limitation of further comprising a sheath at least partly covering said sidewalls adjoining said upper chamber.

Morison '677 teaches: the concept of a sheath (184) at least partly covering said sidewalls adjoining said upper chamber (as shown in Figs. 31-32: Col 16, lines 30-47).

Since all claimed elements were known in the art at the time of the invention, it would have been obvious to one having ordinary skill in the art before the effective filing date of the claimed invention was made to modify the device of Winchell '235 in view of Morison '677 to include a sheath at least partly covering said sidewalls adjoining said upper chamber, in order to impact the accuracy or precision of data gathered or measurements the device.

Therefore, it would have been obvious to one having ordinary skill in the art before the effective filing date of the claimed invention was made to modify the Winchell '235 in view of Morison '677 to obtain the invention as specified in claim 6.

Claims **9 and 11** are rejected under 35 U.S.C. 103 as being unpatentable over *Winchell '235, in view of LEE et al. '551, further in view of* Morison '677.

Regarding claim 9, Winchell '235 discloses the freezer thaw indicator of Claim 1, wherein: said container walls at said lower chamber are transparent (as shown in Fig. 1: Col 1, lines 29-33 and lines 64-65 and Col 2, lines 66-67).

However, Winchell '235 fails to disclose the limitations of said container walls are hydrophobic; and said liquid contains a visual marker.

LEE et al. '551 teach: the concept of wherein said container walls are hydrophobic (31, 32, and 33) (as shown in Figs. 2-3: [0038-0041]).

Since all claimed elements were known in the art at the time of the invention, it would have been obvious to one having ordinary skill in the art before the effective filing date of the claimed invention was made to modify the container of Winchell '235 in view of LEE et al. '551 such that the container walls are hydrophobic, in order to prevent liquid from adhering to the inner surface of the container (LEE et al. '551 – [0040]).

Therefore, it would have been obvious to one having ordinary skill in the art before the effective filing date of the claimed invention was made to modify the Winchell '235 in view of LEE et al. '551 to obtain the invention as specified in claim 9.

Application/Control Number: 14/932,064 Page 9
Art Unit: 3744

Morison '677 teaches: the concept of liquid containing a visual marker (see Col 1, lines 2-12 and Col 18, lines 48-63, wherein soluble dye constitutes a visual marker).

Since all claimed elements were known in the art at the time of the invention, it would have been obvious to one having ordinary skill in the art before the effective filing date of the claimed invention was made to modify the liquid of Winchell '235 in view of Morison '677 such that the liquid containing a visual marker, in order to enable accurate and inexpensive means for furnishing information on melted liquid (Morison '677 – Col 1, lines 13-26).

Therefore, it would have been obvious to one having ordinary skill in the art before the effective filing date of the claimed invention was made to modify the Winchell '235 in view of Morison '677 to obtain the invention as specified in claim 9.

Regarding claim 11, the combination of Winchell '235, LEE et al. '551 and Morison '677 disclose and teach the freezer thaw indicator of Claim 9, Winchell '235 as modified by Morison '677 further disclose the concept of a sheath (184) at least partly covering said sidewalls adjoining said upper chamber (as shown in Figs. 31-32: Col 16, lines 30-47).

Since all claimed elements were known in the art at the time of the invention, it would have been obvious to one having ordinary skill in the art before the effective filing date of the claimed invention was made to modify the device of Winchell '235 in view of Morison '677 to include a sheath at least partly covering said sidewalls adjoining said upper chamber, in order to impact the accuracy or precision of data gathered or measurements the device.

Therefore, it would have been obvious to one having ordinary skill in the art before the effective filing date of the claimed invention was made to modify the Winchell '235 in view of Morison '677 to obtain the invention as specified in claim 11.

Claim 10 is rejected under 35 U.S.C. 103 as being unpatentable over *Winchell '235, LEE et al. '551 and* Morison '677 as applied to claim 9 above, *further in view of Tepfer '558.*

Application/Control Number: 14/932,064
Art Unit: 3744

Page 10

Regarding claim 10, the combination of Winchell '235, LEE et al. '551 and Morison '677 disclose and teach the freezer thaw indicator of Claim 9.

However, Winchell '235 fails to further disclose the limitations of comprising: a first hook connected to said container walls adjacent said lower chamber; and a second hook connected to said container walls adjacent said upper chamber.

Tepfer '558 teaches: the concept of a first hook (20) connected to container walls (12) adjacent said lower chamber (as shown in Fig. 2: Col 2, lines 10-16); and a second hook (19) connected to said container walls (12) adjacent said upper chamber (as shown in Fig. 2: Col 2, lines 10-16).

Since all claimed elements were known in the art at the time of the invention, it would have been obvious to one having ordinary skill in the art before the effective filing date of the claimed invention was made to modify the Winchell '235 to include the use of a first hook connected to said container walls adjacent said lower chamber; and a second hook connected to said container walls adjacent said upper chamber as taught by Tepfer '558, in order to facilitate mounting of the device to desire object or surface (Tepfer '558 – Col 2, lines 13-15).

Therefore, it would have been obvious to one having ordinary skill in the art before the effective filing date of the claimed invention was made to modify the Winchell '235 in view of Tepfer '558 to obtain the invention as specified in claim 10.

Allowable Subject Matter

Claims 18-20 would be allowable if rewritten or amended to overcome the rejections under 35 U.S.C. 112(b) or 35 U.S.C. 112 (pre-AIA), 2nd paragraph, set forth in this Office action.

Conclusion

4. Any inquiry concerning this communication or earlier communications from the examiner should be directed to EMMANUEL DUKE whose telephone number is (571)270-5290. The examiner can normally be reached on Monday - Friday, 6:00am - 2:30pm EST.

Application/Control Number: 14/932,064 Page 11
Art Unit: 3744

If attempts to reach the examiner by telephone are unsuccessful, the examiner's supervisor, Frantz Jules can be reached on 571-272-6681. The fax phone number for the organization where this application or proceeding is assigned is 571-273-8300.

Information regarding the status of an application may be obtained from the Patent Application Information Retrieval (PAIR) system. Status information for published applications may be obtained from either Private PAIR or Public PAIR. Status information for unpublished applications is available through Private PAIR only. For more information about the PAIR system, see http://pair-direct.uspto.gov. Should you have questions on access to the Private PAIR system, contact the Electronic Business Center (EBC) at 866-217-9197 (toll-free). If you would like assistance from a USPTO Customer Service Representative or access to the automated information system, call 800-786-9199 (IN USA OR CANADA) or 571-272-1000.

/EMMANUEL DUKE/
Primary Examiner, Art Unit 3744
01/23/2016

Notice of References Cited	Application/Control No. 14/932,064	Applicant(s)/Patent Under Reexamination KEEFE, PETER DAVID	
	Examiner EMMANUEL DUKE	Art Unit 3744	Page 1 of 1

U.S. PATENT DOCUMENTS

*		Document Number Country Code-Number-Kind Code	Date MM-YYYY	Name	CPC Classification	US Classification
*	A	US-3,063,235 A	11-1962	PAUL WINCHELL	G01K3/04	368/1
*	B	US-3,620,677 A	11-1971	Ayers Morison	B01D15/08	116/200
*	C	US-3,618,558 A	11-1971	Tepfer; Barry	G01K11/08	116/216
*	D	US-2011/0108551 A1	05-2011	LEE; Sang-Joon	B65D45/325	220/212
	E	US-				
	F	US-				
	G	US-				
	H	US-				
	I	US-				
	J	US-				
	K	US-				
	L	US-				
	M	US-				

FOREIGN PATENT DOCUMENTS

*		Document Number Country Code-Number-Kind Code	Date MM-YYYY	Country	Name	CPC Classification
	N					
	O					
	P					
	Q					
	R					
	S					
	T					

NON-PATENT DOCUMENTS

*		Include as applicable: Author, Title Date, Publisher, Edition or Volume, Pertinent Pages)
	U	
	V	
	W	
	X	

*A copy of this reference is not being furnished with this Office action. (See MPEP § 707.05(a).)
Dates in MM-YYYY format are publication dates. Classifications may be US or foreign.

U.S. Patent and Trademark Office
PTO-892 (Rev. 01-2001) | **Notice of References Cited** | Part of Paper No. 20160122

Below is the entire single reference cited under the Section 102 rejection of the Office Action.

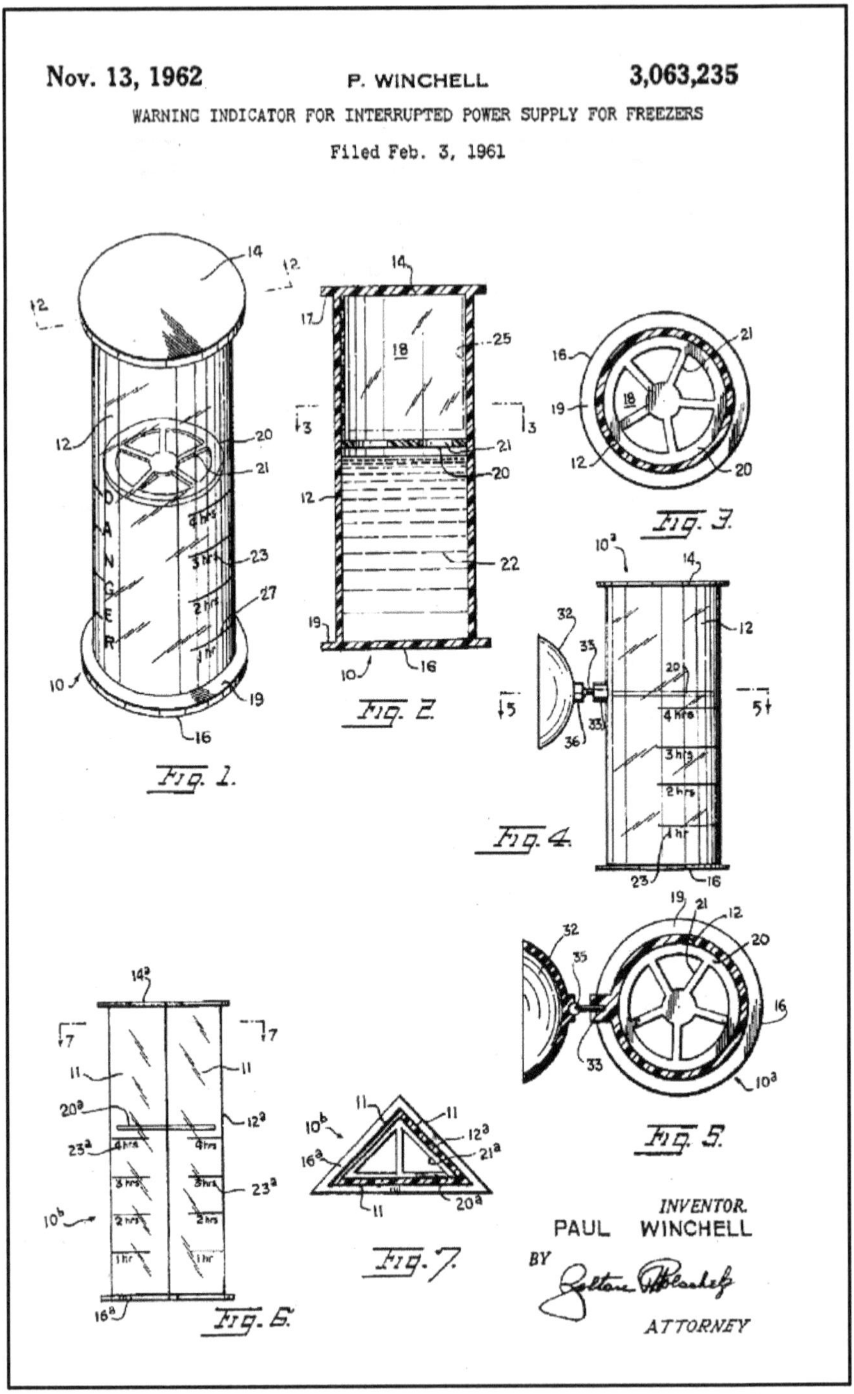
Nov. 13, 1962
P. WINCHELL
3,063,235
WARNING INDICATOR FOR INTERRUPTED POWER SUPPLY FOR FREEZERS
Filed Feb. 3, 1961
DANGER
4 hrs
3 hrs
2 hrs
1 hr
Fig. 1.
Fig. 2.
Fig. 3.
Fig. 4.
Fig. 5.
Fig. 6.
Fig. 7.
INVENTOR.
PAUL WINCHELL
BY
ATTORNEY

3,618,558

1

UNSAFE CONDITION INDICATOR FOR FROZEN FOOD CHESTS

This invention relates to an indicator and more particularly to a thermal indicator for indicating if an unsafe temperature condition has been reached in a cold storage unit such as a frozen food chest.

BACKGROUND OF THE INVENTION

There are many substances which are kept in a frozen state until used. Many of these will spoil if they are permitted to thaw and then refreeze. Frozen foods thawed for long periods of time and then refrozen begin to deteriorate and in some cases may result in bacterial growth in the food and possible food poisoning to the eater. Also, whole blood must be stored under refrigeration below 50° F. and spoils if the temperature gets above the limit.

Ordinarily, the object to be stored is placed in a frozen unit, the desired temperature is pressed and the object is stored for many days. However, during the storage period, either through accident or neglect, the temperature may rise above the pressed maximum limit and damage the contents. When the unit again refreezes, it will not be visible that at some time during the storage period, the object had thawed and then was refrozen.

Many thermal indicators have been used in the prior art. Most of these devices are associated with the particular packed object, i.e., the frozen food or the blood container, rather than the storage unit. Also, with the prior art devices, the indicator is generally prefrozen before it is used and cannot be reused after it has once indicated an unsafe condition. Many of these thermal indicators are complex and relatively expensive devices requiring specially shaped tubes, springs, magnets and other complex parts.

It is accordingly an object of this invention to provide an inexpensive, simple thermal indicator which detects an unsafe temperature condition.

Another object is to provide a thermal indicator which can be reused without resetting the temperature state of the indicator.

A further object is to provide a thermal indicator which can be used in a cold storage unit to detect an unsafe temperature condition.

A still further object is to provide an advertising device having a thermal indicator and presenting advertising indicia on the device.

Yet another object is to provide a card supporting a thermal indicator and having room thereon for advertisements.

These and other objects of our invention will be understood from the following description taken in conjunction with the accompanying drawings.

DESCRIPTION OF THE DRAWING

FIG. 1 is a front view of the indicator on a card; and
FIG. 2 is a side view of the indicator on a card.

DESCRIPTION OF PREFERRED EMBODIMENT(S)

Referring to FIG. 1, a card 10 has place on one side of it the thermal indicator shown generally at 11. The indicator consists of a transparent or translucent plastic tube 12 of about 5/16-inch diameter and about 4 inches long. The ends of tube 12 are flattened and heat sealed at 13, 14 to make the tube waterproof.

Prior to sealing the ends of the tube, approximately seven-eighths of the tube is filled with a transparent solution 15 and with the indicator rod 16. The indicator rod is typically constructed of vinyl material and is about half the length of the tube. Its diameter is sufficiently small to pass freely through the tube. Other materials can be used for the indicator rod, so long as it is clearly visible, will sink in the solution, and be of a size to be free moving in the tube.

The solution used was water with approximately 0.01 percent solution of Dupont "Zonyl," to reduce surface tension. Other solutions with similar freezing, transparency and sur-

2

face tension reducing characteristics could also be used. The type of solution is dependent upon the temperature threshold desired. For a 32° F. maximum temperature, water would be used for the solution. For a lower temperature alcohol or salt would be added to the water in an amount sufficient to depress the melting temperature of the mixture to any desired value below 32° F. For a temperature above 32° F. organic compounds could be used.

The indicator tube 12, when filled and sealed then grommeted to the card by piercing the flattened ends of the tube and inserting grommets 17, 18 through the pierced holes and into the card.

Mounting hooks 19, 20 are attached to the underside of the card 10 and connected to the card using the same grommets 17, 18. Two additional hooks 21, 22 may be affixed to the card 10 at the other end thereof by means of two additional grommets 23, 24. In place of grommets 17, 18, staples or other conventional fastening means may be employed.

The card 10 is constructed of a waterproof material and the area 25 adjacent to the indicator 11 may be imprinted with an advertising message or instructions for the operation of the device.

To operate the indicator, the entire card is placed or suspended, by means of one set of hooks (18, 22 or 20, 21) in a cold storage chest such as the frozen food compartment of a refrigerator. The indicator rod 16 will immediately fall to the bottom of the tube and remain immersed in the solution. The temperature to be monitored will be below the freezing point of the solution so that the liquid will freeze in that portion of the tube that is downward.

When the liquid is frozen, the card is remounted in the freezer unit with the frozen solution containing the indicator rod, in the upward position, as shown in FIGS. 1 and 2. The opposite set of hooks may be used for the mounting. The device is left in a visible place in the freezer unit.

In the event that there is a lowering of the temperature in the freezer unit, sufficient to melt the solution, the indicator rod will be released and it will drop to the lower portion of the tube because it is heavier than the liquid. The presence of the indicator on the bottom of the tube indicates that the temperature has risen above the unsafe condition and the contents of the freezer may have been affected by the defrosting.

Even if the freezer unit had subsequently begun proper operation and the temperature had again dropped below the threshold, the indicator rod will remain on the bottom of the tube indicating that previously there was an unsafe condition.

When an unsafe condition occurs and the indicator rod is on the bottom, as soon as the liquid on the bottom has again refrozen, the card can immediately be used again by inverting it and remounting it from the opposite hooks.

It has been found that if a colored water solution is used without the rod the device is inoperative because the liquid sticks to the wall of the tube and does not drop down to indicate melting. However, if a wetting agent to reduce surface tension is added to the liquid, the liquid will freely drop down. There are many wetting agents commonly available as standard items of commerce. The quantity to be employed is readily determined by experiment and is generally not critical.

It will be seen that this device can be reused constantly without ever opening up the tube to reset the indicator or ever removing the indicator. The entire card and tube are completely waterproof so no liquids from the melting can damage the indicator during normal use.

Having thus disclosed the best embodiment of the invention presently contemplated, it is to be understood that various changes and modifications may be made by those skilled in the art without departing from the spirit of the invention.

What I claim as new and desire to secure by Letters Patent is:

1. An indicator for detecting the occurrence of a temperature rise above a preset maximum in a cold storage unit, said indicator comprising the combination of:

a. a card;

3,083,235

3

brated to indicate the length of time said water flows through said screen from one end of the container to the other, after the water is once frozen to ice in the one end of the container and the ice thereafter thaws temporarily, and a suction cup secured to said body by swivel means so that the body is rotatable in a plane perpendicular to

4

the axis of said cup, said body being cylindrical in form, said screen being in the form of a spider ring.

References Cited in the file of this patent

UNITED STATES PATENTS

2,847,067	Brewer	Aug. 12, 1958

Below are the faces of the other references cited under the Section 103 rejection of the Office Action.

United States Patent [11] **3,618,558**

[72] Inventor **Barry Tepfer**
19 Milburn St., Rockville Center, N.Y. 11570
[21] Appl. No. **33,782**
[22] Filed **May 1, 1970**
[45] Patented **Nov. 9, 1971**

[54] **UNSAFE CONDITION INDICATOR FOR FROZEN FOOD CHESTS**
1 Claim, 2 Drawing Figs.

[52] U.S. Cl. **116/114.5,** 73/371, 99/192
[51] Int. Cl. **G01k 1/02**
[50] Field of Search .... 116/101, 106, 114.5; 73/368.3, 17, 358, 378; 99/192 TT

[56] **References Cited**
UNITED STATES PATENTS

1,779,066	10/1930	Halset	116/114.5 X
2,788,282	4/1957	Hammond, Jr.	99/192
2,852,394	9/1958	Fahringer	99/192
2,915,405	12/1959	Hammond, Jr. et al.	99/192
3,090,236	5/1963	Nicol	73/358
3,290,942	12/1966	Carbaugh et al.	73/358
3,518,961	7/1970	Kovac	116/114

Primary Examiner—Louis J. Capozi
Attorney—Leonard H. King

ABSTRACT: A card having mounted thereon a transparent waterproof tube containing a liquid solution and a short indicator rod. The card is placed in a freezing unit until the liquid, with the rod within it, freezes. The card is then inverted in the freezer unit. When the temperature of the unit rises above the melting point of the liquid, the indicator rod will fall indicating an unsafe condition.

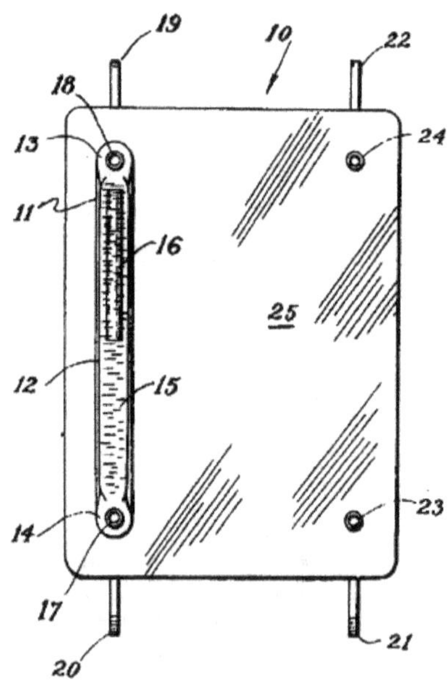

(19) **United States**

(12) **Patent Application Publication** (10) **Pub. No.: US 2011/0108551 A1**

LEE et al. (43) **Pub. Date: May 12, 2011**

(54) **LIQUID CONTAINER**

(75) Inventors: **Sang-Joon LEE**, Pohang-city (KR); **Jung-Yeop Lee**, Pohang-city (KR)

(73) Assignee: **POSTECH ACADEMY-INDUSTRY FOUNDATION**, Pohang-city (KR)

(21) Appl. No.: **12/943,983**

(22) Filed: **Nov. 11, 2010**

(30) **Foreign Application Priority Data**

Nov. 12, 2009 (KR) 10-2009-0109302

Publication Classification

(51) **Int. Cl.**
B65D 51/00 (2006.01)

(52) **U.S. Cl.** **220/212**

(57) **ABSTRACT**

An exemplary embodiment of the present invention relates to a liquid container that prevents a liquid substance from flowing down from the outlet by minimizing surface energy generated between the liquid substance and the outlet, and prevents leakage at a joint between the body and the guide.

A liquid container according to an exemplary embodiment of the present invention includes a body containing a liquid substance and discharging the liquid substance through a mouth and a guide connected to the mouth and having an outlet for discharging the liquid substance, wherein a first hydrophobic layer is formed by hydrophobic treatment on the surface of the outlet.

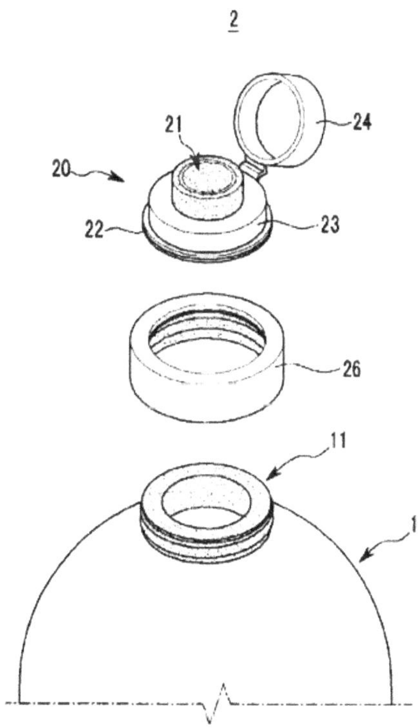

United States Patent [11] **3,620,677**

[72] Inventor **Ayers Morison**
Gross Pointe, Mich.
[21] Appl. No. **160,127**
[22] Filed **Dec. 18, 1961**
[45] Patented **Nov. 16, 1971**
[73] Assignee **Miles Laboratories, Inc.**
Elkhart, Ind.

[54] **INDICATING DEVICE**
21 Claims, 46 Drawing Figs.

[52] **U.S. Cl.** **23/253,** 116/114, 252/425.5

[51] **Int. Cl.** **G01n 29/02**

[50] **Field of Search** .... 73/53, 29, 358, 335; 58/1; 99/192 TI; 116/114.19, 114, 114.20; 158/96; 67/53, 70, 71, 69; 117/121.2, 140 R; 252/425.5; 23/253 TP, 254; 55/387; 261/99, 107

[56] **References Cited**

UNITED STATES PATENTS

161,118	3/1875	Halvorson	252/425.5
197,902	12/1877	Scott	117/121.2
580,308	4/1897	Fenby	252/425.5
1,238,123	8/1917	Freeman	23/253
2,337,534	12/1943	Barber	58/1
2,459,042	1/1949	Nave et al.	67/53
2,555,294	5/1951	Reilly	67/69
2,560,537	7/1951	Anderson	99/192
2,567,445	9/1951	Parker	23/253
2,681,866	6/1954	Auchterlonie	117/140
2,708,896	5/1955	Smith et al.	116/114
2,714,571	8/1955	Irion et al.	117/140
2,823,984	2/1958	Mavrodineanu	23/253
2,915,405	12/1959	Hammond et al.	99/192
2,918,893	12/1959	Norton	116/114
2,939,311	6/1960	Booth	73/29
2,943,594	7/1960	Price	116/114
2,951,764	9/1960	Chase	99/192
2,986,936	6/1961	Vernet	73/358
2,605,634	8/1952	Lewis	116/114
2,998,306	8/1961	Huyck et al.	23/254
3,015,228	1/1962	Shuttleworth et al.	73/29
3,018,611	1/1962	Biritz	58/1
3,041,870	7/1962	Levine	73/53

Primary Examiner—Joseph Scovronek
Attorney—Harness, Dickey & Pierce

CLAIM: 1. An indicating device comprising in combination a porous capillary material characterized by connected voids of sufficiently small size to induce the progressive absorption of a fluid, and an impervious covering material enclosing at least the major portion of the exterior surfaces of said capillary material and disposed in intimate contact therewith defining an absorptive cavity of a preselected volume, said device constructed to provide directional guidance through said absorptive cavity of a fluid contacting an exposed surface of said capillary material, indicating means on said indicating device, said capillary material within said absorptive cavity operable in conjunction with a fluid absorbed to evidence in combination with said indicating means a characteristic of the fluid absorbed therein.

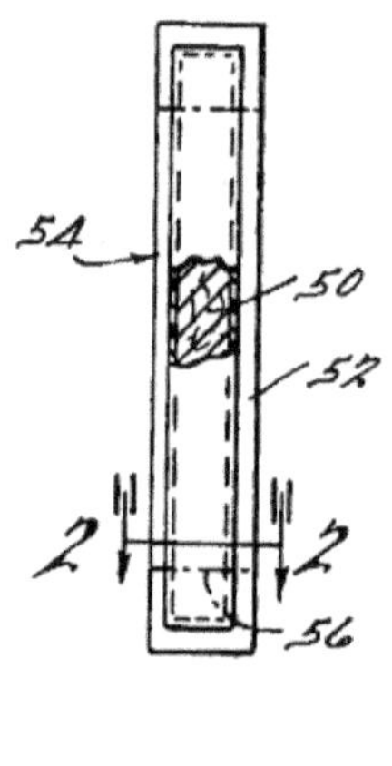

Images credit: USPTO.gov database.

Analysis of the Office Action

When I started out, apprenticing at a very successful patent law firm, I was given a file having a first Office Action that needed an Amendment to be prepared. My task was to prepare an Amendment for the senior partner to review. When the review came, I was asked a lot of questions by the partner to ferret out my command of the patent laws, rules and my ability to perform the task at hand. He looked at my time record, and asked me, "What is this entry, analysis?" I responded, "I took that hour and a half after reading through everything to analyze my best approach to writing the Amendment." He replied, "Nobody does that!"

Let's now look at the analysis I did before writing the Thawometer Amendment.

Rejection under Section 112:

The Examiner raised a rejection under Section 112b of Claims 18-20, in that he pointed out Claim 18 failed to interrelate the element "computer based simulation" to the Specification. Here the Examiner made a mistake because it was actually Claim 19 that introduced this element. At any rate, there was clear support at Figure 27 and paragraphs 72-80. So, this rejection was going to be no problem to overcome in my forthcoming Amendment.

Rejection under Section 102:

To say that I was shocked to learn Paul Winchell, God bless him, got the idea for the Thawometer over 50 years before me is an understatement. But there it was, irrefutably, unarguably, unavoidably. Sweet spot 1 of the Thermometer was rendered D.O.A.

Never think your idea is so rare that it's impossible someone could have earlier invented it!

I was curious to learn the prosecution record of Winchell's patent application, but his patent was too early to do this online. For patents issued after 1980, go to https://PatentCenter.USPTO.gov/search. Type in the document's number and, voila, its USPTO examination "file history" will appear; try it to view the file history of the Thawometer.

It was clear as the day is long that the Examiner was proper in his use of Winchell to reject independent Claims 1 and 15, as well as dependent Claims 4, 5, 8, 12, 13, 14, 16 and 17. This was a case of "you can't fight city hall."

Rejection under Section 103:

You'll notice on page 5 of the Office Action, at the beginning of the Section 103 rejection, the Examiner says, "*This application currently names joint inventors.*" While each and every item of objection/rejection must be responded to, this is not one of them. It was clear that the Examiner had simply used USPTO "boiler plate" language. It was unambiguous on the face of the Application and the acknowledging Filing Receipt that I was the sole inventor. As they say, why beat a dead horse? So I decided to ignore this.

The Examiner addressed each of the remaining dependent claims of base Claim 1, Claims 2, 3, 6, 7, 9, 10 and 11, with a Section 103 rejection.

In each of the Section 103 grounds for rejection, the Examiner combined Winchell with the disclosures in Tepfer, Lee and Morrison to show the claimed subject matter was obvious to a person of ordinary skill in the art.

In so doing, the Examiner did his job exactly as required by the USPTO. He cited Winchell, and then the specific drawing figure and/or passage in the text of the Specification of each of the other applied references where the claimed element is found. If he had failed to do this, or if he misspoke, then I could have challenged his conclusions. But he was on-point, dead on target, and there was no wiggle room for me to argue for allowance of any of these rejected dependent claims.

Nonetheless, I considered to amend base Claim 1 regarding specificity of the "porous support member." In Claim 1, I had recited a functional limitation of the structure, "Wherein … said porous support member supports said frozen liquid and said liquid passes through said porous support member and collects in said lower chamber." I considered to add a limitation that, "wherein the porosity of said porous support member allows said liquid to freely pass into said bottom chamber." But in all honesty, in keeping with my experimentation about this, Winchell's ring 20 had openings 21 spacious enough to do this. It would be another rejection under Section 102 or Section 103. Further, while Winchell did not show my "cross-hairs" type of porous support member, I had doubts this would be robust enough for everyday use, and claiming it would only open up a new Section 103 rejection, as cross-hairs are notoriously well known.

I decided not to amend Claim 1 (nor 15) on the basis I'd almost certainly not win, and arguments on the record can adversely affect the scope of allowed claims.

Allowable Subject Matter:

With regard to Claims 18, 19 and 20, no prior art was found that anticipated them or rendered them obvious.

In view Claims 18-20 were indicated to be allowable if the rejection under Section 112 could be overcome, I resolved that's the road I'd take: preservation of Sweet Spot 2.

* * *

Patent Office Statistics

Curious to know how well the USPTO handles its pending patent applications?

The USPTO provides a performance dashboard which tells at a glance how it is doing. Just click on the relevant box to obtain information on:

- Unexamined Application Inventory;
- Total Application Inventory;
- First Office Action Pendency;
- Traditional Total Pendency;
- Traditional Total Pendency (incl. RCEs)
- Other Data including: Patent Term Adj., After Final Response, Design, Quality, Production, Pendency, Track One, Petition, and Reexamination.

* * *

Below is my responsive Amendment from the USPTO file history of U.S. Patent 9,410,730. Note: page 9 is omitted, being merely an optional certificate of submission.

Responsive Amendment of April 21, 2016:

IN THE UNITED STATES PATENT AND TRADEMARK OFFICE

Patent Application of: Peter David Keefe

For: Freezer Thaw Indicator

Serial Number: 14/932,064

Filed: 11/04/2015

Group Art Unit: 3744

Confirmation No.: 6261

Examiner: Emmanuel E. Duke

Atty. Ref. No.: PDK-775

AMENDMENT

Commissioner for Patents
P.O. Box 1450
Alexandria, VA 22313

Dear Sir:

In response to the Office Action dated 01/28/2016, please amend the above identified patent application as follows.

US Serial No. 14/932,064
Page 2 of 9

IN THE CLAIMS:

Please cancel without prejudice Claims 1 through 17, as follows.

1. – 17. (canceled)

18. (original) A method for adjusting thermal sensitivity of a freezer thaw indicator to match a thermal cross-section of a freezer, said method comprising the steps of:

providing container walls defining a closed inner space;

providing a porous support member disposed in the closed inner space and fixed in positional relation to the container walls such that on one side of the porous support member is an upper chamber of the closed inner space and on the other side of the porous support member is a lower chamber of the closed inner space;

providing a freezer thaw indicator by introduction of a liquid into the closed inner space, wherein the liquid partly fills the inner space;

providing a cold zone of a freezer having a thermal cross-section, the thermal cross-section including at least one frozen object;

orienting the container to a first orientation such that the lower chamber is vertically above the upper chamber with respect to gravity, wherein the liquid is disposed in the upper chamber;

freezing the liquid in the first orientation;

orienting the container to a second orientation such that the upper chamber is vertically above the lower chamber with respect to gravity, wherein the frozen liquid remains in the upper chamber;

inducing a thaw episode of the cold zone;

US Serial No. 14/932,064
Page 3 of 9

indicating occurrence of the thaw episode of the cold zone of the freezer by presence of the liquid in the lower chamber; and

determining whether the indication of occurrence matches thaw of the at least one frozen object;

wherein if said step of determining determines a match, then the freezer thaw indicator has a correct sensitivity; and

wherein if said step of determining determines a mismatch, then the freezer thaw indicator has an incorrect sensitivity and said step of providing container walls is repeated until said step of determining determines a match.

19. (original) The method of Claim 18, wherein said steps are carried out electronically by a computer based simulation.

20. (original) The method of Claim 18, wherein the repeating of said step of providing container walls further comprises adjusting a sheath, wherein the sheath at least partly covers the container walls adjoining the upper chamber.

US Serial No. 14/932,064
Page 4 of 9

REMARKS

The above identified Office Action has been reviewed, the references carefully considered, and the Examiner's comments carefully weighed. In this regard, Claims 1 through 17 have been canceled without prejudice.

It is contended that by the present Amendment, all bases of rejection set forth in the Office Action have been traversed and overcome. Accordingly, reconsideration and withdrawal of the rejection is respectfully requested.

Rejection under 35 U.S.C. 112

Ground for Rejection:

According to the Office Action, Claims 18-20 are rejected as being indefinite in that Claim 18 fails to interrelate an essential element, to wit: the computer based simulation as defined in the Specification.

Applicant's Response:

Applicant respectfully submits that base Claim 18 is definite as originally submitted in that the Disclosure clearly indicates the method can be carried out empirically or by electronic computer simulation.

Claim 18 requires, inter alia:

"providing container walls defining a closed inner space;

US Serial No. 14/932,064
Page 5 of 9

providing a porous support member disposed in the closed inner space and fixed in positional relation to the container walls such that on one side of the porous support member is an upper chamber of the closed inner space and on the other side of the porous support member is a lower chamber of the closed inner space;

providing a freezer thaw indicator by introduction of a liquid into the closed inner space, wherein the liquid partly fills the inner space;

providing a cold zone of a freezer having a thermal cross-section, the thermal cross-section including at least one frozen object;

orienting the container to a first orientation such that the lower chamber is vertically above the upper chamber with respect to gravity, wherein the liquid is disposed in the upper chamber;

freezing the liquid in the first orientation;

orienting the container to a second orientation such that the upper chamber is vertically above the lower chamber with respect to gravity, wherein the frozen liquid remains in the upper chamber;

inducing a thaw episode of the cold zone;

indicating occurrence of the thaw episode of the cold zone of the freezer by presence of the liquid in the lower chamber; and

determining whether the indication of occurrence matches thaw of the at least one frozen object;"

Claim 18 does not recite a step requiring a "computer based simulation. However, this requirement is recited in Claim 19, which recites, inter alia:

"wherein said steps are carried out electronically by a computer based simulation."

Using Applicant's Disclosure for guidance as to the completeness and definiteness of base Claim 18, Drawing Sheet 8 contains a flow chart of the algorithm at Figure 27, and the Specification recites the methodology at Paragraphs [0072] through [0080].

Figure 27 does not indicate a step requiring a "computer based simulation".

In addition, the Specification alludes to an alternative use of simulation at Paragraph [0075], in reciting:

US Serial No. 14/932,064
Page 6 of 9

> *"At Block 208, a thermal cross-section for a cold zone of a freezer is determined. For example, a freezer is provided (or simulated)..."*

Further, the Specification alludes to empirical testing at Paragraph [0076], in reciting:

> "In this regard, the test empirically examines whether ice melt in the freezer thaw indicator matches with thaw of the objects in the cold zone."

Finally, the Specification makes clear the method can be carried out as an empirical test or a computer simulation at Paragraph [0080]:

> *"It is to be noted the above steps may be carried out empirically or by electronic computer simulation."*

In view an electronic computer simulation is not essential to the steps recited in base Claim 18, base Claim 18 meets the requirements of 35 U.S.C. 112.

Accordingly, Applicant respectfully requests the Examiner to withdraw the rejection under 35 U.S.C. 112 and allow pending Claims 18 through 20.

Rejection under 35 U.S.C. 102

Grounds for Rejection:

According to the Office Action, Claims 1, 4, 5, 8 and 12-17 are rejected as being anticipated by Winchell.

Applicant's Response:

In view of the present amendment in which Claims 1-17 have been canceled without prejudice, Applicant courteously submits this ground for rejection is now moot.

US Serial No. 14/932,064
Page 7 of 9

Rejection under 35 U.S.C. 103

Grounds for Rejection:

According to the Office Action, Claim 2 is rejected a being unpatentable over Winchell in view of Tepfer.

According to the Office Action, Claim 3 is rejected a being unpatentable over Winchell in view of Lee, et al.

According to the Office Action, Claims 6 and 7 are rejected a being unpatentable over Winchell in view of Morison.

According to the Office Action, Claims 9 and 11 are rejected a being unpatentable over Winchell in view of Lee, et al and further in view of Morison.

According to the Office Action, Claim 10 is rejected a being unpatentable over Winchell in view of Morison and further in view of Tepfer.

Applicant's Response:

In view of the present amendment in which Claims 1-17 have been canceled without prejudice, Applicant courteously submits this ground for rejection is now moot.

Allowable Subject Matter

According to the Office Action, Claims 18-20 would be allowable if rewritten or amended to overcome the rejection under 35 U.S.C. 112.

US Serial No. 14/932,064
Page 8 of 9

Applicant courteously submits the above response to the rejection under 35 U.S.C. 112 fully addressed and overcame all outstanding issues.

Accordingly, Applicant respectfully submits Claims 18-20 are presently in condition for immediate allowance.

Conclusion

It is respectfully submitted that Applicant has responded in a fully satisfactory manner to all matters at issue in this Application, and that this Application is now in condition for allowance. In this regard, Applicant has made every effort to comply with the requirements set forth in the Office Action as well as the statutory requirements. Accordingly, Applicant respectfully requests that the Examiner enter this Amendment, allow the presently pending claims, and pass this Application on to issue.

Respectfully submitted,

/Peter D. Keefe/
Peter D. Keefe
Reg. No. 31,114

Dated: April 21, 2016

Peter D. Keefe
Keefe and Associates
24405 Gratiot Ave.
Eastpointe, MI 48021

Tel. (586) 775-5680

After considering my Amendment, the Examiner issued a second Office Action, dated May 9, 2016. It was a Notice of Allowance—every inventor's prize!

Below is the Examiner's Notice of Allowance/Allowability from the USPTO file history of U.S. Patent 9,410,730.

UNITED STATES PATENT AND TRADEMARK OFFICE

UNITED STATES DEPARTMENT OF COMMERCE
United States Patent and Trademark Office
Address: COMMISSIONER FOR PATENTS
P.O. Box 1450
Alexandria, Virginia 22313-1450
www.uspto.gov

NOTICE OF ALLOWANCE AND FEE(S) DUE

23592 7590 05/09/2016
PETER D KEEFE
KEEFE AND ASSOCIATES
24405 GRATIOT AVENUE
EASTPOINTE, MI 48021

EXAMINER	
DUKE, EMMANUEL E	
ART UNIT	PAPER NUMBER
3744	

DATE MAILED: 05/09/2016

APPLICATION NO.	FILING DATE	FIRST NAMED INVENTOR	ATTORNEY DOCKET NO.	CONFIRMATION NO.
14/932,064	11/04/2015	Peter David Keefe	PDK-775	6261

TITLE OF INVENTION: Freezer Thaw Indicator

APPLN. TYPE	ENTITY STATUS	ISSUE FEE DUE	PUBLICATION FEE DUE	PREV. PAID ISSUE FEE	TOTAL FEE(S) DUE	DATE DUE
nonprovisional	SMALL	$480	$0	$0	$480	08/09/2016

THE APPLICATION IDENTIFIED ABOVE HAS BEEN EXAMINED AND IS ALLOWED FOR ISSUANCE AS A PATENT. PROSECUTION ON THE MERITS IS CLOSED. THIS NOTICE OF ALLOWANCE IS NOT A GRANT OF PATENT RIGHTS. THIS APPLICATION IS SUBJECT TO WITHDRAWAL FROM ISSUE AT THE INITIATIVE OF THE OFFICE OR UPON PETITION BY THE APPLICANT. SEE 37 CFR 1.313 AND MPEP 1308.

THE ISSUE FEE AND PUBLICATION FEE (IF REQUIRED) MUST BE PAID WITHIN THREE MONTHS FROM THE MAILING DATE OF THIS NOTICE OR THIS APPLICATION SHALL BE REGARDED AS ABANDONED. THIS STATUTORY PERIOD CANNOT BE EXTENDED. SEE 35 U.S.C. 151. THE ISSUE FEE DUE INDICATED ABOVE DOES NOT REFLECT A CREDIT FOR ANY PREVIOUSLY PAID ISSUE FEE IN THIS APPLICATION. IF AN ISSUE FEE HAS PREVIOUSLY BEEN PAID IN THIS APPLICATION (AS SHOWN ABOVE), THE RETURN OF PART B OF THIS FORM WILL BE CONSIDERED A REQUEST TO REAPPLY THE PREVIOUSLY PAID ISSUE FEE TOWARD THE ISSUE FEE NOW DUE.

HOW TO REPLY TO THIS NOTICE:

I. Review the ENTITY STATUS shown above. If the ENTITY STATUS is shown as SMALL or MICRO, verify whether entitlement to that entity status still applies.

If the ENTITY STATUS is the same as shown above, pay the TOTAL FEE(S) DUE shown above.

If the ENTITY STATUS is changed from that shown above, on PART B - FEE(S) TRANSMITTAL, complete section number 5 titled "Change in Entity Status (from status indicated above)".

For purposes of this notice, small entity fees are 1/2 the amount of undiscounted fees, and micro entity fees are 1/2 the amount of small entity fees.

II. PART B - FEE(S) TRANSMITTAL, or its equivalent, must be completed and returned to the United States Patent and Trademark Office (USPTO) with your ISSUE FEE and PUBLICATION FEE (if required). If you are charging the fee(s) to your deposit account, section "4b" of Part B - Fee(s) Transmittal should be completed and an extra copy of the form should be submitted. If an equivalent of Part B is filed, a request to reapply a previously paid issue fee must be clearly made, and delays in processing may occur due to the difficulty in recognizing the paper as an equivalent of Part B.

III. All communications regarding this application must give the application number. Please direct all communications prior to issuance to Mail Stop ISSUE FEE unless advised to the contrary.

IMPORTANT REMINDER: Utility patents issuing on applications filed on or after Dec. 12, 1980 may require payment of maintenance fees. It is patentee's responsibility to ensure timely payment of maintenance fees when due.

Page 1 of 3

PTOL-85 (Rev. 02/11)

UNITED STATES PATENT AND TRADEMARK OFFICE

UNITED STATES DEPARTMENT OF COMMERCE
United States Patent and Trademark Office
Address: COMMISSIONER FOR PATENTS
P.O. Box 1450
Alexandria, Virginia 22313-1450
www.uspto.gov

APPLICATION NO.	FILING DATE	FIRST NAMED INVENTOR	ATTORNEY DOCKET NO.	CONFIRMATION NO.
14/932,064	11/04/2015	Peter David Keefe	PDK-775	6261

23592 7590 05/09/2016
PETER D KEEFE
KEEFE AND ASSOCIATES
24405 GRATIOT AVENUE
EASTPOINTE, MI 48021

EXAMINER	
DUKE, EMMANUEL E	
ART UNIT	**PAPER NUMBER**
3744	

DATE MAILED: 05/09/2016

Determination of Patent Term Adjustment under 35 U.S.C. 154 (b)
(Applications filed on or after May 29, 2000)

The Office has discontinued providing a Patent Term Adjustment (PTA) calculation with the Notice of Allowance.

Section 1(h)(2) of the AIA Technical Corrections Act amended 35 U.S.C. 154(b)(3)(B)(i) to eliminate the requirement that the Office provide a patent term adjustment determination with the notice of allowance. See Revisions to Patent Term Adjustment, 78 Fed. Reg. 19416, 19417 (Apr. 1, 2013). Therefore, the Office is no longer providing an initial patent term adjustment determination with the notice of allowance. The Office will continue to provide a patent term adjustment determination with the Issue Notification Letter that is mailed to applicant approximately three weeks prior to the issue date of the patent, and will include the patent term adjustment on the patent. Any request for reconsideration of the patent term adjustment determination (or reinstatement of patent term adjustment) should follow the process outlined in 37 CFR 1.705.

Any questions regarding the Patent Term Extension or Adjustment determination should be directed to the Office of Patent Legal Administration at (571)-272-7702. Questions relating to issue and publication fee payments should be directed to the Customer Service Center of the Office of Patent Publication at 1-(888)-786-0101 or (571)-272-4200.

Page 3 of 3

PTOL-85 (Rev. 02/11)

Notice of Allowability	Application No. 14/932,064	Applicant(s) KEEFE, PETER DAVID	
	Examiner EMMANUEL DUKE	Art Unit 3744	AIA (First Inventor to File) Status Yes

-- The MAILING DATE of this communication appears on the cover sheet with the correspondence address--
All claims being allowable, PROSECUTION ON THE MERITS IS (OR REMAINS) CLOSED in this application. If not included herewith (or previously mailed), a Notice of Allowance (PTOL-85) or other appropriate communication will be mailed in due course. **THIS NOTICE OF ALLOWABILITY IS NOT A GRANT OF PATENT RIGHTS.** This application is subject to withdrawal from issue at the initiative of the Office or upon petition by the applicant. See 37 CFR 1.313 and MPEP 1308.

1. ☒ This communication is responsive to *Claims filed on 04/21/2016*.
   ☐ A declaration(s)/affidavit(s) under **37 CFR 1.130(b)** was/were filed on______.
2. ☐ An election was made by the applicant in response to a restriction requirement set forth during the interview on _____; the restriction requirement and election have been incorporated into this action.
3. ☒ The allowed claim(s) is/are *18-20*. As a result of the allowed claim(s), you may be eligible to benefit from the **Patent Prosecution Highway** program at a participating intellectual property office for the corresponding application. For more information, please see http://www.uspto.gov/patents/init_events/pph/index.jsp or send an inquiry to PPHfeedback@uspto.gov.
4. ☐ Acknowledgment is made of a claim for foreign priority under 35 U.S.C. § 119(a)-(d) or (f).
   Certified copies:
   a) ☐ All b) ☐ Some *c) ☐ None of the:
   1. ☐ Certified copies of the priority documents have been received.
   2. ☐ Certified copies of the priority documents have been received in Application No. _____.
   3. ☐ Copies of the certified copies of the priority documents have been received in this national stage application from the International Bureau (PCT Rule 17.2(a)).

   * Certified copies not received: _____.

Applicant has THREE MONTHS FROM THE "MAILING DATE" of this communication to file a reply complying with the requirements noted below. Failure to timely comply will result in ABANDONMENT of this application.
THIS THREE-MONTH PERIOD IS NOT EXTENDABLE.

5. ☐ CORRECTED DRAWINGS (as "replacement sheets") must be submitted.
   ☐ including changes required by the attached Examiner's Amendment / Comment or in the Office action of Paper No./Mail Date _____.

   Identifying indicia such as the application number (see 37 CFR 1.84(c)) should be written on the drawings in the front (not the back) of each sheet. Replacement sheet(s) should be labeled as such in the header according to 37 CFR 1.121(d).
6. ☐ DEPOSIT OF and/or INFORMATION about the deposit of BIOLOGICAL MATERIAL must be submitted. Note the attached Examiner's comment regarding REQUIREMENT FOR THE DEPOSIT OF BIOLOGICAL MATERIAL.

Attachment(s)
1. ☒ Notice of References Cited (PTO-892)
2. ☐ Information Disclosure Statements (PTO/SB/08), Paper No./Mail Date _____
3. ☐ Examiner's Comment Regarding Requirement for Deposit of Biological Material
4. ☐ Interview Summary (PTO-413), Paper No./Mail Date _____.
5. ☒ Examiner's Amendment/Comment
6. ☒ Examiner's Statement of Reasons for Allowance
7. ☐ Other _____.

/EMMANUEL DUKE/
Primary Examiner, Art Unit 3744

U.S. Patent and Trademark Office
PTOL-37 (Rev. 08-13) **Notice of Allowability** Part of Paper No./Mail Date 20160504

Application/Control Number: 14/932,064 Page 2
Art Unit: 3744

DETAILED ACTION

Notice of Pre-AIA or AIA Status

The present application, filed on or after March 16, 2013, is being examined under the first inventor to file provisions of the AIA.

EXAMINER'S AMENDMENT

1. An examiner's amendment to the record appears below. Should the changes and/or additions be unacceptable to applicant, an amendment may be filed as provided by 37 CFR 1.312. To ensure consideration of such an amendment, it MUST be submitted no later than the payment of the issue fee.

- In Claim 18, line 8; the phrase "a freezer thaw indicator" has been changed to --the freezer thaw indicator--.
- In Claim 18, line 10; the phrase "a thermal cross-section" has been changed to --the thermal cross-section--.

REASON FOR ALLOWANCE

2. The following is an examiner's statement of reasons for allowable: The prior art of record when consider as a whole, alone or in combination, neither anticipates nor renders obvious: the method for adjusting thermal sensitivity of a freezer thaw indicator to match a thermal cross-section of a freezer, said method comprising the steps of: providing container walls defining a closed inner space; providing a porous support member disposed in the closed inner

Application/Control Number: 14/932,064 Page 3
Art Unit: 3744

space and fixed in positional relation to the container walls such that on one side of the porous support member is an upper chamber of the closed inner space and on the other side of the porous support member is a lower chamber of the closed inner space; providing a freezer thaw indicator by introduction of a liquid into the closed inner space, wherein the liquid partly fills the inner space; providing a cold zone of a freezer having a thermal cross-section, the thermal cross-section including at least one frozen object; orienting the container to a first orientation such that the lower chamber is vertically above the upper chamber with respect to gravity, wherein the liquid is disposed in the upper chamber; freezing the liquid in the first orientation; orienting the container to a second orientation such that the upper chamber is vertically above the lower chamber with respect to gravity, wherein the frozen liquid remains in the upper chamber; inducing a thaw episode of the cold zone; indicating occurrence of the thaw episode of the cold zone of the freezer by presence of the liquid in the lower chamber; and determining whether the indication of occurrence matches thaw of the at least one frozen object of instant claim 1.

The following references (US 4137049 A) to Couch et al., (US 3220259 A) to Beyer, (US 3618558 A) to Tepfer, (US 3063235 A) to Paul, (US 20080026110 A1) to Cooper et al., (US 4114443 A) to Clark, (US 6357383 B1) to Al harshani, and (US 3414415 A) to Broad; are the most relevant references. However, above mentioned references fail to anticipate or render obvious the invention of independent claim 1. Therefore, the independent claim and dependent claims thereof have been found to be allowable.

Any comments considered necessary by applicant must be submitted no later than the payment of the issue fee and, to avoid processing delays, should preferably accompany the issue

Application/Control Number: 14/932,064 Page 4
Art Unit: 3744

fee. Such submissions should be clearly labeled "Comments on Statement of Reasons for Allowance.

Any inquiry concerning this communication or earlier communications from the examiner should be directed to EMMANUEL DUKE whose telephone number is (571)270-5290. The examiner can normally be reached on Monday - Friday; 6:00am - 2:30pm EST.

If attempts to reach the examiner by telephone are unsuccessful, the examiner's supervisor, Frantz Jules can be reached on 571-272-6681. The fax phone number for the organization where this application or proceeding is assigned is 571-273-8300.

Information regarding the status of an application may be obtained from the Patent Application Information Retrieval (PAIR) system. Status information for published applications may be obtained from either Private PAIR or Public PAIR. Status information for unpublished applications is available through Private PAIR only. For more information about the PAIR system, see http://pair-direct.uspto.gov. Should you have questions on access to the Private PAIR system, contact the Electronic Business Center (EBC) at 866-217-9197 (toll-free). If you would like assistance from a USPTO Customer Service Representative or access to the automated information system, call 800-786-9199 (IN USA OR CANADA) or 571-272-1000.

/EMMANUEL DUKE/
Primary Examiner, Art Unit 3744
05/04/2016

Notice of References Cited	Application/Control No. 14/932,064	Applicant(s)/Patent Under Reexamination KEEFE, PETER DAVID	
	Examiner EMMANUEL DUKE	Art Unit 3744	Page 1 of 1

U.S. PATENT DOCUMENTS

*		Document Number Country Code-Number-Kind Code	Date MM-YYYY	Name	CPC Classification	US Classification
*	A	US-3,063,235 A	11-1962	PAUL WINCHELL	G01K3/04	368/1
*	B	US-3,220,259 A	11-1965	BEYER STUART E	G01K3/04	116/217
*	C	US-3,414,415 A	12-1968	BROAD JR ROBERT L	G01K3/04	116/219
*	D	US-3,618,558 A	11-1971	Tepfer; Barry	G01K11/08	116/216
*	E	US-4,114,443 A	09-1978	Clark; Trevor Percival	G01K11/06	116/217
*	F	US-4,137,049 A	01-1979	Couch; Thomas W.	G01K3/02	116/206
*	G	US-6,357,383 B1	03-2002	Al harshani; Mubarak Dakeel	G01K11/06	116/216
*	H	US-2008/0026110 A1	01-2008	Cooper; Shay	G01K11/06	426/88
	I	US-				
	J	US-				
	K	US-				
	L	US-				
	M	US-				

FOREIGN PATENT DOCUMENTS

*		Document Number Country Code-Number-Kind Code	Date MM-YYYY	Country	Name	CPC Classification
	N					
	O					
	P					
	Q					
	R					
	S					
	T					

NON-PATENT DOCUMENTS

*		Include as applicable: Author, Title Date, Publisher, Edition or Volume, Pertinent Pages)
	U	
	V	
	W	
	X	

*A copy of this reference is not being furnished with this Office action. (See MPEP § 707.05(a).)
Dates in MM-YYYY format are publication dates. Classifications may be US or foreign.

U.S. Patent and Trademark Office
PTO-892 (Rev. 01-2001) **Notice of References Cited** Part of Paper No. 20160504

The Examiner corrected Claim 18 by "Examiner's Amendment" to change in two places the article "a" for the article "the." "The" or "said" refers to an element of a claim first introduced by an "a." The Examiner considered the first introduction to be in the preamble. The preamble is not ordinarily considered a recitation of elements. Nonetheless, there are a number (under fifty percent) of patent attorneys who would use an "a" instead of "the" in this situation. So, I simply accepted it.

I paid the Issue Fee on July 6, 2016. Below is the Issue Notification from the USPTO file history of U.S. Patent 9,410,730.

UNITED STATES PATENT AND TRADEMARK OFFICE

UNITED STATES DEPARTMENT OF COMMERCE
United States Patent and Trademark Office
Address: COMMISSIONER FOR PATENTS
P.O. Box 1450
Alexandria, Virginia 22313-1450
www.uspto.gov

APPLICATION NO.	ISSUE DATE	PATENT NO.	ATTORNEY DOCKET NO	CONFIRMATION NO.
14/932,064	08/09/2016	9410730	PDK-775	6261

23592 7590 07/20/2016

PETER D KEEFE
KEEFE AND ASSOCIATES
24405 GRATIOT AVENUE
EASTPOINTE, MI 48021

ISSUE NOTIFICATION

The projected patent number and issue date are specified above.

Determination of Patent Term Adjustment under 35 U.S.C. 154 (b)
(application filed on or after May 29, 2000)

The Patent Term Adjustment is 0 day(s). Any patent to issue from the above-identified application will include an indication of the adjustment on the front page.

If a Continued Prosecution Application (CPA) was filed in the above-identified application, the filing date that determines Patent Term Adjustment is the filing date of the most recent CPA.

Applicant will be able to obtain more detailed information by accessing the Patent Application Information Retrieval (PAIR) WEB site (http://pair.uspto.gov).

Any questions regarding the Patent Term Extension or Adjustment determination should be directed to the Office of Patent Legal Administration at (571)-272-7702. Questions relating to issue and publication fee payments should be directed to the Application Assistance Unit (AAU) of the Office of Data Management (ODM) at (571)-272-4200.

APPLICANT(s) (Please see PAIR WEB site http://pair.uspto.gov for additional applicants):

Peter David Keefe, Roseville, MI;

The United States represents the largest, most dynamic marketplace in the world and is an unparalleled location for business investment, innovation, and commercialization of new technologies. The USA offers tremendous resources and advantages for those who invest and manufacture goods here. Through SelectUSA, our nation works to encourage and facilitate business investment. To learn more about why the USA is the best country in the world to develop technology, manufacture products, and grow your business, visit SelectUSA.gov.

IR103 (Rev. 10/09)

Important information indicated included: the patent was to issue on August 9, 2016, which is essential to know because any patent application that requires "co-pending" status needs to be filed before then; the Patent Number of 9,410,730; and the determination of Patent Term Adjustment, which was zero days in view extra days of patent term are granted for USPTO delays (in absence of Applicant delays), and there were none.

Post Issuance Issues/Concerns

1. Correction:

Correction of clerical errors made by the Applicant or errors in printing made by the USPTO which show nonconformity with the prosecution record are easily rectified by a Certificate of Correction.

Substantive errors by the Applicant, for example, under-claiming or over-claiming, fatal mistakes in the Drawing, and substantive misstatements in the Specification cannot be rectified by a Certificate of Correction, but must go through a process called "Reissue," in which an Examiner decides if the correction can be made so that the defective patent can be corrected and then reissued.

Reissue can be used by inventors who find during the marketing phase that their product has acquired modifications that need to be covered by revised claims of broader scope. This must be done within two years of the issuance date of the patent.

2. Enforceability Issues:

In the event a patent document is uncovered that casts a patentability shadow on one or more claims, a request for "Reexamination" can be made with the USPTO. The claims in question will be examined in light of the newly found patent.

3. Maintenance Fees:

As inevitable as death and taxes, every four years during the life of your patent you are required to pay maintenance fees. An idea of European patent practice, it is now a cash cow for the USPTO. Failure to pay results in an early expiration of your patent.

The USPTO will send you a Notice of Maintenance Fees Due, but don't count on it. Ask your patent attorney to keep track for you.

Payments are simple to do online at the USPTO.gov website using a credit card.

I once had a client who delayed to pay, no matter my reminders. Then suddenly he decided to pay on the last day possible. He got in his car and drove from Detroit to Washington, D.C. to pay it in person at the USPTO. Those were the days when online payments weren't possible, but there were certificates of mailing that sufficed. Note: I did not provide the address of the USPTO, above, for you to do this. ☺

4. Charge of Infringement by Another:

The fact that you have a patent does not mean you're going to be able to keep it enforceable all the way through to its expiration date. If you have a high demand product covered by your patent, and/or if a company or another entity is of the opinion you are infringing on its products and/or its intellectual property, you can fall victim to a law suit challenging the validity of your claims.

At the first whiff of trouble, don't wait for that faint aroma to blossom into a stink bomb, seek out your patent attorney immediately.

5. Charge of Infringement by You:

Copycats seem to come out of the woodwork when you have a best selling product. Overseas production facilities can flood the market with knockoffs.

Once you get wind of infringing products on the market, see your patent attorney. If he/she agrees infringement is occurring, he/she will write a letter to the alleged infringer to cease and desist. This will either end happily with an acceptable arrangement, such as a license, or, less happily, in litigation.

If the infringement is coming from overseas, your patent attorney can seek the U.S. Customs and Border Protection agency to impound the infringing goods at the port of entry into the USA.

6. Challenges to Patent Validity at the USPTO:

In the name of reducing litigation costs, the America Invents Act created three avenues for challenge to your patent at the USPTO:

- Inter Partes Review: someone other than the patent owner may petition the Patent Trial and Appeal Board to cancel one or more claims because of unpatentability under Sections 102 or 103;
- Ex-Parte Reexamination: anyone can initiate Reexamination if there is a newly uncovered patent document that a reasonable Examiner would have considered when doing his/her original examination; and
- Post Grant Review: within nine months of issuance, a patent is subject to challenge on any ground of validity.

* * *

PART III

MARKETING

Chapter 1

How to Sell Your Invention

Yes, you can do this even with limited funds and limited experience, as there are time-tested techniques that really work: all you need is to be informed of how to do it—then do it.

Before you begin, there is one *essential* requisite: you MUST be patent pending or have a patent that describes and claims the structure and function of your best and basic embodiments. Having a prototype is a plus, but as you'll see, it's not essential.

For the QR codes for each of the organizations mentioned in Part III, please refer to "Quick Links" in the Appendix.

Turning your Invention into a Product

Surely after perfecting your invention and then patenting it, you should know all there is to know about it. No. Why? Because now you're entering into unchartered territory, embarking on a journey that will take you from invention to product.

A product differs from an invention in a number of ways. Inventions are typically sterile, lacking the sex appeal of a product. The mechanics that got you that patent may be an engineer's dream, but it's very likely also a consumer's nightmare. Consumers are motivated to buy pretty things, not unsightly things; easy to use things, not Rube Goldberg things.

Most often, the task at hand is to reimagine the look, the materials, and the functionality of your invention with the consumer in mind. In view we are all consumers, this should not be so hard. But do not hesitate to inquire of others their thoughts. Sometimes the perspective of a housewife, a child, or a handyman can open otherwise closed doors of your imagination.

Practicality should be your first consideration. Obviously, your invention is operable, but is it practical? Practicality blends structure and function into a neat package that infuses operation with ease of use.

Simplicity is a close second. Simplicity involves a minimization of parts, yes, but it includes streamlining those parts into a cohesive whole that exudes elegance.

Beauty is yet another consideration. Beauty is more than "skin deep" physical attractiveness, it imbues a cast of emotive responses: alluring, appealing, enticing, inviting, engaging, pleasing, enchanting, gratifying, compelling, seducing, dazzling, winning, intriguing, exciting, glittering, refreshing, provoking, tempting, welcoming, captivating, outstanding, satisfying. You get the idea.

With these considerations in mind, you have to take the road less travelled through this uncharted territory you've embarked upon to get to not just a product, but an optimal product.

Don't fly down the road so fast that you blow past the weigh-station of cost. While a patented invention can be composed of impractically expensive components and be fabricated using utopian methods, that's not going to suffice for a product. For an invention, the USPTO does not care about impracticalities or utopian visions so long as you are able to describe to a person of ordinary skill in the art how to make and use. Cost of materials and production are make or break for a product and the paramount consideration for consumer acceptance.

In revising your invention into a product, you must be careful not to so modify it that you create something outside the scope of your patent claims. If that happens, consult your patent attorney whether you can file for a reissue or a new patent application protecting the revision.

> *Turning an invention into a product often involves as much effort as turning an idea into an invention.*

Product Development Help

Perhaps the best path to a product is via the University of Wisconsin at Whitewater (located southwest of Milwaukee), which operates the Wisconsin Innovation Service Center (WISC). With over twenty years of tradition, the experts there are readily available to assist inventors and entrepreneurs in three areas of specialty:

- New Product Assessment;
- Market Landscape Study; and
- Technology Viability Assessment.

The WISC web page is https://uww.edu/wisc. Professor of Economics Russ Kashian heads WISC. His mission is to provide nothing less than a transformative collaboration. The e-mail and phone contacts are: innovate@uww.edu and (262) 472-1365.

Another path is via consultation with a prototype shop in your locality. If there's balking about signing a nondisclosure agreement, find another. Be wary, be careful, be cautious, but don't be overly paranoid.

Don't overlook the nuts and bolts help that joining an inventor group can provide for you. For example, the Inventors' Association of Metro Detroit, which I created in 1986, has provided invaluable help to a ton of individual inventors—and still does. These wonderful and committed organizations are located all over the country; go online to find one in your area.

The USPTO provides assistance to individual inventors, not only by posts on its website, but by periodic online seminars on a vast number of topics. See https://www.uspto.gov/learning-and-resources/support-centers/inventors-assistance-center-iac.

The PatentApplication.com Reader Support portal is your exclusive online resource for readers of this handbook.

A wonderful nonprofit resource partner of the Small Business Administration is the Service Corps of Retired Executives (SCORE), which provides a mentorship program for aspiring entrepreneurs that has helped thousands get a business going.

For those of you who are concerned the U.S. patent system is not everything that it could be, then have a look at the USInventor.org website. A creation of Paul Morinville and Randy Landreneau, US Inventor is committed to educational programs and legislation reforms aimed at restoring American innovation.

> *Help is out there. While you do not need to fear scrupulous sources, keep an ounce of caution and a pinch of paranoia just in case a distasteful concoction comes your way.*

Finding a Prospective Buyer/Licensee

Going to retail outlets and perusing the aisles is a great way to see what's out there, glean how the products are packaged, and learn how competitors compete with each other. You'll walk away with a treasure-trove of info.

Using Google to search prospective companies for sale/license is a great way to familiarize yourself with the market landscape.

Perhaps the best resource for researching prospective companies for sale/license of your invention is The Thomas Register of North American Manufacturing. You can find it online at https://thomasnet.com. For over 125 years, this has been the go to—and it still is. With over 500,000 companies, you can filter your search by location, company type, etc.

> *Unless you find potential buyers/licensees, your marketing efforts will make as much progress as a hamster running on an exercise wheel.*

Marketing Techniques

For inventors, there are basically two markets, consumer and commercial. The consumer market involves point of sale transactions, revolving around retail sales. The commercial market, on the other hand, involves point of production transactions, revolving around organizational sales. If your invention has commercial application, then cost, practicality and simplicity trump beauty. In consumer products, beauty sells.

The vast majority of inventors pursue a deal with a company that is already established in the marketplace. There is also a fraction of inventors who go it alone.

A. Making a Deal with an Existing Company

1. The Commercial Market:

Returning to our friends, Joe and Rita, let's see how they would do this.

Joe has a working grasp of the faucet marketplace, so he is able to quickly zero-in on manufacturers. His big unknown, however, is their corporate cultures. Do they accept outside ideas? What are their plans for new products and does a washerless single handle faucet fit into those plans? Are they fair in their dealings? He'll only know the answers if he can talk to someone at each of these manufacturers. But who?

This is best answered by a peek online at the website of each of the prospective manufacturers. The corporate officers are usually indicated and means to contact them also provided. If Joe is making the contact on his own, I would recommend the V.P. of marketing. If Joe's patent attorney is involved, he/she would first approach the company's in-house patent counsel.

Cold calls can work great, but far more often than not they're an unadulterated disaster. This is particularly true if your targeted executive has a gate-keeper secretary. Here, schmooze coupled with intrigue may carry the day. If you're not good at it, then forget about it. I recommend to simply forget about it.

The Query Letter

The time-tested method of making a cold approach to a company is not a phone call, but a letter. This is called a "query." The job of a query letter is to sell the sizzle, not the steak.

While a postal letter was once standard for a query submission, this has been replaced by e-mail.

The query letter is just that, a missive sent to inquire if there is interest. The perfect crafting of this all important missive cannot be over emphasized.

The specifics as to the information provided and the layout of the query letter vary to suit each particular situation. If you are credentialed in the field of your invention, like Joe, then establishing this up front is a wise approach. But if you're not credentialed, like Rita, then you need to use an alternate approach (discussed in the next section), called a "logline."

In any event, a query letter has a general format that includes the following elements:

- a sentence or two describing who you are and to what extent you are an expert (even if not credentialed) in the field of the invention;
- a brief statement of a problem in the art and how the invention meritoriously solves that problem—without divulging the structure and function of the invention; and
- a courteous conclusion that requests permission to submit the invention for evaluation.

While the hoped for reply would almost certainly be by reply e-mail, it's a good idea to include your phone number.

Below is a query letter by e-mail that Joe composes and e-mails to a targeted company prospect, directly to its vice president of marketing.

Subject: Licensing Query for New Faucet Product

Dear Mr. James,

I'm a master plumber who has developed a patented product that is a perfect fit for the Acme Faucet Company.

The Achilles heel of your single handle faucet line is the center washer, which takes wear and tear each time the handle is moved. Over time, it is the first component to fail. Homeowners see leakage and think poorly of your faucet. When called, I replace the washer. But eventually the homeowner needs a new faucet, and inevitably says "No leaky Acme faucet!"

My patented faucet eliminates this problem and ensures a leak-free seal at the joint that lasts the life of the faucet.

I would like to discuss my faucet improvement with you at your earliest convenience.

Thank you for your kind consideration.

Best wishes,
Joe Plumber
123-456-7890

If Acme's V.P. of Marketing, Mr. James, responds favorably, it is not too soon for Joe to get his patent attorney involved.

Rita, on the other hand, has no credentials, just a patent and a prayer. Well, she also has Abby, whose engineering credentials are impeccable. However, let's say for our illustration that Abby is out of the game. What is Rita to do?

She has two classes of candidates: the OEMs (car manufacturers) and their suppliers, who are rated by tiers, tier 1 being the big boys. In view of the lack of her credentials, she is not going to command a response like Joe was able to get from his query e-mail. On top of that, she has no prototype; her "product" is her patent.

Her best approach is to talk to her patent attorney to make the intros necessary to get the ball rolling. An alternative she could explore is to contact a manufacturer's representative. These professionals have a plethora of industry contacts and they know who among those contacts are most likely to bite.

> *If you are credentialed, then by all means send out your own query letters. If not, your patent attorney is a good bet.*

2. The Consumer Market:

Joe and Rita are targeting the commercial market, and in so doing the need to have a prototype product is useful, but not necessary. Most inventors will be targeting the consumer market and the further along they are having a presentable prototype product the better.

When you begin your marketing efforts, the first thing you want to do is learn how your product fits into the marketplace and which companies are making similar types of consumer products. If your product is unique, then your task is to sleuth around for product lines that your invention complements. Googling is your most productive avenue, but a walk down store aisles should definitely be on your to do list.

When you've got in your mind the lay of the land, make yourself a list of prospects and an action plan *in writing*. Keep it current: a running log of contacts and plan revisions as events develop.

Example: The Diver's Sight Saver

In 1968, another of my ideas was "The Diver's Sight Saver." It solved the problem of a diver who needs eyeglasses while wearing a diving mask. The concept I envisioned had a pair of rubbery gaskets, each with a center slit through which a temple of a pair of eyeglasses is passed. The gaskets were located on the temples so that they would press against the skirt of the mask and a diver's head when both the eyeglasses and the mask were worn by the diver. Gasket compression onto the temples would complete the seal. Below are two pictorial illustrations of the invention.

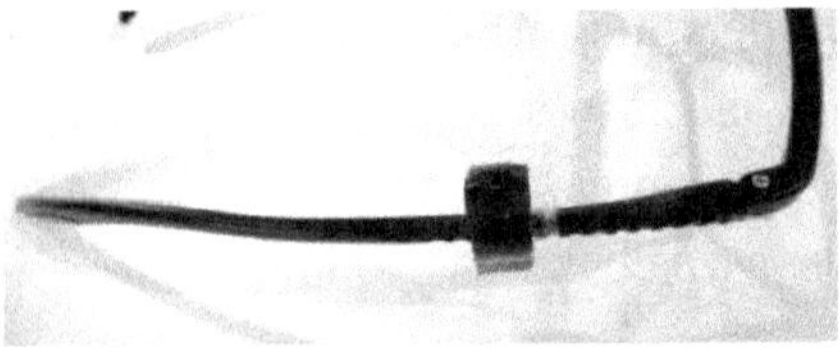

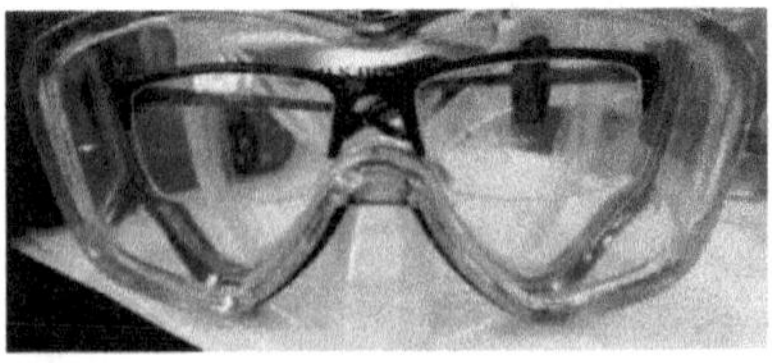

How would an inventor market The Diver's Sight Saver?

The first thing is to assess whether it's a potentially marketable product. It definitely solves a problem that a large proportion of the diving public has to deal with. No one wants to go on a dive and not be able to clearly see all the beauty below the surface. So it looks promising ... but does it work, and if so, does it work reliably?

With a prototype, as the figures show, testing is required to clearly ascertain the sealing reliability of the gaskets, and while it's clear the lenses, themselves, look to be positioned to provide improved sight, testing for that is also necessary: testing at typically deep depths many divers go down to, testing the gaskets with different masks and different eyeglasses, evaluating the clarity of sight through the lenses, and making sure the gaskets are optimized for reliable, long term use.

I always recommend to find a patent attorney and discuss both your invention and your plans with him/her as soon as you have a clear grasp of your invention. He/she will conduct a patentability search and if it comes back clean, then you've got a green light to move ahead. Even as your patent attorney is preparing your patent application, you can continue your testing. If testing is taking an extended amount of time, he/she will file one or more provisional patent applications to secure your priority.

Before approaching a manufacturer, you must do a deep soul search to determine if there are other ways to accomplish the invention. For example, take a pair of eyeglasses, remove the temples, and either use the bridge of the nose to secure the glasses when the mask is worn, or, one way or another, mount the eyeglasses frame to the inside of the mask. Of course, these alternatives require the eyeglasses to be modified, but they are alternatives a competitor could consider to get around the patent.

The Diver's Sight Saver is a simple product that can be manufactured, packaged and shipped inexpensively. This is a big marketing plus. While for a consumer product beauty sells, for the Diver's Sight Saver gaskets, cost and functionality will carry the day (it's pretty hard to impart gaskets with sex appeal but would neon colors do the trick?).

After perfecting The Diver's Sight Saver and establishing patent pending covering the basic and best mode embodiments, it's time to seek a manufacturer for it.

First determine what sort of manufacturers would be likely to buy/license the patent application. In this regard, a patent application is as powerful as a patent. The reason is that the rights of a patent to exclude others from making, using and selling are on the way. The best fit manufacturers are those manufacturing and selling dive products, most particularly the masks used by divers. A Google search accompanied by a visit to a dive shop will quickly and effortlessly reveal them.

Make a log of these companies (particularly the most relevant division, if any), including the officers, the physical address, the e-mail addresses and phone numbers of the officers, and the most relevant products by name and product number.

Next, determine how the Diver's Sight Saver would interface with the products. Make a sketch. Better yet, buy the most relevant product from the each manufacturer and apply the Diver's Sight Saver to each of them. Do tests. Take photos.

Additional prep would advisably include talking to the pro of several dive shops to get his/her opinion. Indeed, why not let the pro borrow a prototyped mask to try. The feedback he/she will give is invaluable. Get permission from each pro to use his/her comments in your marketing efforts. These are independent expert evaluations, and as such, speak with a megaphone when told to a manufacturer.

It's now time to contact a company. Determine if your first targeted company has an invention submission process. If so, follow that exactly. If not, prepare your e-mail query and send it to the V.P. of marketing. Alternatively, you can have your patent attorney make the query for you.

Unlike Joe, who is credentialed in the subject matter of his invention and who introduces this at the beginning of his query, most inventors, like Rita, are not credentialed. They need to provide a commanding replacement: a "logline."

The Logline

A logline concisely sums up the merits of an invention without saying how it works. This is key, and here's why: at this initial stage you want to arouse interest and intrigue that will compel a favorable response to your request to submit. On the other hand, if you reveal to the company what you have, you're just throwing cold water on the company's burning desire to find out what you have. It's a matter of applied psychology.

For The Diver's Sight Saver, a logline could be: "*Eyeglasses and diving masks go together like oil and water, but the Diver's Sight Saver joins them together like bread and butter.*"

Below is a query e-mail example for The Diver's Sight Saver.

> Subject: Invention submission query, *The Diver's Sight Saver*
>
> Dear Vice President Daniels,
>
> Eyeglasses and diving masks go together like oil and water, but *The Diver's Sight Saver* joins them together like bread and butter.
>
> It has been a longstanding problem for poor sighted divers to correct their vision for a dive. *The Diver's Sight Saver* accomplishes this effectively in the form of a product that these divers will flock to.
>
> I'm a diver myself with nearsightedness. *The Diver's Sight Saver* has been my best friend on dives. John Hodges, owner of B&J Diving Shop says, "This is a godsend for the sight impaired diver. It's a must have!"
>
> *The Diver's Sight Saver* would be a perfect fit for your SeaGoer Mask Series.
>
> I am currently patent pending and look forward to discussing how *The Diver's Sight Saver* would be a mega sales winner for the Acme Dive and Sport Co.
>
> Thank you.
>
> Best wishes,
> John J. Inventor,
> 109-876-5432

If you get a positive response, call your patent attorney pronto.

B. Producing and Marketing Yourself

The other side of the coin is the inventor who has a consumer product and is capable of getting it to retail outlets. Assuming the start-up costs can be overcome by personal funds, investors and/or a loan, it is the exceptional inventor who can design, produce, package and market his/her patented or patent pending product.

My experience is that these exceptional inventors all have in common a catalogue of inner qualities: single-minded drive, endless energy, an over-active imagination, clever and artistic hands-on skills, and a solid dose of chutzpa.

Besides creating a product suitable for the consumer market (including the accompanying literature and packaging), you'll need to set up a business (see Chapter 3), get product liability insurance and market the product to retailers.

Not an easy task, but I've had clients who did just that—and made it BIG!

Douglas Stewart came to my office seeking a patent on an idea he got during a dream. His dream was to put a picture of a person celebrating his/her birthday on the icing of a birthday cake: not just a photo, but an edible photo. He researched the possibilities and mated an edible film to an inkjet printer: not just an inkjet printer but a food certified edible ink inkjet printer. I prepared his patent application while he was setting up an assembly line to make and package his "*Cake Decals.*"

Image credit/permission:
Douglas Stewart

Doug contacted a major Michigan retailer, Meijer (a chain of supercenters selling groceries and general merchandise), requesting shelf space for *Cake Decals*. Meijer has a tradition of helping inventors and entrepreneurs, so they readily agreed. The fruits of Doug's production line soon made it into the homes of very happy kids from 1 to 120 years of age.

Doug's eyes saw far beyond his local production operation, and as a result of his untiring and exceptional efforts he made serious money. His *Cake Decals*, now sold in other forms under other names and made by other producers, lives on and has become the industry standard.

> *Doug's story is not for the faint of heart. He put his whole being into Cake Decals. If you can't do that, don't try it.*

How to Bargain

"It's a dog-eat-dog world, and only the meanest of junk-yard dogs make it." No! The world is full of decent people and business is not in the least dog-eat-dog. If a deal goes bad, it is usually because one party agreed to language in a contract that he/she should have read, thought about carefully and objected to when the contract was being negotiated. It is almost never because the wool was deceitfully pulled over his/her eyes. Keep in mind, however, I did use the word, "almost."

Bargaining happens when negotiations are conducted among equals. This is why a union negotiates a contract for the employees; strength in numbers creates a balance to the economic might of a company. Inventors rarely enjoy bargaining equality. Most often, they are ill-equipped to negotiate, and even less equipped to make demands. In such unequal situations, there's really no bargaining; the inventor is left with only two choices, take it or leave it.

There are two ways to equalize the playing field.

First, have your patent attorney speak for you beginning with the earliest stages of negotiations. This ensures there will be nothing misspoken or inadvertently promised that's against your interest.

Be involved and confer with your patent attorney, just make certain that he/she is your spokesperson. Never volunteer anything during negotiations, and before speaking make certain your patent attorney assents. Once a contract is negotiated, read it over carefully before discussing it with your patent attorney. Make a list of all your questions. Mark-up the contract with margin notes and highlight any questionable passages. In particular, if you do not understand something, make a note of that.

After renegotiation, if the contract is fair and equitable, then sign it with the assent of your patent attorney. Remember, haste makes waste. Keep in mind that when you *assume* something and don't speak up before it's too late, your patent attorney can only retort, "You made an *ass* of *you* and *me*."

Second, offer a product of enough value to a company that the worth of that product speaks for itself in negotiations. To accomplish this, you must not only have a great product, you'll need to mate it with a company that understands, needs, and seeks your product.

Inventors tend to think of their inventions as a beautiful baby. But beauty is in the eye of the beholder, and it is the eye of the company you're seeking to do business with that will observe either a beautiful baby or an ugly duckling. Quite honestly, if your invention is not so great, don't pretend that it is. Modesty is your best route, and going for a field goal instead of a touchdown may be your best call. Be accepting that your invention is what it is: the most delightful wrapping paper you package it with will not change things, only delay the inevitable.

The key is to bargain with a company that shares a mutual goal with you: to achieve a deal. No matter the intrinsic excellence of your invention, unless you pair it with a company that will appreciate it and need it, you are wasting everyone's time and setting yourself up for failure. No one likes rejection and the surest way to avoid it is to approach a receptive company.

How do you know a receptive company? If online it looks like one and reads like one, then most likely it is one. It would be great if it was that easy, but it's not. In reality, you have to do your homework. One of the most telling aspects is the product line of the company you have in mind. Does it encompass everything but your invention? Does it have a product that could be revolutionized by your invention? Has it just released a product that is similar to your invention, but woefully missed the benefits your invention offers?

> *There are two ways to achieve bargaining equality: your patent attorney and the intrinsic worth of your product coupled to a receptive company.*

* * *

Chapter 2

Types of Deals

Deals are business transactions involving a written contract signed between you and a buyer/licensee defining the patent rights being transferred and the terms and conditions under which those patent rights are transferred to the buyer/licensee in consideration of the payment of money to you.

There are three types of deals:

- Sale/Assignment;
- Exclusive license; and
- Non-exclusive license.

Sales and Assignments

A sale/assignment is an agreement entered into between a seller/assignor (you, the inventor) and a purchaser/assignee (a company or other entity), which for consideration (the payment of money) from the purchaser/assignee, a transfer of ownership of the invention, as defined by the claims, from the owner/assignor to the purchaser/assignee is consummated.

An assignment is a transfer of ownership without strings, without any residual rights withheld, without restrictions. The purchaser acquires unfettered rights in the inventor's invention as disclosed and claimed in the patent. Generally speaking, the sphere of ownership includes obvious variants beyond the scope of the patent claims, as per the terms of the agreement of sale.

Assignments of one hundred percent of all rights are sales.

Assignments of a percentage of all rights can also occur. For example, the grant of assignment could recite, "By these presents I do hereby grant to (Assignee Name) twenty percent (20%) of all my rights in U.S. Patent …"

Sales and assignments command the most money, as compared with deal types that involve licensing.

Exclusive Licenses

An exclusive license is an agreement between a licensor (you, the inventor) and a single licensee (a company or other entity), which for consideration (the payment of a royalty) from the licensee, an exclusive right to make, use and sell the invention, as defined by the patent claims, from the licensor to the licensee is consummated.

An exclusive license differs from an assignment in that in an exclusive license the licensor retains ownership. Think of it analogously to renting out a home as compared to selling it. When you sell, you no longer have any rights to the home. The new homeowner can do whatever he/she wants to the home. Not so if you rent it out to a tenant. Now the homeowner is a landlord, retaining ownership of the home, but losing the right to use it in favor of the tenant.

An exclusive license transfers the patent rights to make, use and sell to a single entity, while some residual ownership rights are retained by the licensor. These retained rights are spelled out in the license agreement. Most often, these include the right to terminate the license if some predetermined event occurs, retention of making, using and selling rights for the personal use of the licensor, territorial limitations, and quality assurance guarantees made by the licensee to the licensor.

Non-exclusive Licenses

A non-exclusive license is an agreement between a licensor (you, the inventor) and a licensee (a company or other entity), which for consideration (the payment of a royalty) from the licensee, a non-exclusive right to make, use and sell the invention, as defined by the patent claims, from the licensor to the licensee is consummated.

In a non-exclusive license, unlike an exclusive license, the licensor can license to any number of other licensees.

As with the exclusive license, the licensor transfers the right to make, use and sell the invention to the licensee, while some residual ownership rights are retained by the licensor. In view a number of licensees may be involved, this deal type commands the least amount of money. On the other hand, this lesser sum can be multiplied.

> *A sale/assignment commands the most money. In an exclusive license you retain an ownership interest. A non-exclusive license commands less money, but can be replicated.*

* * *

Chapter 3

Business Entities

If you decide not to assign or license, but would rather commercially sell your product, then you'll need to set-up an entity for doing business. Remember to mark your product with "Patent Pending," or the patent number, if you have it. Ordinarily, you will also need to obtain product liability insurance.

There are a number of business entities to choose from, each with advantages and disadvantages. These are:

- Proprietorship;
- Partnership;
- Corporation; and
- Limited Liability Company.

Whichever of these is best for you is a decision that must be made between you and your patent attorney, as well as your accountant. Don't make this decision on your own without the advice and counsel of licensed/credentialed professionals.

Proprietorship

A proprietorship is a business run by an individual. The business owner calls all the shots and assumes all the risk, including his/her personal assets outside of the business.

The biggest advantage of this type of business is that it is easy to set-up, usually by going to the county clerk's office and registering it. If you do nothing, your business is a proprietorship by default. Other advantages include: little to no government hassles, ease of reporting on your personal income tax return, and ability to make decisions without interference.

The biggest disadvantage of being a proprietor is unlimited exposure in the event things go sour. If you have little assets outside of the business, or if you're a risk taker, then this can work. Otherwise, a business entity with limited risk is the better choice. Another disadvantage is loss of continuity in the event of death of the proprietor, wherein the proprietor's testamentary provisions will be determinative.

Partnership

As the word implies, this form of business entity is one entered into among two or more partners. This is effected under a partnership agreement among the partners, and, as in the case of the proprietor, the partnership is registered in the county.

There are two forms of partnership: general and limited. In a general partnership, all the partners have a say in the business, as per the partnership agreement, and each has an exposure of their personal assets in the event things go south. In a limited partnership, at least one of the partners is a general partner, who has all the say, and there is at least one additional limited partner whose assets exposure is limited to his/her partnership investment, but who has no say in the business.

The major advantage of a partnership is that its business functions with the ease of a proprietorship. Other advantages include shared capital contribution and shared loss risk among the general partners. For limited partners, the major advantage is the limitation on liability.

The major disadvantage for the general partners is the risk of unlimited loss of personal assets. Another major disadvantage is that when a general partner dies, the partnership likewise could cease to exist unless the partnership agreement provides for this contingency.

Corporation

A corporation is a "person" in the eye of the law, created by filing of an "Articles of Incorporation" with the secretary of state of a selected state. A corporation operates according to its "Bylaws" which spell-out the structural and operational aspects of the corporation. In this regard, a corporation has at least one shareholder owning shares in the corporation. Shares, depending on the provisions in the bylaws, have voting rights and rights to profit sharing, referred to as "dividends." A corporation is administered by officers who are elected by the shareholders.

Publicly traded corporations are an animal outside the scope of this handbook. For our purpose of examining inventor-based businesses, we'll discuss aspects of private corporations.

There are two types of corporations arising from the Internal Revenue Service code: a "C corporation" and a "Sub-chapter S corporation." A C corporation is required to report its own income tax return, and each shareholder receives a "K-1" form for reporting on his/her income tax return. A Sub-chapter S corporation is treated for income tax purposes as if it were a partnership.

The main reason for setting-up a corporation is that the shareholders are not personally exposed to liability. The corporation is treated legally as a separate entity from the shareholders; only the corporate assets are at risk. Another advantage is that the shareholders can come and go; a corporation can potentially enjoy immortality. Also, one person can be the only shareholder and sole officer.

The main disadvantage is the paperwork at the state level in the form of annual reports, as well as at the federal level in terms of income tax reporting.

Limited Liability Company

A limited liability company (LLC) has limited liability, like a corporation, and is created by filing of an "Articles of Organization" with the secretary of state of a selected state. An LLC operates according to its "Operating Agreement," which names a Manager, lists its Members and specifies the structure and operating arrangement of the company. The Manager runs the business, assisted by officers, while the Members each have an ownership interest in the LLC based upon their ownership of "units." The Operating Agreement spells out the classes of the units.

The major advantages of an LLC are the ease of set-up, freedom from onerous reporting and taxation requirements, and the enjoyment of limited liability. Another advantage is that an LLC can be created by a single person, who serves as both Manager and Member.

The major disadvantage of an LLC is the inability to easily withdraw as a Member, which event should be provided for in the Operating Agreement.

Of the types of business entities, these days the LLC is most popular. But what is best for you is a decision made between you, your patent attorney and your accountant.

* * *

Chapter 4

The Ten Maxims of Marketing

The ten maxims of marketing may seem at first glance to be straightforward, but careful consideration will reveal their inscrutably nuanced character. If you master them, you'll be able to navigate with sly confidence the rocky shoals and stormy seas of the unforgiving waters you must traverse to sell your invention.

Maxim 1: ***Your patent attorney is your best go to.***

If you're a sales person, an attorney and credentialed in the field of your invention, then you may very well go it alone and succeed quite nicely with the marketing of your product. If you are not all three of those, do not go it alone. I can't stress enough the need to consult with your patent attorney.

Maxim 2: ***A good patent title is a bad product title.***

Patent titles are required to be succinct and a technically accurate description of the subject matter of the Disclosure. There are few times a technical description of an invention can serve as a sexy product title.

To illustrate, the title of my patent was the technically dry, but accurate, "Freezer Thaw Indicator." It's true that I could use this as the name of my product. But products need spicy names that uniquely resonate. Thus, I coined the name, "Thawometer." I had a dual thought in mind. It sounded like "thermometer" and it conveyed the idea that it was a "meter that measures thawing."

Coined names have the advantage that they can (usually) be trademarked somewhat easily, depending on uniqueness.

Maxim 3: ***Your patent is a wonderful marketing tool.***

A patent is first and foremost a grant of monopoly, which immediately commands respect. In addition, the Drawing and the Specification delineate how to make and use your invention, while the claims warn others not to infringe.

Maxim 4: ***Your patent is a terrible marketing tool.***

A patent is a formal, legal document meant to convey exclusive rights in an invention to its inventor. When you go to market, you have to show a product not an invention. This can be accomplished by way of an illustration and/or a prototype.

An example of the illustration approach is the Thawometer instructions sheet.

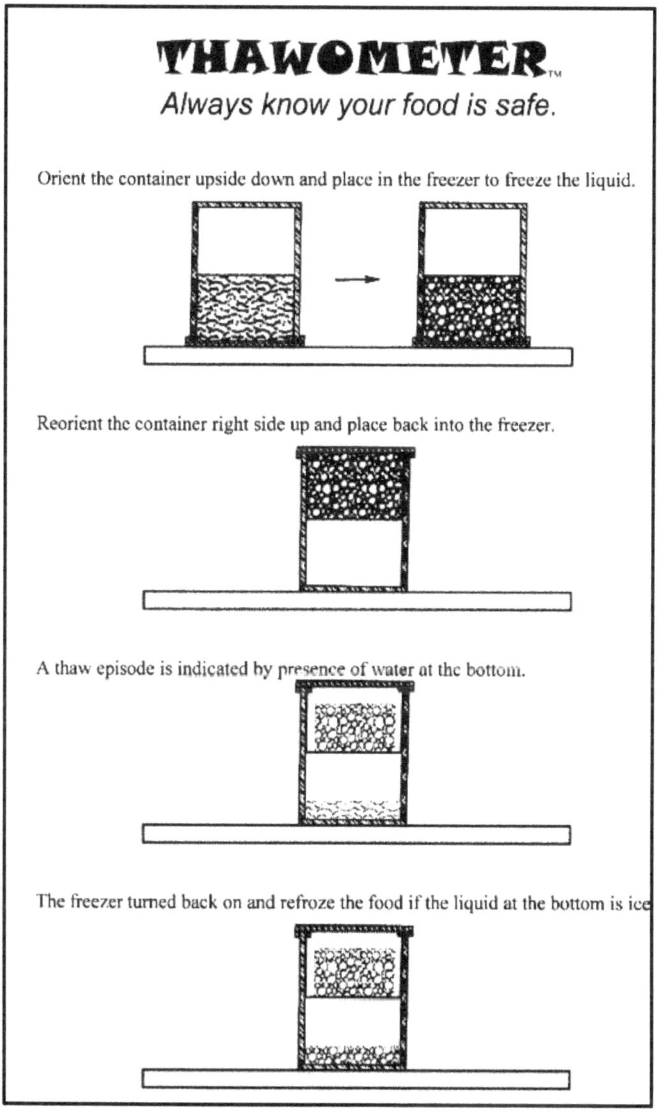

Maxim 5: ***Prototypes are the best.***

A prototype, if close to the look and feel of a finished product ready for market, is nothing less than a dazzling sales tool. The ability to show and tell to a prospective buyer or licensee can be the very thing that effects closure of a deal.

If it's something you can make yourself in the garage or basement, then by all means do so. The experimentation and beautification that results from going through an iteration process will only help you to market. Indeed, this is what I did with the Thawometer, where the product pictured in my instructions sheet was the very sales prototype I had made.

If making a product is technically beyond your skill set, available tools, and/or available materials/components, then consultation with the Wisconsin Innovation Service Center or a local prototype shop can get this accomplished.

Maxim 6: ***Prototypes are the worst.***

When you go into the office of a prospective buyer or licensee, confidently carrying your prototype and begin your spiel with the prototype as your centerpiece, things may go south fast. Why? I have been in such meetings, and what I've observed is that when you show a prototype, the prospective buyer/licensee sees only the prototype. While visions of sugar-plumb variations of your prototype dance in your head, all the buyer/licensee is thinking about is the prototype. This is so much the case, that even if you stress your sugar-plumb variations, they won't consider them.

Bottom-line: a prototype is great, but it must be accompanied by a convincing exposition of the variations you have in mind. A second, different, prototype could do this. A set of artistic drawings showing variations could suffice, as well.

Maxim 7: ***Maximize your intellectual property portfolio.***

Remember, a patent is one form of intellectual property. Additionally, there are trademarks, copyrights and trade secrets. Try to touch on as many forms of intellectual property as possible before embarking on your marketing campaign.

Trademarks protect names and symbols that identify the origin of goods and services. If you have a really great name for your product, then by all means file for a trademark on it. Your patent attorney can get this done for you. Trademarks add value and can be a deal maker. By way of example, I filed for an "Intent to Use" trademark with the USPTO for "Thawometer" and received U.S. Registration No. 8,7320,638. Intent to Use requires interstate use within six months or within a limited number of six month extensions.

Copyrights include drawings and write-ups, as for example the instructions sheet for the Thawometer. Copyright ownership is created by affixing the work, so ask your patent attorney if you need to file with the Copyright Office.

Everything, well most everything, you know and have in your possession outside the disclosure of your patent is game for trade secret status. Indeed, one of the best ways to enhance a deal is to offer your know-how. A lucrative consulting gig can be yours if you're able to assist the buyer/licensee to bring your product to market and help grow that market.

<u>Maxim 8:</u> ***Target your queries.***

Do not be tempted to send out a shot gun blast of query letters. A shot gun is intended to project a wide pattern of buckshot that will hit something generally in the direction of aim. That may work for duck hunting, but not buyer/licensee hunting. For that, you need a rifle, a high power round in the chamber and a sighted-in scope, the combination of which being able to take down the largest of buyer/licensee game with a single shot.

You must carefully research your very best prospects and the best person to contact within each of those contacts. This can be done by diligently searching online. The query letter you send to each must be crafted to uniquely approach that particular prospect. That means you need to specify in your query letter aspects that show you did your research and you are contacting the prospect for clearly articulated reasons, as for example why the prospect is a good fit for your product, the strength and reputation of the prospect, and your willingness to cooperate with the prospect.

<u>Maxim 9:</u> ***Be prepared for success.***

You may be surprised, maybe even shocked, to hear this, but I have seen time and again people who plan and plan, but avoid consummation of the plan. Why would anyone plan, but never finalize? I think there are a number of reasons. High among them are obsessive behavior, fear of success/failure/rejection, discomfort associated with change and perceived issues with friends and family. There is repose within one's cubby-hole, and jumping out of it can be terrifying.

There is a difference between success in marketing and winning the lottery. The lottery is faceless and nonjudgmental; you win or you don't. Marketing your product is a face-to-face, fraught with biased opinion affair that can be quite intimidating.

Maxim 10: ***Business is business.***

The marketing of your product should not be a contest, a validation or a pastime: it should be to make money. If you glory in the pursuit, gloat over favorable outcomes, or dally just to have something to do, you are missing the mark. The bull's-eye is to walk away from the closing of a sale or license with a fistful of cash.

Whatever can be said of the thrill of the rollercoaster ride that is inventing, the ride is for the purpose of business. Business.

> *The tactics of marketing involve smarts, diligence, patience and a whole lot of chutzpah.*

* * *

Chapter 5

Invention Marketing Firms

There are companies that exist for the express purpose of assisting inventors to market their inventions. They have been around for a long time, and have evolved with the times.

You can find them in advertisements in the back of magazines. You can find them online. You'll hear from them by mail even before you get your Notice of Allowance; their letters of introduction can be your first indication of when your patent will issue and what your patent number will be.

Some offer only marketing assistance, and these are the firms you'll hear from when your patent issues. Others offer "full service," including the preparation and filing of a patent application.

Marketing Only Firms

These companies assert they have in-house staff, or alternatively outside contractors, of artistic and literary skill who can illustrate a product version of your patented invention and write it up in product style. They also boast databases in various markets, as well as contacts within those markets with whom their team can introduce the inventions of their clientele.

My experience is that, while these firms have slick literature that attest to their capabilities and accomplishments, few measure up to their boasts.

Generally speaking, an inventor hires an invention marketing firm by paying an upfront fee, followed by other fees and perhaps a royalty share. I suspect the upfront fee carries the day for them, rendering the incentive to follow through to the rigors they proclaimed in their literature dubious.

I recommend an invention marketing firm as a last resort. If you've made an honest try to market your invention and failed, then you have nothing to lose except your upfront payment, and other payments as long as you stay in.

If you decide marketing is not your thing, then an invention marketing company might assist you. I would caution to be cynical and insist on accountability. Try to find an invention marketing firm that works solely on a royalty share basis, not a fee basis. I'm not sure if there are any that work that way, but maybe one or two can be found.

Full Service Firms

You already know what I'm going to say here. Use a patent attorney, not an invention marketing firm, to prepare, file and prosecute your patent application with the USPTO. I have listened to the wails of inventors who went to a full service firm to get a patent, only to later find out what they got was a design patent, not a utility patent.

USPTO Involvement

Complaints against invention marketing firms are legion. Under the Inventor's Rights Act of 1999, the USPTO has the power to accept complaints and forward them to the subject invention marketing firms for a response. While the USPTO does not investigate, it lists these complaints and responses from the marketing firms at https://www.uspto.gov/patents/basics/using-legal-services/scam-prevention/published-complaints/published.

> *Invention marketing firms have a dubious reputation.*

* * *

Epilogue

Marketing of the Thawometer

To be honest, the Section 102 rejection destroyed any real chance for me to make serious money with the Thawometer. Indeed, Winchell's patent has been around for over fifty years, yet it's sage advice is nowhere to be seen in a store! Pretty discouraging stuff.

I decided to dabble in the marketing side of the inventing process for the purpose of learning what inventors face at this stage in their roller coaster ride.

I settled upon a prototype that made good sense from a consumer stand point. Then I utilized that prototype in my instructions sheet to provide an easily understandable description of the Thawometer that did not rely on my patent disclosure. This was important to do because in any sales situation you want to have an easily read and immediately understandable description that avoids the use of *patentese*.

A local manufacturing company considered to partner with me, but in the end they declined. The Thawometer was a bit outside of their automotive roots, though they were looking to expand into other areas. It was a quite pleasant experience.

Curious about invention marketing firms, I responded to an out-of-state firm that talked a good game. I met with them personally. They knew I was a patent attorney. Still, when it came to showing me the beef, there was none between the buns. The fee structure was such that I could pullout before committing if I was unhappy. I was unhappy.

The one thing they did do was alert me to U.S. Patent 9,217,676. A quick look at the face of the patent showed it was Thawometer-like. A deeper dive revealed the claims recited many elements that enabled "The Freezer Failure Indicator" to get around Winchell.

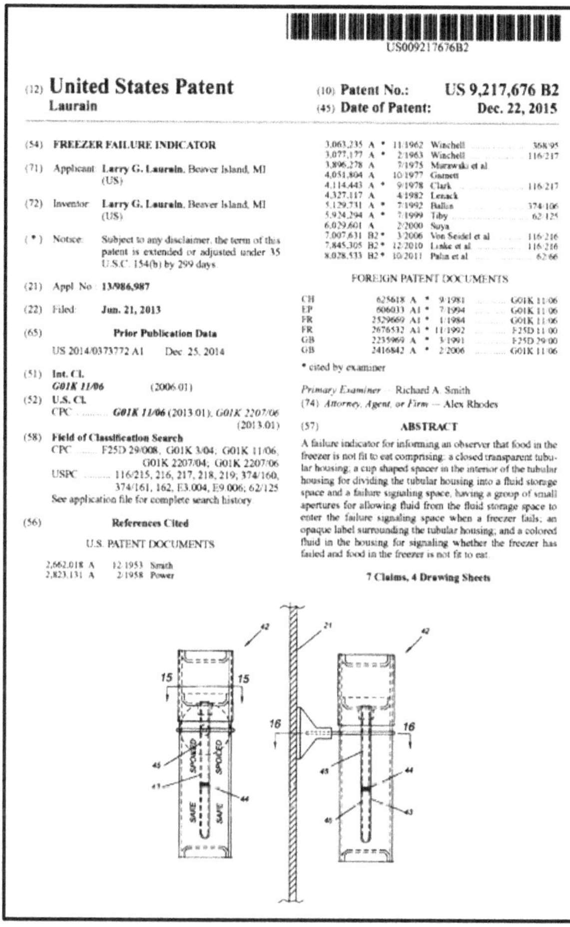

US009217676B2

(12) **United States Patent**
Laurain

(10) **Patent No.: US 9,217,676 B2**
(45) **Date of Patent: Dec. 22, 2015**

(54) **FREEZER FAILURE INDICATOR**

(71) Applicant: **Larry G. Laurain**, Beaver Island, MI (US)

(72) Inventor: **Larry G. Laurain**, Beaver Island, MI (US)

(*) Notice: Subject to any disclaimer, the term of this patent is extended or adjusted under 35 U.S.C. 154(b) by 299 days.

(21) Appl. No.: **13/986,987**

(22) Filed: **Jun. 21, 2013**

(65) **Prior Publication Data**

US 2014/0373772 A1 Dec. 25, 2014

(51) **Int. Cl.**
G01K 11/06 (2006.01)

(52) **U.S. Cl.**
CPC *G01K 11/06* (2013.01); *G01K 2207/06* (2013.01)

(58) **Field of Classification Search**
CPC F25D 29/008; G01K 3/04; G01K 11/06; G01K 2207/04; G01K 2207/06
USPC 116/215, 216, 217, 218, 219; 374/160, 374/161, 162, E3.004, E9.006; 62/125
See application file for complete search history.

(56) **References Cited**

U.S. PATENT DOCUMENTS

2,662,018 A 12/1953 Smith
2,823,131 A 2/1958 Power
3,063,235 A * 11/1962 Winchell 368/95
3,077,177 A * 2/1963 Winchell 116/217
3,896,278 A 7/1975 Murawski et al.
4,051,804 A 10/1977 Garnett
4,114,443 A * 9/1978 Clark 116/217
4,327,117 A 4/1982 Lenack
5,129,731 A * 7/1992 Ballin 374/106
5,924,294 A * 7/1999 Tiby 62/125
6,029,601 A 2/2000 Suya
7,007,631 B2 * 3/2006 Von Seidel et al. 116/216
7,845,305 B2 * 12/2010 Linke et al. 116/216
8,028,533 B2 * 10/2011 Palm et al. 62/66

FOREIGN PATENT DOCUMENTS

CH 625618 A * 9/1981 .... G01K 11/06
EP 606033 A1 * 7/1994 .... G01K 11/06
FR 2529669 A1 * 1/1984 .... G01K 11/06
FR 2676532 A1 * 11/1992 .... F25D 11/00
GB 2235969 A * 3/1991 .... F25D 29/00
GB 2416842 A * 2/2006 .... G01K 11/06

* cited by examiner

Primary Examiner — Richard A. Smith
(74) *Attorney, Agent, or Firm* — Alex Rhodes

(57) **ABSTRACT**

A failure indicator for informing an observer that food in the freezer is not fit to eat comprising: a closed transparent tubular housing; a cup shaped spacer in the interior of the tubular housing for dividing the tubular housing into a fluid storage space and a failure signaling space, having a group of small apertures for allowing fluid from the fluid storage space to enter the failure signaling space when a freezer fails; an opaque label surrounding the tubular housing; and a colored fluid in the housing for signaling whether the freezer has failed and food in the freezer is not fit to eat.

7 Claims, 4 Drawing Sheets

Image credit: USPTO.gov database.

A Google search led me to find out the inventor, Larry Laurain, had a product on the market aptly called "Freezer Alert."

By the way, Laurain, a fellow Michigander, was patent pending at the same time I was. Small world!

I bought a Freezer Alert from his online store and experimented with it. It worked pretty well, but I thought it could be improved using my Thawometer technology. However, all my efforts to contact Larry Laurain failed.

My curiosities satiated, I decided to shelve the project.

* * *
* *
*

APPENDIX

Quick Links

Government Agencies:

U.S. Patent & Trademark Office

Events

Fee Schedule

Forms

International Patent Cooperation

Invention Marketing Firm Complaints

Inventor/Entrepreneur Resources

Legal Assistance Programs: Pro Bono/Pro Se

Maintenance Fees

Manual of Patent Examining Procedure

Online Filing Portal: Patent Center

Online Training

Patent Basics

Patent FAQs

Patent Laws

Patent Resource Libraries

Patent Rules

Patent Search

Patent Statistics

Prosecution Record

Provisional Patent Applications

Roster of Patent Practitioners

System of CPC Symbols (Classification)

Trademarks

USPTO Offices

British Intellectual Property Office

Canadian Intellectual Property Office

China National Intellectual Property Administration

European Patent Office

Japan Patent Office

U.S. Copyright Office

World International Patent Organization (WIPO)

Non-Government Organizations:

American Intellectual Property Law Association

Carrier, Shende and Associates (patent law firm)

Google Patents

Google Scholar

Inventor Associations (UIA)

Inventors Digest Magazine

Keefe and Associates (patent law firm)

ProQuest

Prototype Shops (Design Rush)

Service Corps of Retired Executives (SCORE)

Thomas Register of American Manufacturers

University of Maryland Plant Patent Database

University of Wisconsin Innovation Service Center

US Inventor (patent rights advocacy)

Wizcom, Ltd. (Technologists™)

Detailed Table of Contents

PATENTAPPLICATION.COM

Helping inventors shed their downy feathers, break out of their shell, and bring their ideas to light since 1983.

The Inventor Handbook

2nd Edition, 2025

www.ingramcontent.com/pod-product-compliance
Lightning Source LLC
LaVergne TN
LVHW052319200926
848481LV00002B/605